Fairies
in Colored Pencil

Learn to draw imaginative fairies
in vibrant color

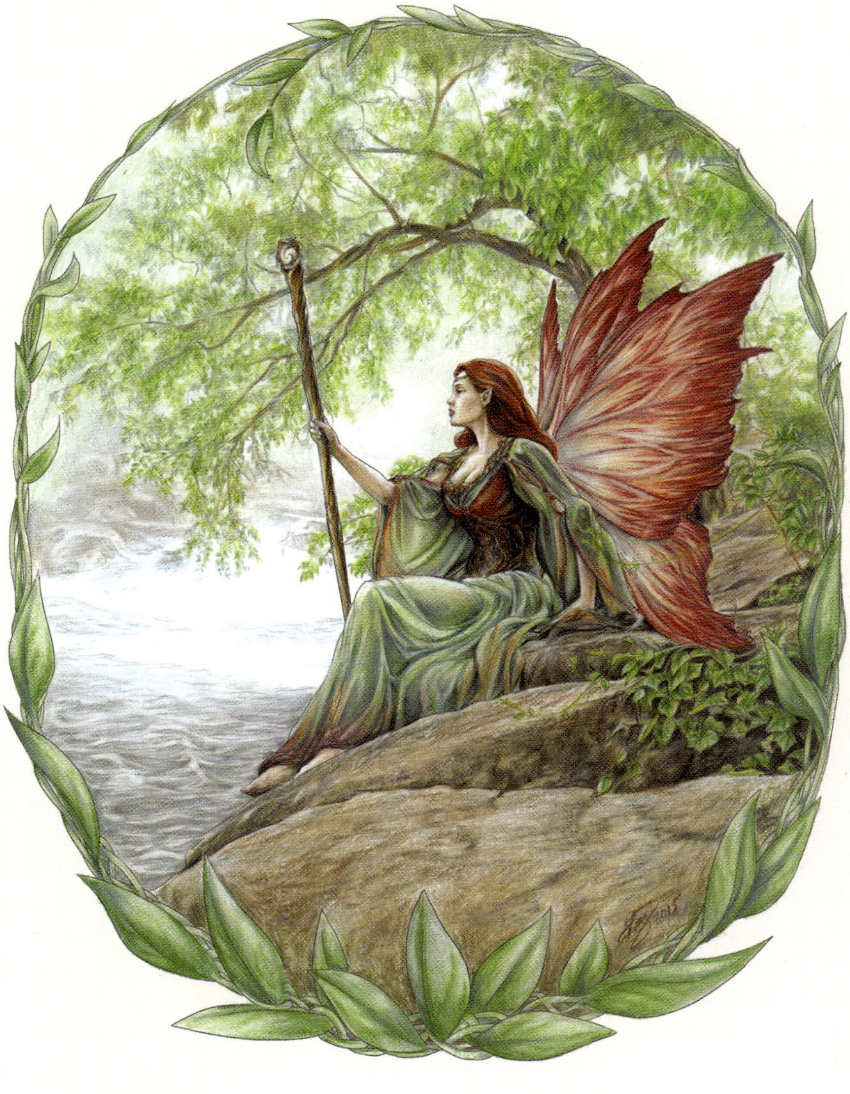

Walter Foster

with Lindsay Archer, Sara Burrier,
and Cynthia Knox

Quarto is the authority on a wide range of topics.
Quarto educates, entertains, and enriches the lives of our readers—
enthusiasts and lovers of hands-on living.
www.quartoknows.com

Project Editor: Elizabeth T. Gilbert
Page Layout: Kirstin McDougall

6 Orchard Road, Suite 100
Lake Forest, CA 92630
quartoknows.com
Visit our blogs at @quartoknows.com

Printed in China
3 5 7 9 10 8 6 4 2

Table of Contents

Introduction

THE FAIRY WORLD ENCHANTS ARTISTS OF ALL AGES AND SKILL LEVELS. It evokes the magic of youth and celebrates the mystery and beauty of nature. Whether you're drawn to their mythical roots or simply their petite, graceful figures, fairies connect us to stories told throughout human history.

In this book, you will learn how to draw 15 different fairies—from a forest guardian to a snow and a flower fairy. Accomplished artists Lindsay Archer, Sara Burrier, and Cynthia Knox guide you through each project, step by beautiful step. You'll find that colored pencil is a versatile medium that is ideal for rendering the fairy world. This medium can yield rich color, wispy strokes, and everything in between, making it suitable for both dreamy, atmospheric effects and fanciful details.

Leave the real world behind and immerse yourself in the uncharted realm of fairies. Your inner artist will not regret it!

"The world is full of magic things, patiently waiting for our senses to grow sharper."

—W. B. YEATS

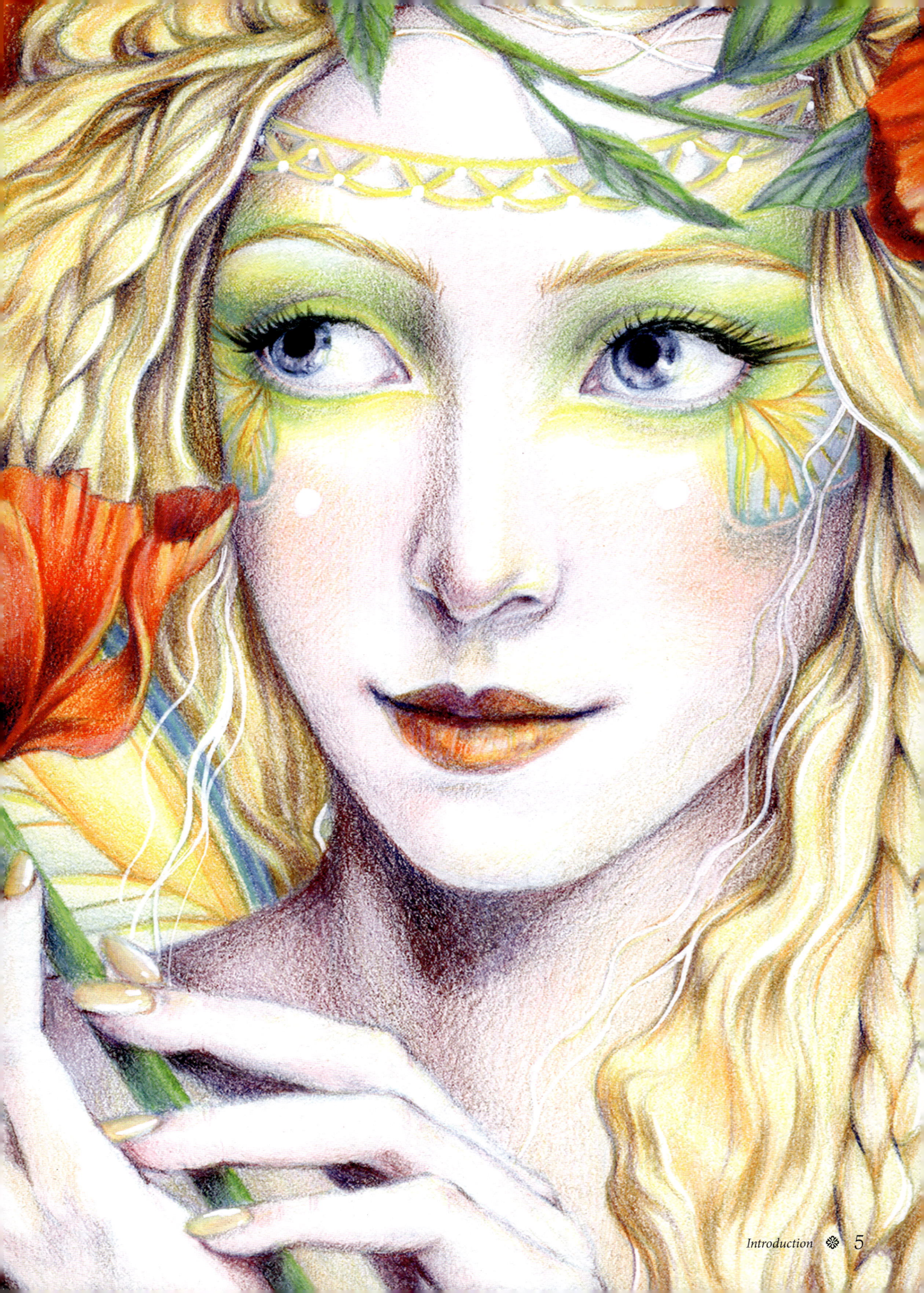

Tools & Materials

WORKING IN COLORED PENCIL is one of the simplest ways to create colorful artwork. Unlike working with pastels or paints, colored pencils don't require many supplies, and your fingers stay clean in the process! The following pages show what materials you should gather before beginning the techniques and projects in this book.

Supports

Most artists find it best to use colored pencil on a paper with a bit of *tooth* (or textured surface). This surface catches and holds the pigment to create rich colors. Examples of suitable paper for colored pencil include medium or fine-toothed drawing paper and Bristol board. Some artists choose to work on toned paper, as shown in the project on page 82.

Colored Pencils

Colored pencils are wood-encased leads made of pigment and wax, kaolin clay, or oil. Wax is the most common and affordable; these leads are soft and allow for smooth, controlled blends. Oil-based pencils are harder and great for producing fine lines, and they do not create wax *bloom* (or foggy buildup) on the drawing's surface. Colored pencil works well on multiple supports, from smooth to rough to toned surfaces.

Sharpener

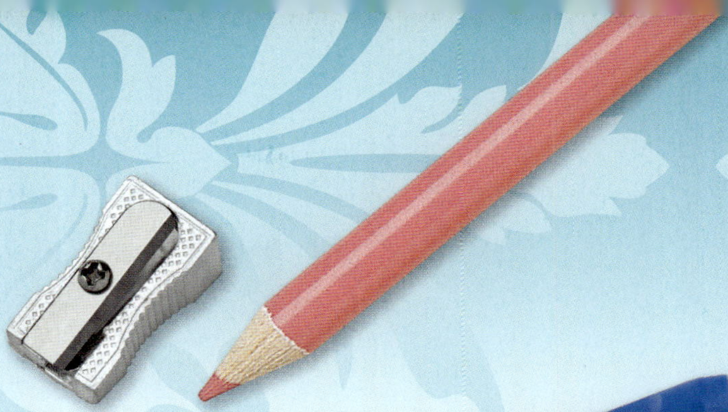

Keep a handheld or electric sharpener on hand for maintaining clean, sharp points.

Erasers

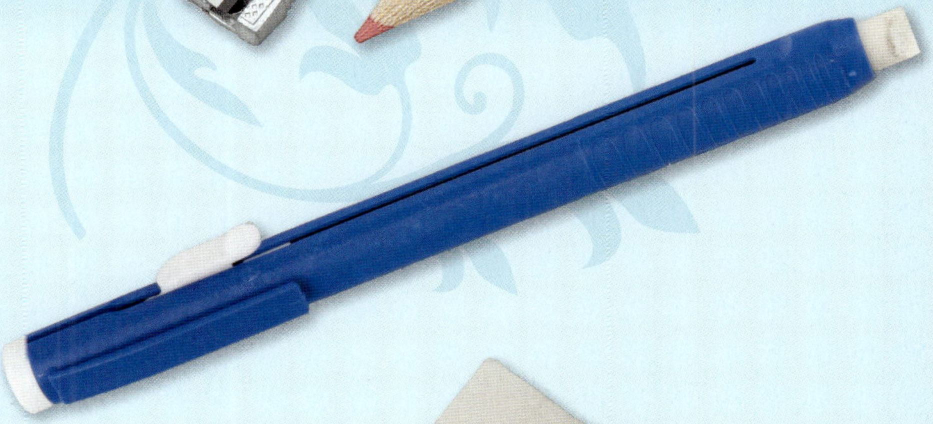

The best erasers for colored pencil are vinyl or plastic. To have maximum control as you work in small areas, you may want to try a stick eraser or electric eraser. Remember that, due to the staining nature of some pigments, you may not be able to erase every hint of color.

Other Materials

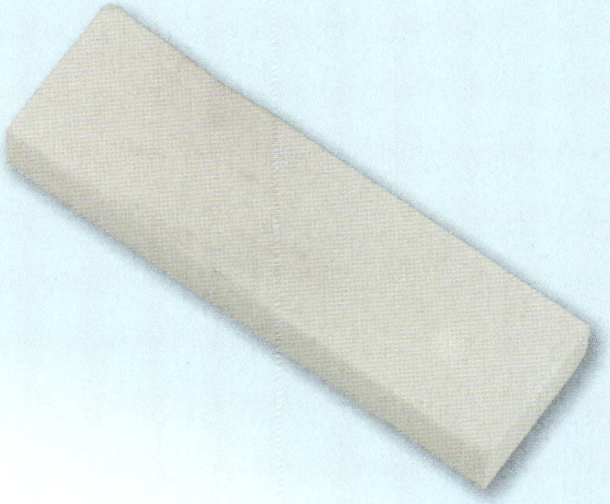

Additional supplies to keep on hand include a trash can or cup for pencil shavings and a soft cloth or brush for gently wiping away eraser crumbs and colored dust. Also, gather a range of graphite pencils to use for sketching (such as B, HB, and 6H), and purchase some workable spray fixative to protect your finished pieces.

Tip

When using wax-based pencils, your work may develop bloom—a light fog over the drawing as a result of wax rising to the surface. To eliminate this, let the drawing sit for two weeks and then rub a tissue, cotton ball, or cotton pad gently over the blooms, which will catch and remove the wax.

Basic Drawing

BEFORE YOU DELVE INTO THE FAIRY PROJECTS, it's a good idea to acquaint (or reacquaint) yourself with the basics of drawing. Practicing stroke styles and building convincing form will help you achieve depth and realism in your work.

Practicing Lines

When drawing lines, it is not necessary to always use a sharp point. In fact, sometimes a blunt point may create a more desirable effect. When using larger lead diameters, the effect of a blunt point is even more evident. Play around with your pencils to familiarize yourself with the different types of lines they can create. Make every kind of stroke you can think of, using both a sharp point and a blunt point. Practice the strokes below to help you loosen up.

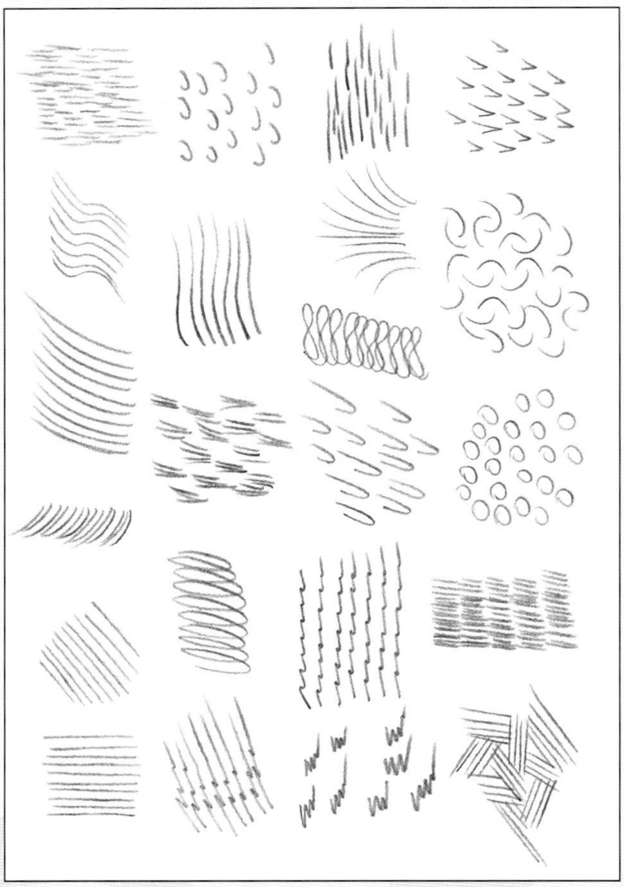

Drawing with a Sharp Point First draw a series of parallel lines. Try them vertically; then angle them. Make some of them curved, trying both short and long strokes. Try some wavy lines at an angle and some with short, vertical strokes.

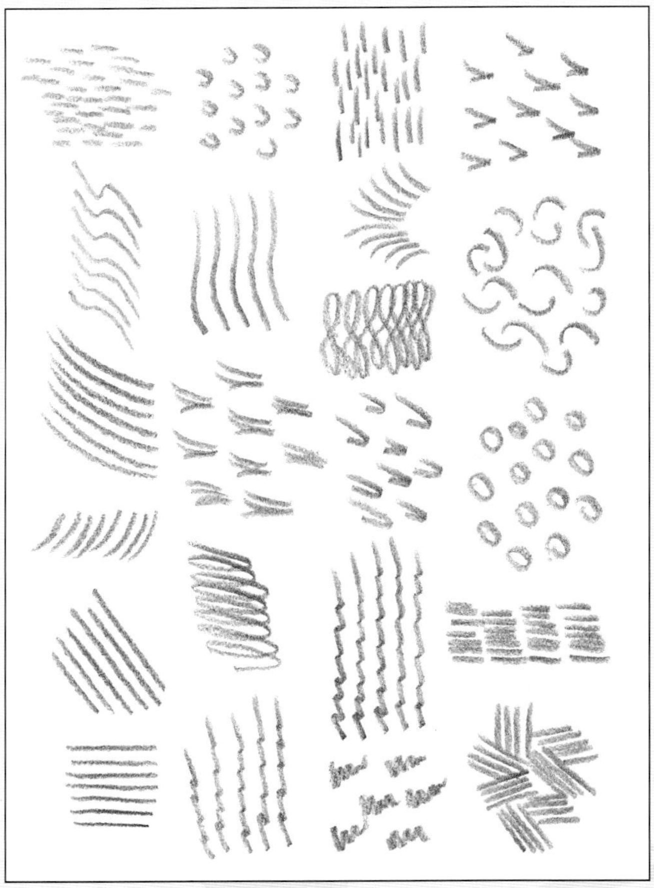

Drawing with a Blunt Point It is good to take the same exercises and try them with a blunt point. Even if you use the same hand positions and strokes, the results will be different when you switch pencils.

Creating Form

The first step when creating an object is to establish a line drawing to delineate the flat area that the object takes up. This is known as the "shape" of the object. The four basic shapes—the rectangle, circle, triangle, and square—can appear to be three-dimensional by adding a few carefully placed lines that suggest additional planes. By adding ellipses to the rectangle, circle, and triangle, you've given the shapes dimension and have begun to produce a form within space. Now the shapes are a cylinder, sphere, and cone. Add a second square above and to the side of the first square, connect them with parallel lines, and you have a cube.

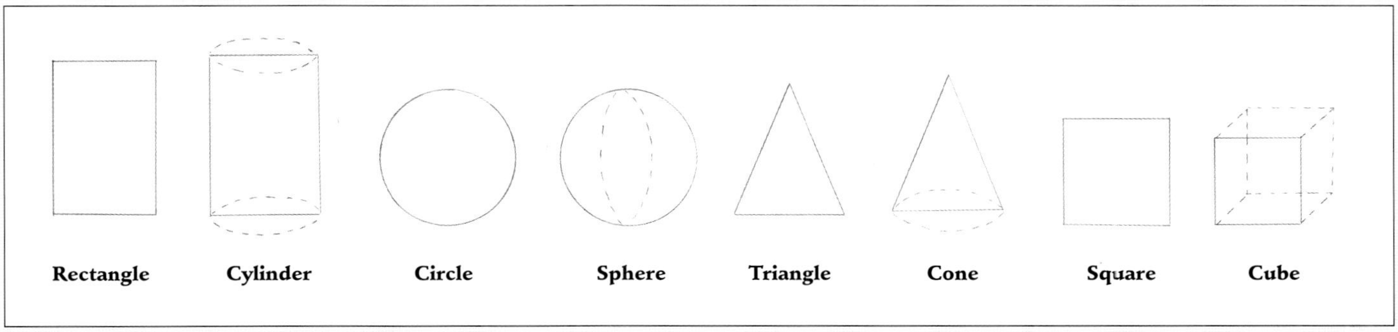

Adding Value to Create Form

A shape can be further defined by showing how light hits the object to create highlights and shadows. First note from which direction the source of light is coming. (In these examples, the light source is beaming from the upper right.) Then add the shadows accordingly, as shown in the examples below. The core shadow is the darkest area on the object and is opposite the light source. The cast shadow is what is thrown onto a nearby surface by the object. The highlight is the lightest area on the object, where the reflection of light is strongest. Reflected light, often overlooked by beginners, is surrounding light that is reflected into the shadowed area of an object.

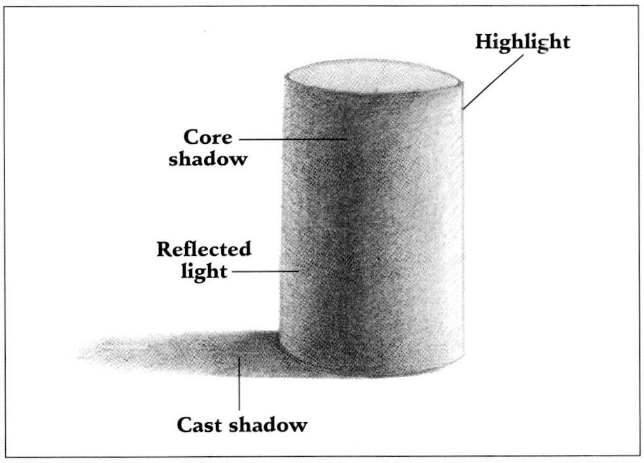

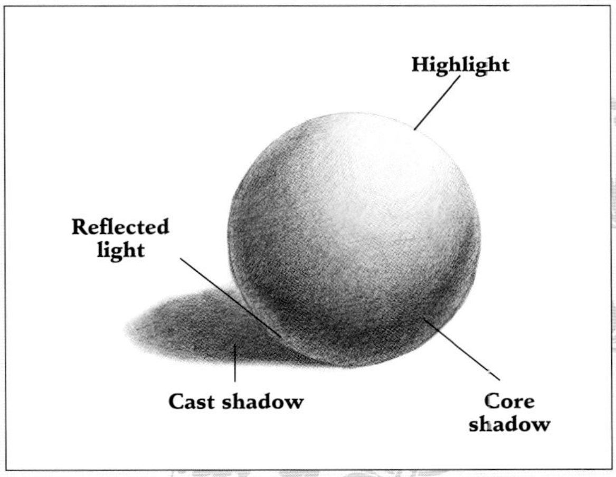

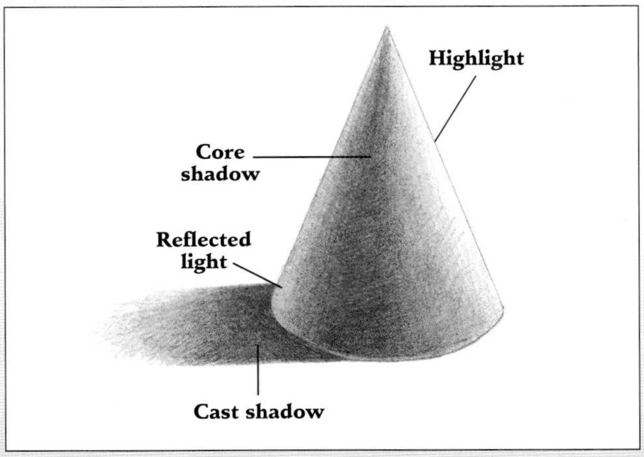

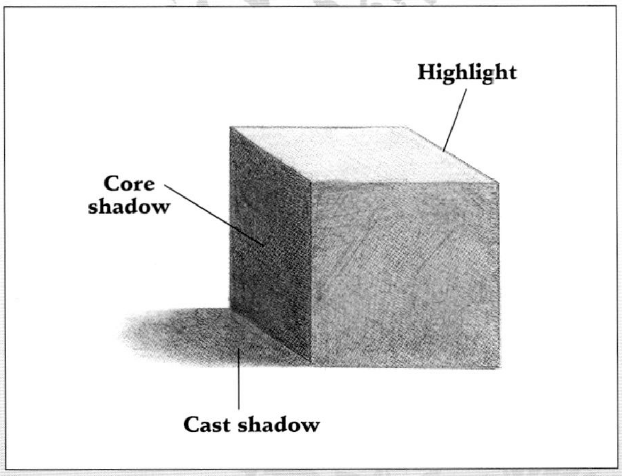

Colored Pencil Techniques

ONCE YOU'RE FAMILIAR WITH THE BASICS OF DRAWING IN GRAPHITE, try your hand at colored pencils. Experiment with strokes and various forms of application, as recommended on the following pages.

Pressure

Colored pencil is not like paint: You can't just add more color to the tip when you want it to be darker. Because of this, your main tool is the amount of pressure you use to apply the color. It is always best to start light so that you maintain the tooth of the paper for as long as you can.

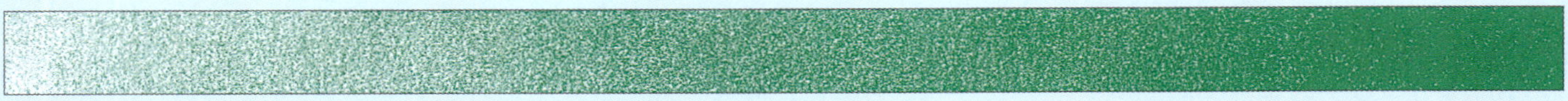

Light Pressure Here color was applied by just whispering a sharp pencil over the paper's surface.

Medium Pressure This middle range creates a good foundation for layering. This is also the pressure you might want to use when signing your drawings.

Heavy Pressure Really pushing down on the pencil flattens the paper's texture, making the color appear almost solid.

Tip

EXPERIMENT WITH THE ANGLE AT WHICH YOUR PENCIL TIPS CONTACT THE PAPER. HOLDING THE PENCIL NEARLY PERPENDICULAR TO THE PAPER IS GREAT FOR DOTS AND THIN LINES, WHEREAS HOLDING AT A STEEP ANGLE CAN PRODUCE BROAD, TEXTURED STROKES.

Varying Strokes

Experiment with the tip of your pencil as you create a variety of marks, from lines and dots to circular scribbles.

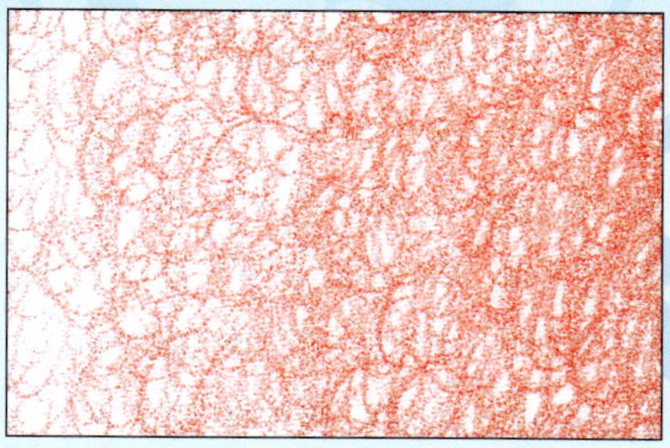

Circular Move your pencil in a circular motion, either in a random manner or in patterned rows. For denser coverage, overlap circles. You can also vary the pressure throughout for a more random appearance.

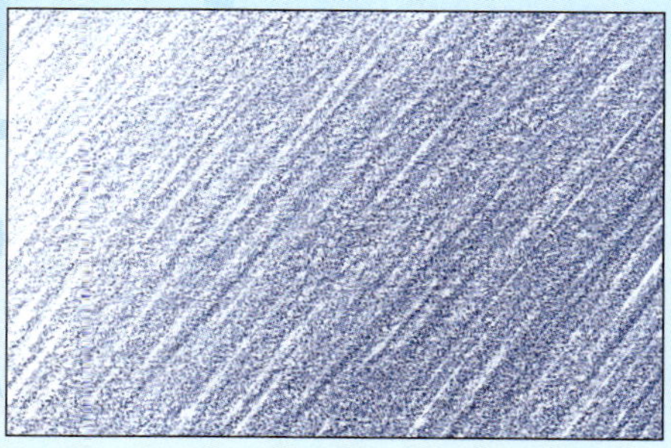

Linear It may be more comfortable for you to work in a linear fashion: vertically, horizontally, or diagonally, depending on your preference. Your strokes can be short and choppy or long and even, depending on the texture desired.

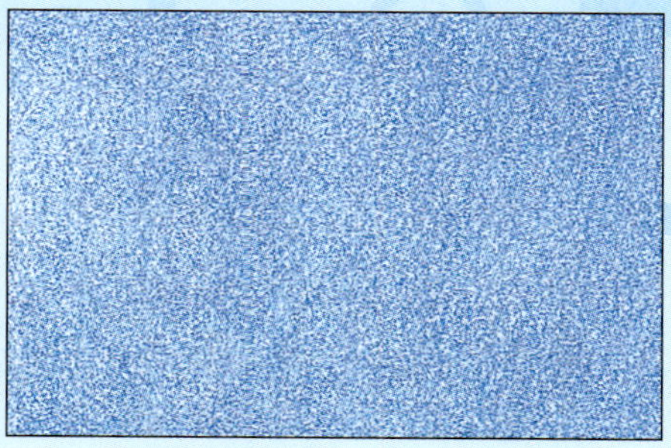

Smooth Always strive to control the pencil so that you apply a smooth, even layer of color regardless of the technique you used to apply it.

Gradating To create a gradation with one color, stroke side to side with heavy pressure and lighten your pressure as you move away, exposing more of the white paper beneath the color.

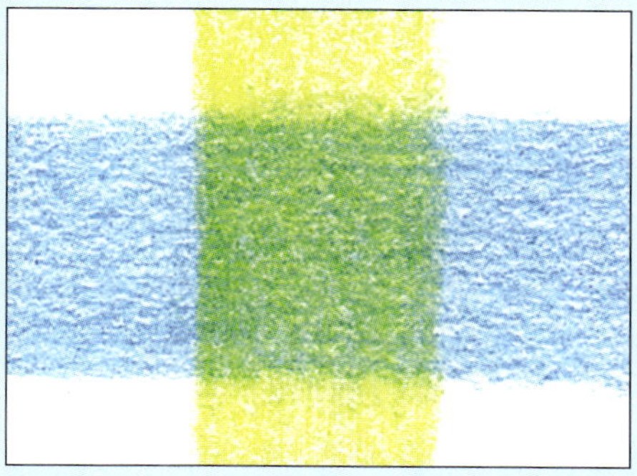

Layering You can optically mix colored pencils by layering them lightly on paper. In this example, observe how layering yellow over blue creates green.

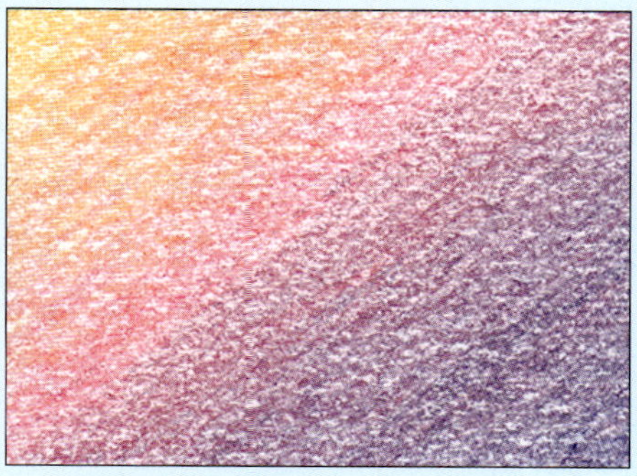

Blending To blend one color into the next, lighten the pressure of your pencil and overlap the strokes where the colors meet.

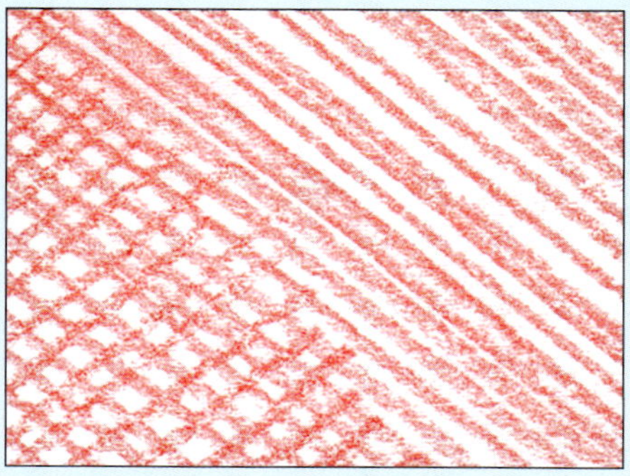

Hatching & Crosshatching Add shading and texture to your work with hatching (parallel lines) and crosshatching (layers of parallel lines applied at varying angles).

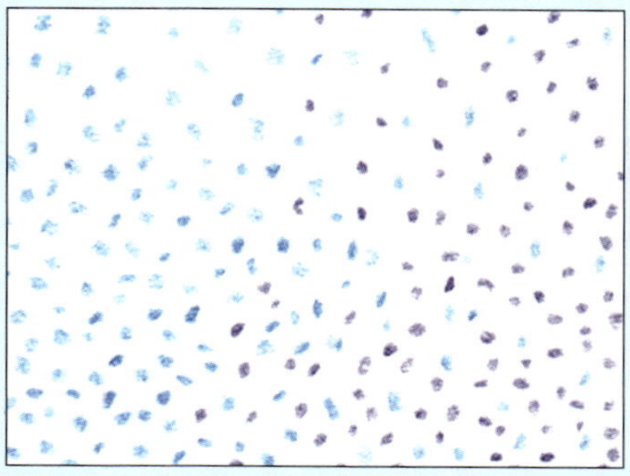

Stippling Apply small dots of color to create texture or shading. The closer together the dots, the darker the stippling will "read" to the eye.

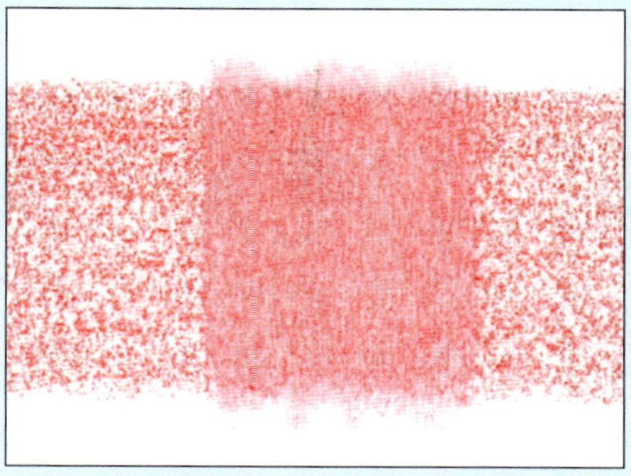

Burnishing Colored pencil catches in the tooth of the paper, therefore the layers can appear rough. For a smooth, shiny effect, burnish the layer by stroking over it with a colorless blender, a white colored pencil (to lighten), or another color (to shift the hue) using heavy pressure. Burnishing pushes the color into the tooth and distributes the pigment for smooth coverage.

Fairy Types

with Sara Burrier

IN AN IMAGINATIVE WORLD FULL OF MAGICAL PLACES, it is no surprise there are many different types of fairies. Ranging from tiny to life-sized, there are fairies that dwell overhead and fairies that dwell below—fairies that are considered evil and fairies that shine light. To explore all the fairies of the world's folklore would take a book in its entirety, so what follows is a very small selection of the most common classifications found in the everyday fairytale.

Brownies

Brownies are solitary sprites who takes up residence in small, unused corners of human homes. If gifts, such as food, are left for them, they will assist with household chores. Brownies, sometimes called "Brown Men," are commonly seen wearing brown clothes (hence their name) and do not have wings. Brownies are part of the House and Hearth group of fairies, as they live with humans (although usually unseen) and provide help around their homes.

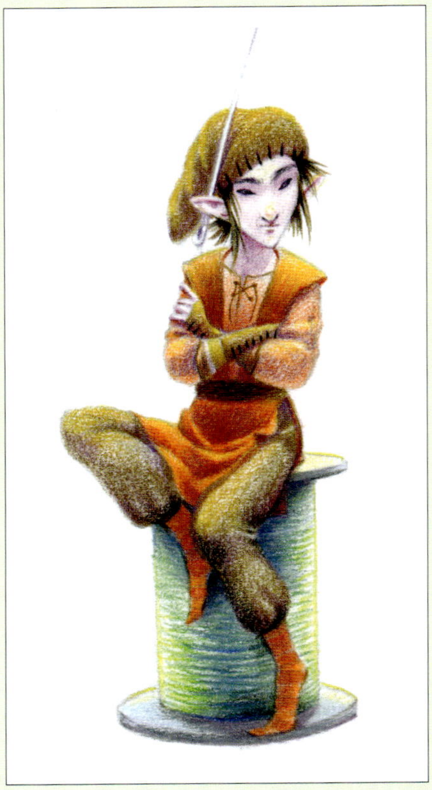

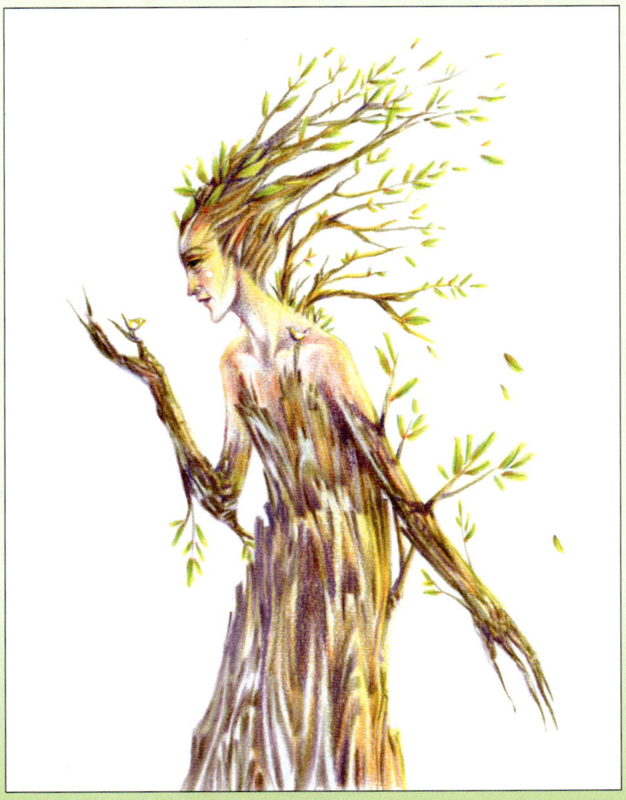

Dryads

The dryad is a type of tree fairy, or spirit, who bears the form of a tree and woman combined. Dryads are confined to their bodies and cannot wander about. There is a different fairy type for each tree species, and each helps keep the air clean, shelters animals, and helps regenerate those who come to sit with them. Because these fairies have a long lifespan, they are known for their wisdom.

Leprechauns

As part of the Earth Elemental fairy group, the leprechaun is another solitary type. He is a very skilled shoemaker and is usually seen either mending shoes or counting his gold. If caught, the leprechaun will grant its captor three wishes. This Irish fairy is about three feet tall and wears shiny, buckled shoes and a red coat symbolizing his solitary classification.

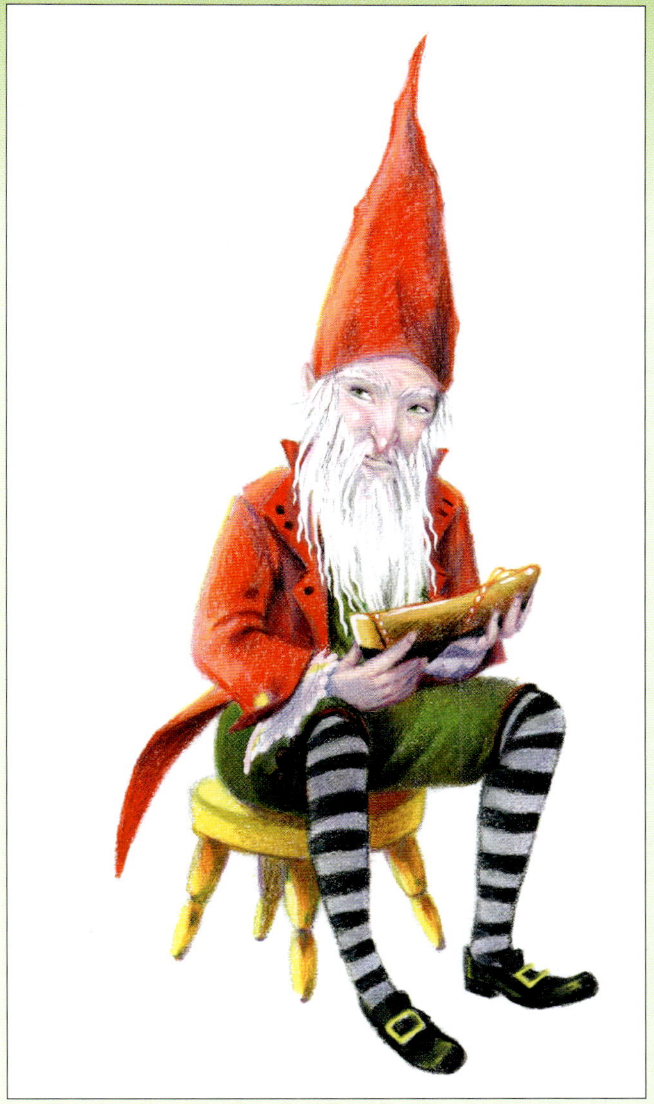

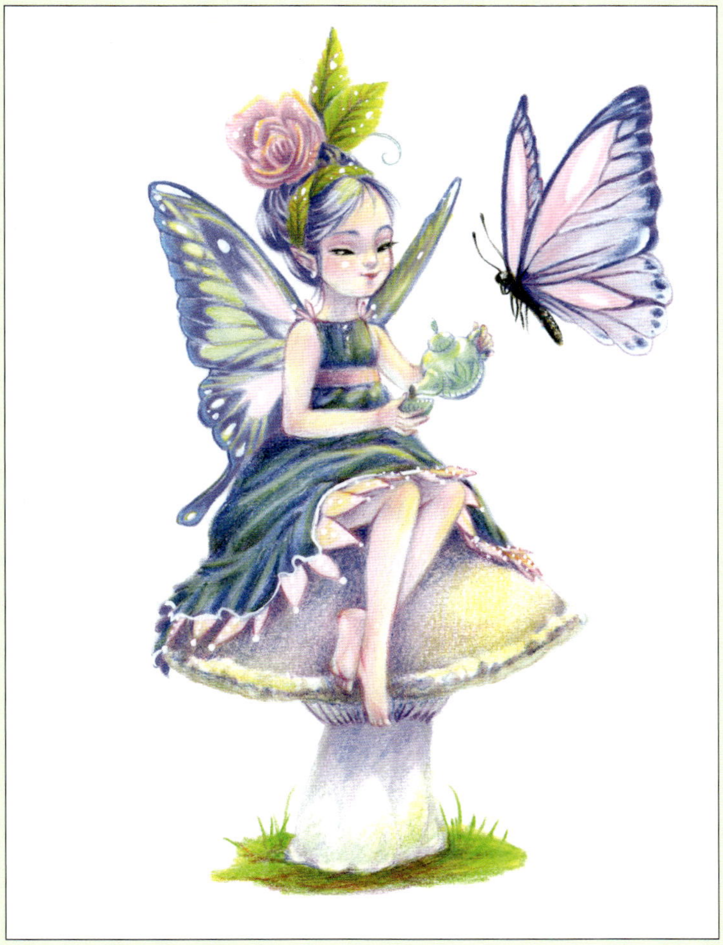

Flower Fairies

The Flower fairy group is know as the kindest, most entertaining, and most innocent of all the fairy groups. They nurture all flowers and pollinate them alongside bees and butterflies, and many flower fairies wear colors as bright as the flowers they represent. You can find flower fairies living in gardens, sleeping inside closed flower buds, nesting under mushrooms, and sometimes residing in small birdhouses.

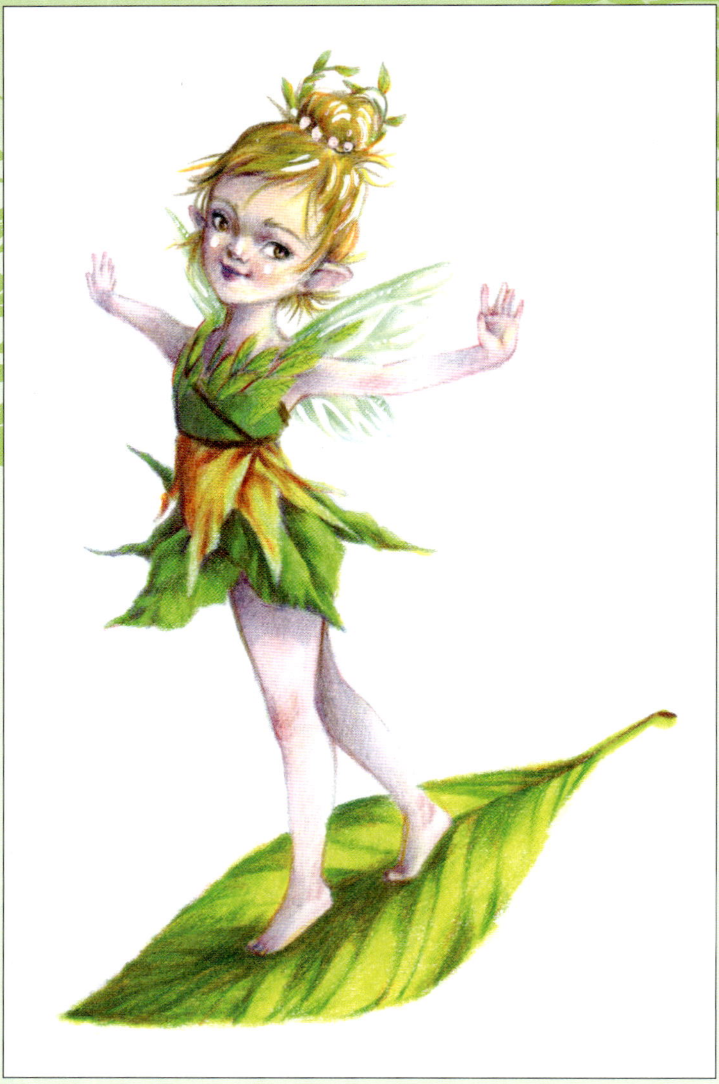

Pixies

Nearly invisible to the naked human eye, pixies are the smallest of the fairies. They are also the most mischievous. They enjoy playing practical jokes and teasing humans, but they are never out to really hurt anyone. You can find pixies dancing and singing all night long together, or you can find them helping a human with a health or home matter. They are members of the Earth Elemental fairy group, and yet they can also be a part of the Weather fairy group, which controls wind.

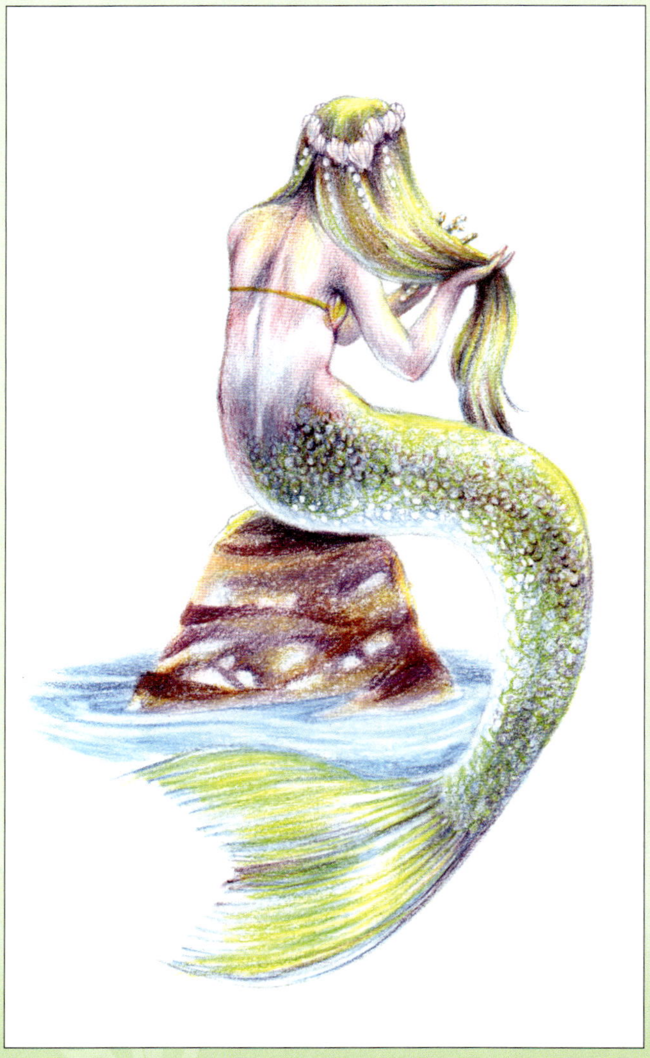

Mermaids

The mermaid is part of the Water Elemental group of fairies. This fairy is half young maiden (on the top) and half fish (on the bottom). The mermaid is commonly seen sitting on a shoreline rock, singing and brushing her hair. She can also symbolize bad weather at sea or a shipwreck—and she is known to lure sailors to meet her in the water. She is often paired with the siren, another Water Elemental fairy who bring sailors to their death.

Salamanders

Light a flame and you may find a salamander. These fairies are part of the Fire Elemental group and hold control over all aspects of fire. The salamander is often linked with a smoke fairy, along with the physical form of an amphibian, lizard, or dragon. Their breath is thought to be poisonous; in addition to controlling the element of fire, they can bring death to all things on which they breathe.

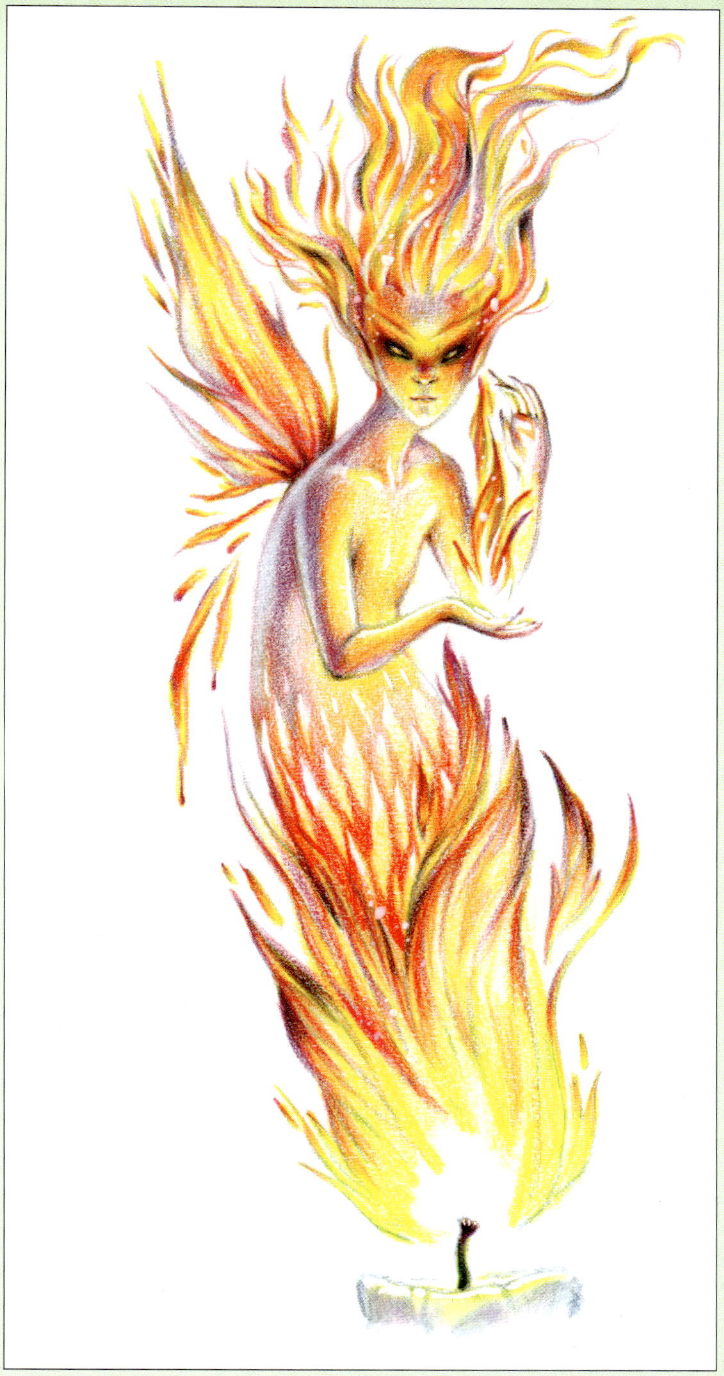

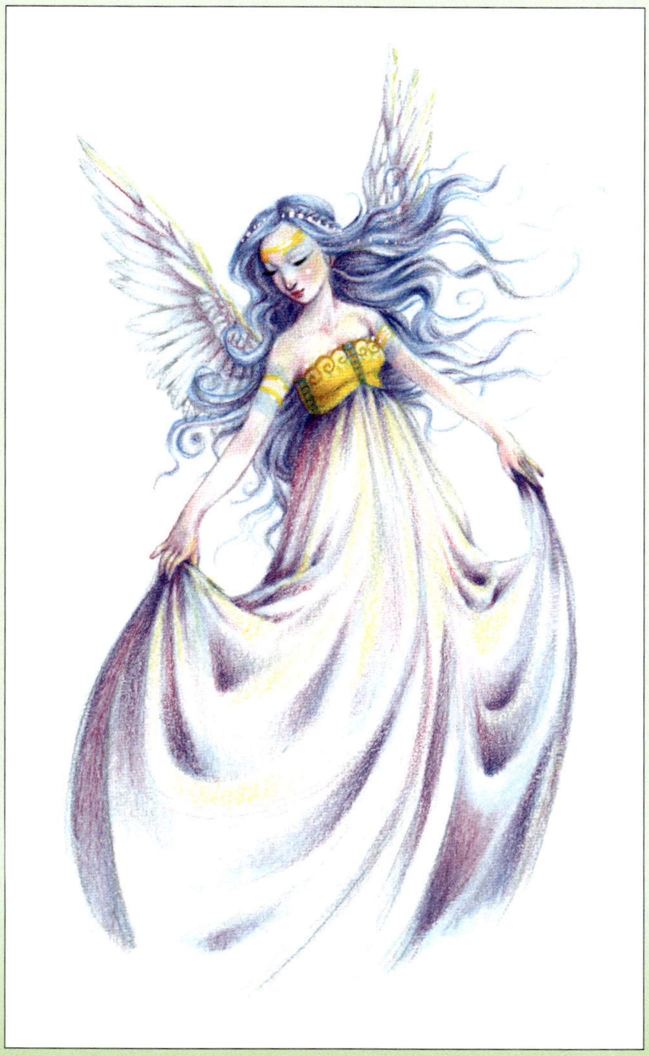

Sylphs

The sylph is part of the Air Elemental group. She controls the winds, air, and clouds and is stronger and wilder than humans or pixies. Because her wings are made of feathers, she is sometimes referred to as an angel. This fairy type lives closest to humans, as humans breathe and exist in air. (The other elements can be harmful to humans.)

Fairy Features

with Lindsay Archer

ON THE FOLLOWING PAGES, focus on developing features specific to fairies, from delicate wings and pointy ears to long locks of hair.

Eyes

Notice that the shape of the eye changes when the face is viewed at an angle. The placement of the iris and pupil determine the direction of the fairy's glance. Compare the placement in the wistful, distant gaze of the top eye to the languid, direct look of the bottom eye.

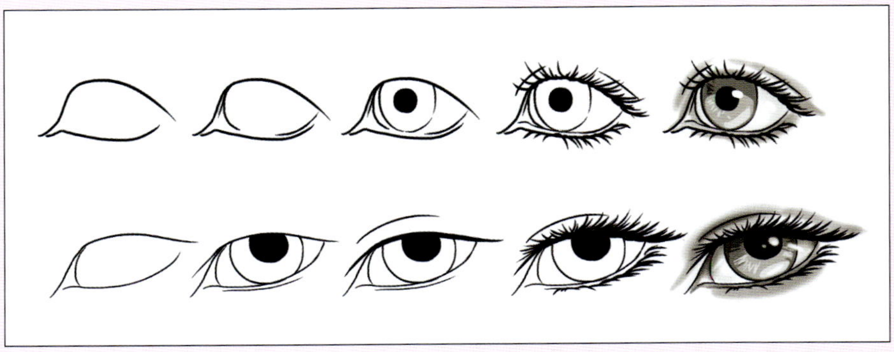

Wings

Because fairies exist in the imagination, there is no right or wrong way to draw the wings. I base my wings on the general shapes of butterfly wings, but I rarely draw them the same way twice. In addition to the two main wing sections, I like to add a third section for aesthetics.

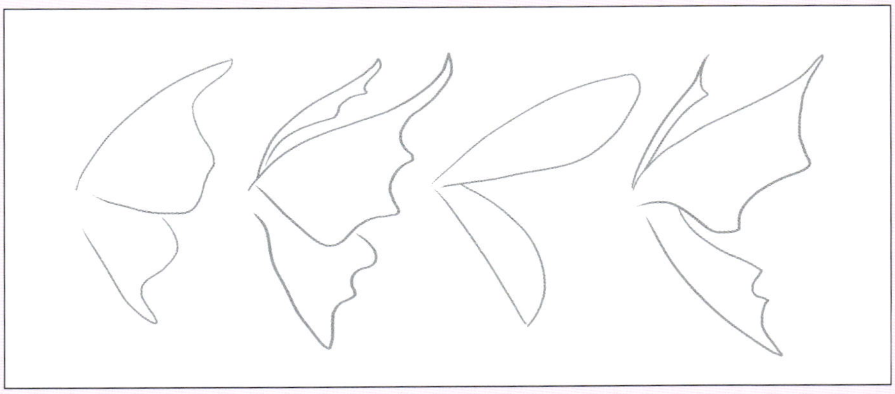

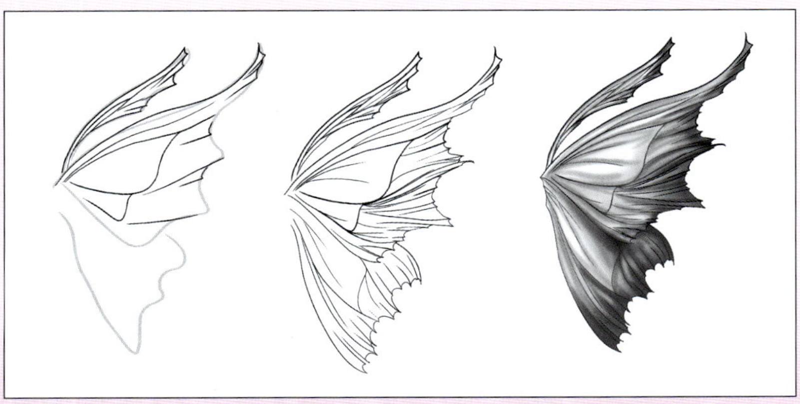

Once you choose a general shape, create the outline of the main wing. Consider giving the wing a ragged edge for texture. For an elegant, elongated look, extend points here and there. The wing meets the body at the center. As you move away from this point toward the wing's edges, make the veins and membranes smaller. Do not connect all the lines; simply hint at some, which keeps the wings from appearing flat. When applying color, I always leave the wing's interior light and the edges dark, which gives them a luminescent quality.

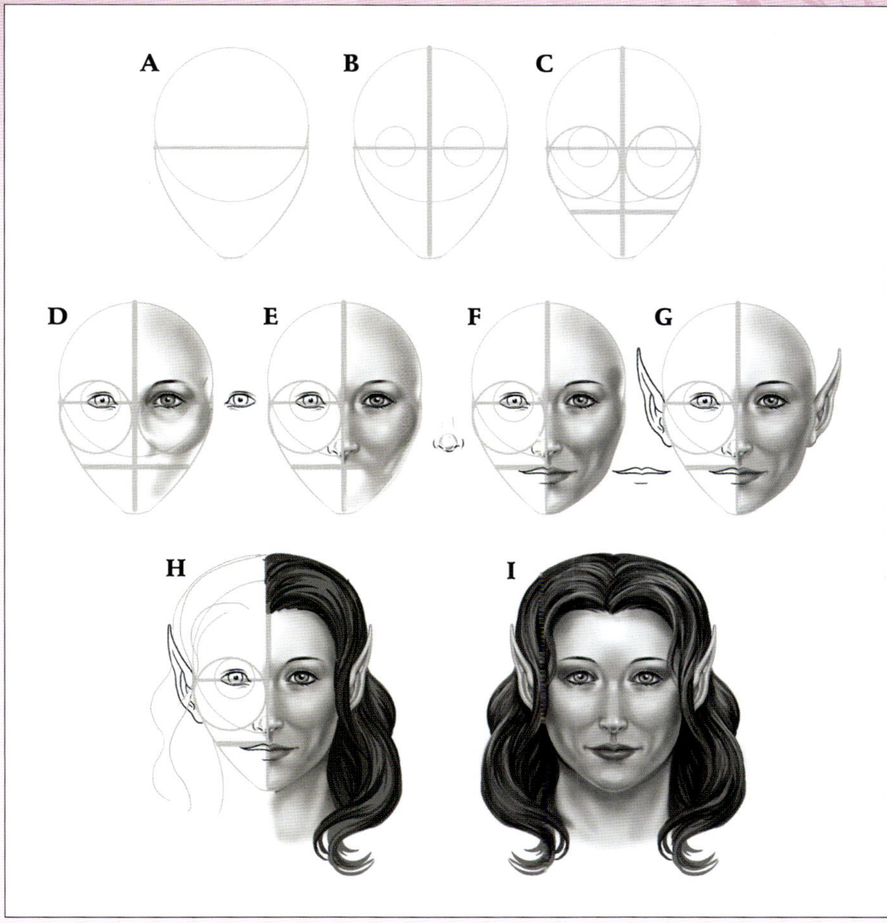

Faces

A Draw a circle, and then extend it into an egg shape to suggest the jaw and chin. Mark the eyeline using a horizontal line that lies halfway between the chin and top of the head.

B Now add a vertical line down the face and mark the placement of the eye sockets with circles.

C Add two larger circles around the eyes, meeting the top of the eye socket, side of the face, and vertical centerline. The bottoms of these circles serve as a guideline for the cheekbones. Now add a line halfway between the chin and the eyeline, which marks the position of the top of the mouth.

D Position the nose between the two larger eye circles, aligning the bottom of the nose with the bottoms of the circles. Begin developing the face with shading and detail, focusing on the rounded forms and subtle gradations of shadow.

E Develop the nose with shadow. Note that the outsides of the nostrils often line up with the interior corners of the eyes—but remember that this isn't always the case, especially if you are creating a fairy with very delicate features. Use a simple line for the nostril opening. A highlight under the tip of the nose and one on top of the nose will instantly add depth.

F Now work on the mouth area. Move the jawline out from the egg shape a bit. Align the top of the lip with your guideline, and align the bottom of the lip about halfway between the guideline and the chin. The corners of the mouth should never pass the pupils of the eye.

G Fairy ears have tops that taper to a point. Although they are often well hidden by hair, the ears usually poke through. Aside from their points, the ears resemble those of humans.

H When you draw hair, focus on the general shapes and locks rather than on each strand.

I Try to keep the fairy's face symmetrical as you develop the shading, particularly when viewing the fairy straight on.

Daisy Fairy

with Cynthia Knox

FLOWER FAIRIES GENERALLY RESEMBLE THE FLOWERS in which they dwell, with garments that reflect their environment. These delicate creatures also have butterfly or dragonfly wings. In this drawing of a daisy fairy, use the burnishing technique to create a smooth, polished finish that reflects the silky textures of a floral scene.

50% French gray	Beige	Black	Black grape	Burnt ochre	Burnt umber	Chartreuse	Chocolate	Cloud blue	Cobalt turquoise	Cream
Crimson red	Dark brown	Dark green	Dark purple	Dark umber	Kelp	Light umber	Limepeel	Magenta	Marine green	Nectar
Peach	Peach beige	Permanent red	Pink	Poppy red	Rosy beige	Sienna brown	Terra cotta	Tuscan red	White	Yellow ochre

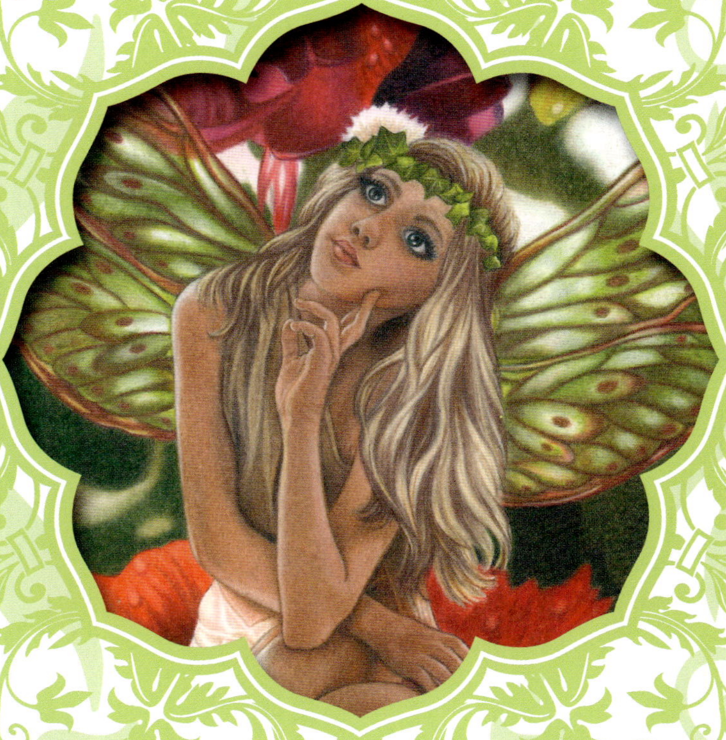

SKETCH Sketch the composition using a 50% French gray pencil, which will blend well with the rest of the colors in the palette. Consider sketching the details of the face and wing in graphite for easy erasing.

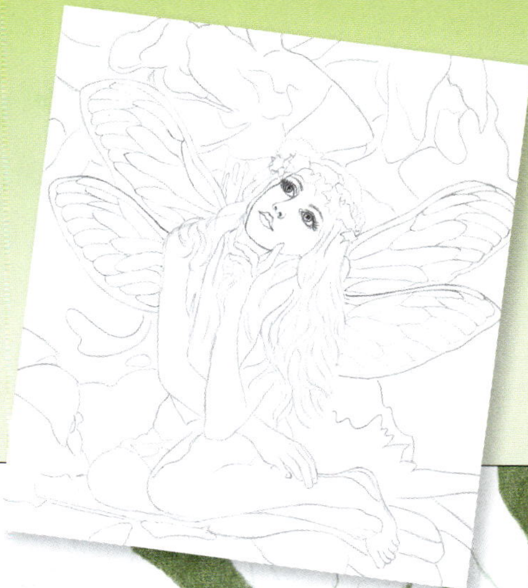

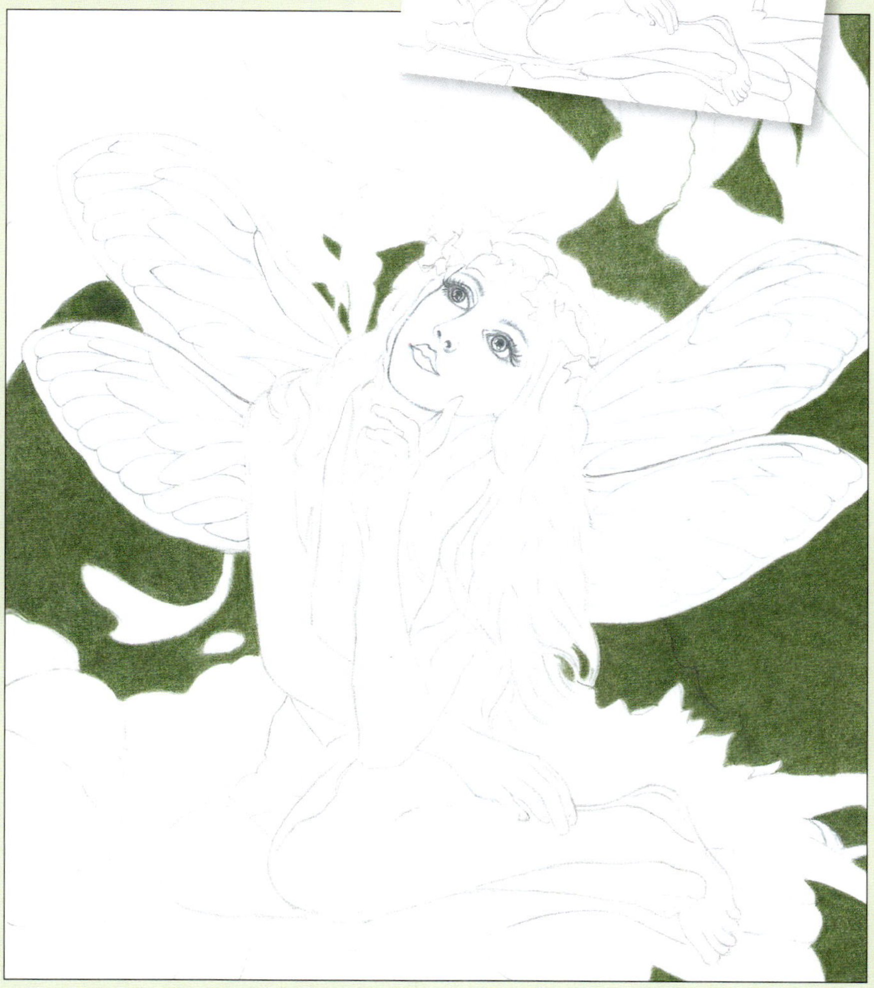

STEP 1 Begin adding the green background foliage using a layer of kelp and moderate pressure, working in small, elliptical strokes.

STEP 2 Now darken the large section of the left using black and dark green, warming areas with yellow ochre. Inside the lower curved shape, apply peach beige followed by yellow ochre. Using the blunt tip of yellow ochre, drag some of the neighboring green into the shape and blur the outline with small, elliptical strokes. Lighten the center with white. In the upper left, apply marine green, limepeel, and yellow ochre, burnishing the edges with white. Use peach beige, nectar, and yellow ochre to suggest the warm branch.

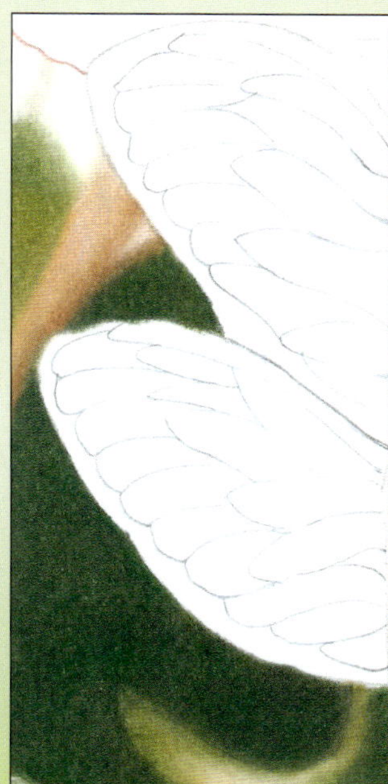

Tip

BURNISHING YOUR BORDERS AND EDGES IN THE BACKGROUND CREATES A DREAMY, SOFT-FOCUS LOOK, WHICH CONTRASTS WELL WITH THE SHARP CLARITY OF THE FAIRY AND HER WINGS.

Step 3 Working from left to right and top to bottom, apply various shades of greens, yellows, and browns to achieve complex, layered hues that suggest leaves and distant foliage. Begin with marine green and kelp, darkening with black and burnt umber. For the bright yellow leaf, use yellow ochre, chartreuse, and marine green, adding veins with dark umber. Blur your strokes with yellow ochre (within the yellows) and marine green (within the greens). For the dark leaf, apply yellow ochre, chocolate, and kelp. Use peach beige and white to blur your edges. Within the lower right, layer black, dark umber, and kelp, lightening with yellow ochre.

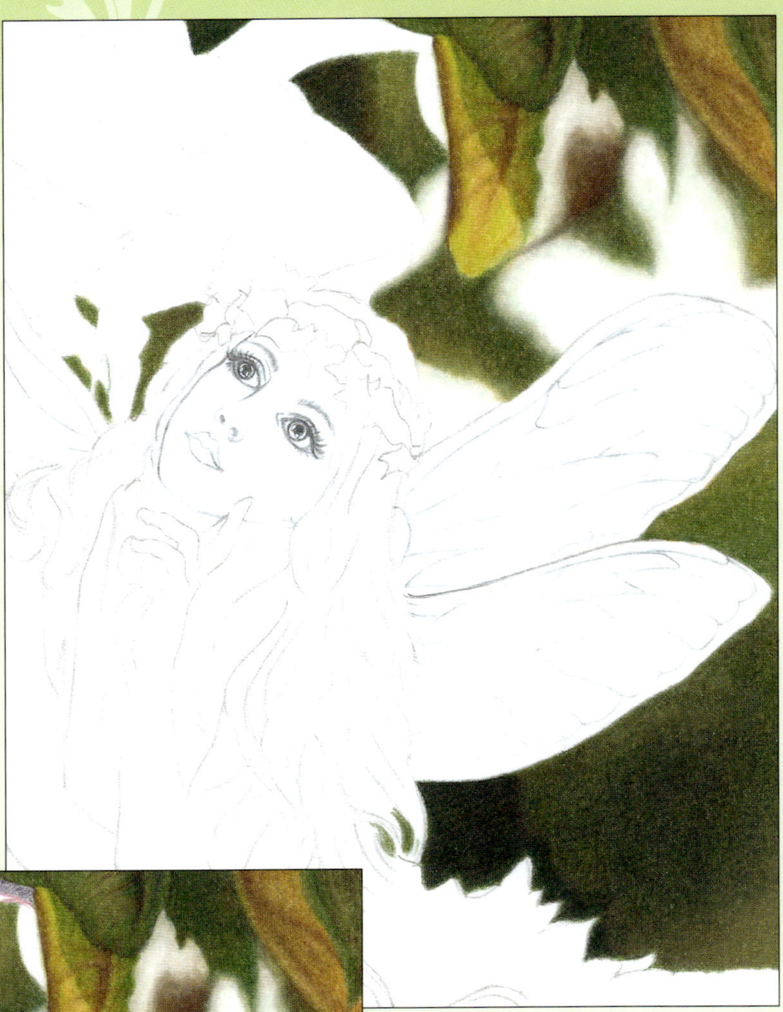

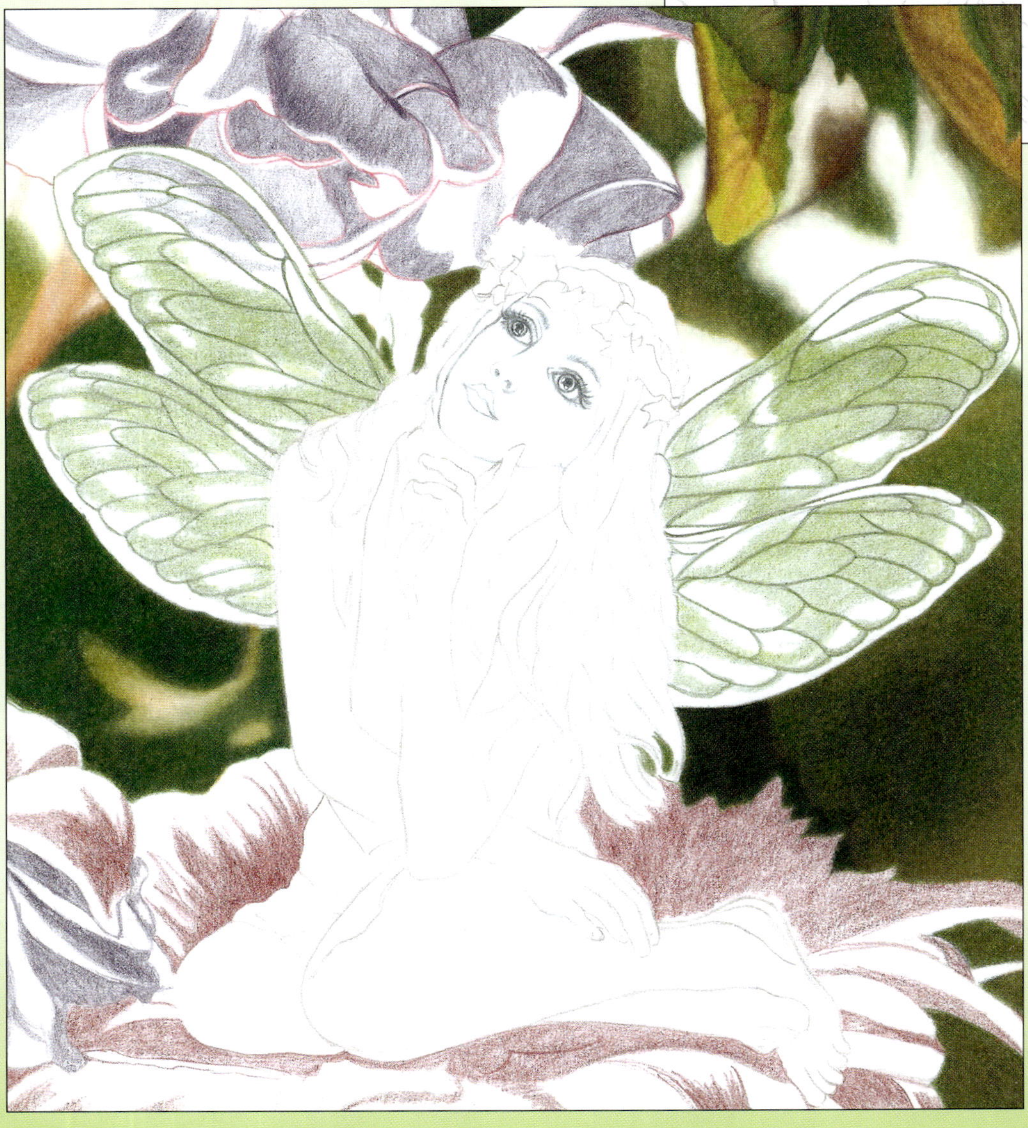

Step 4 Block in the shadows of the reddish-purple flower with a light layer of black grape, following the form of the flower's petals. For the bright red petals, block in the shadows with Tuscan red. Then outline the veins of the wings with kelp using moderate pressure. To achieve a translucent look, add light layers of kelp and limepeel, retouching the veins where necessary. Add a touch of black grape to the upper left wing to reflect the flower behind it.

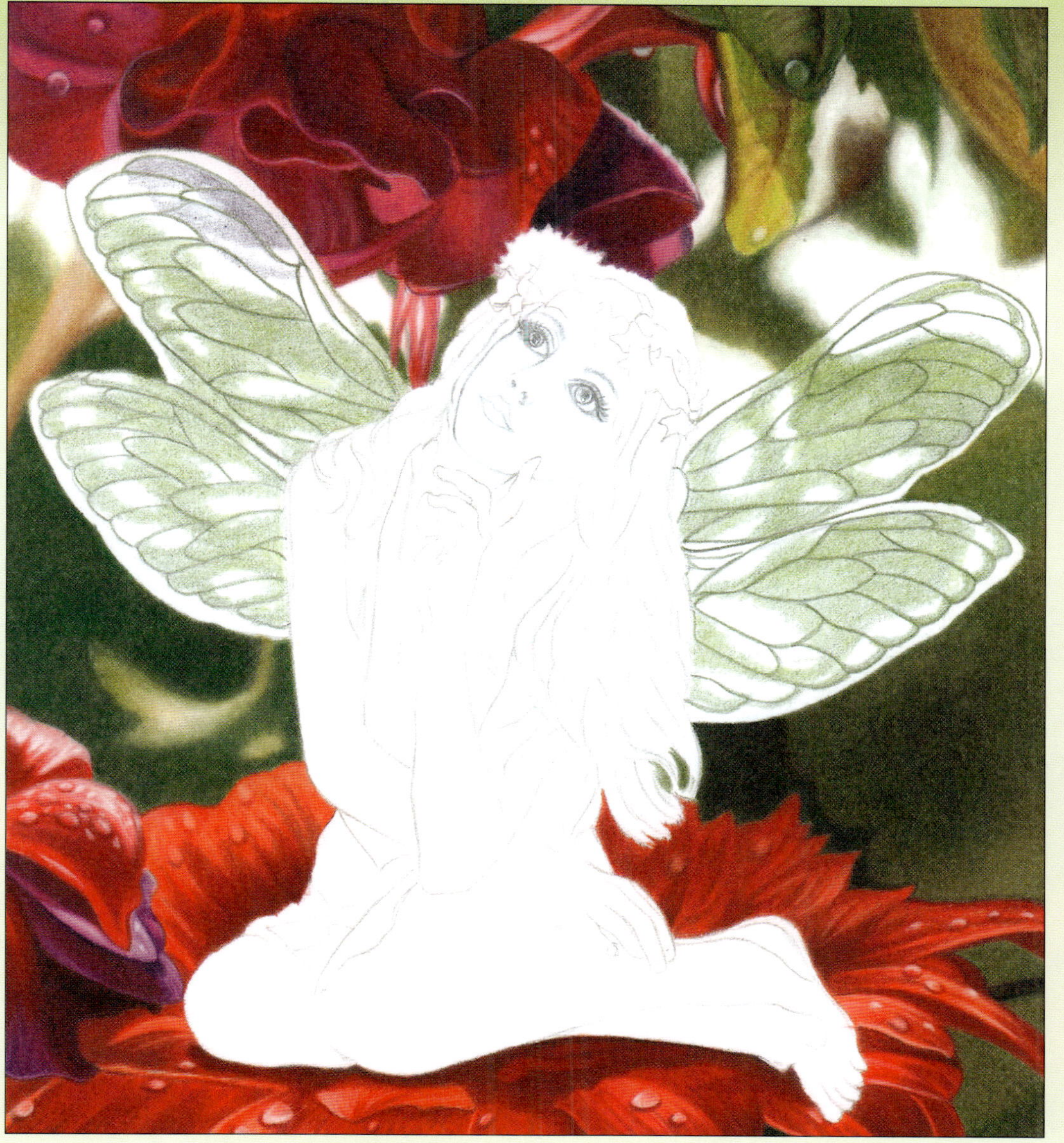

Step 5 For the red Gerbera daisy, use medium pressure to coat the flower with poppy red followed by permanent red. Darken the shadows with Tuscan red, adding black in the darkest areas. Smooth out your strokes using crimson red or poppy red with a dull point and diagonal strokes. For the brightest reds, apply several layers of crimson red; for the sunlit areas, add yellow ochre. Burnish the highlights with white and bring a little color back in using yellow ochre or poppy red. For the remaining red and purple flowers, apply crimson red to the red petals and burnish with white, using Tuscan red for the shadows. Apply dark purple over the purple petals, using white to lighten along with black and Tuscan red to darken.

Tip

If color applications are not blending smoothly, press hard with the dull tip of your white pencil to blend them together using small, elliptical strokes. This creates a smooth surface upon which you can restore color with additional layers.

Step 6 Suggest a recent rain shower by adding water drops throughout. First use a dull white point to carve out a basic elliptical shape, and then add shadow beneath the shape to give it dimension. Use Tuscan red for the drops on the red and orange flowers, black grape for the drops on the magenta flower, and black for the drops on the leaf. Then add color within each drop, blur, and lighten with white.

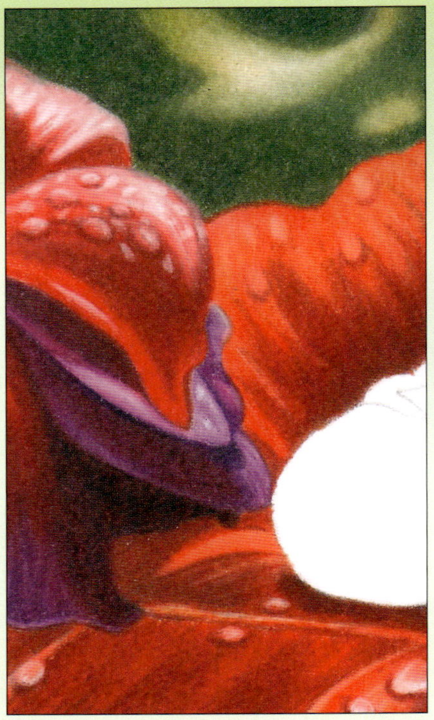

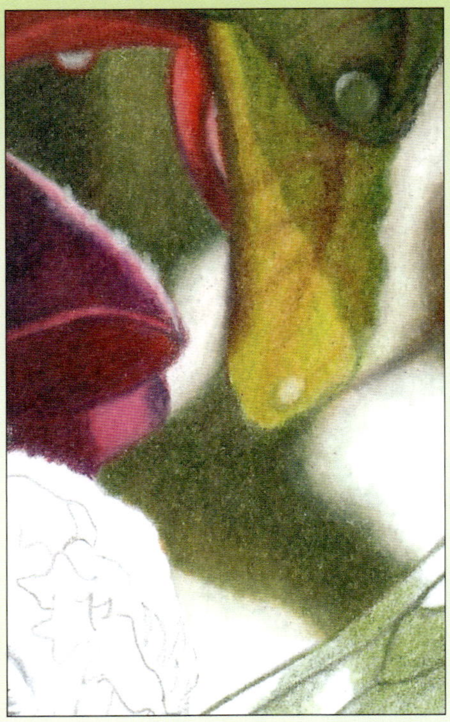

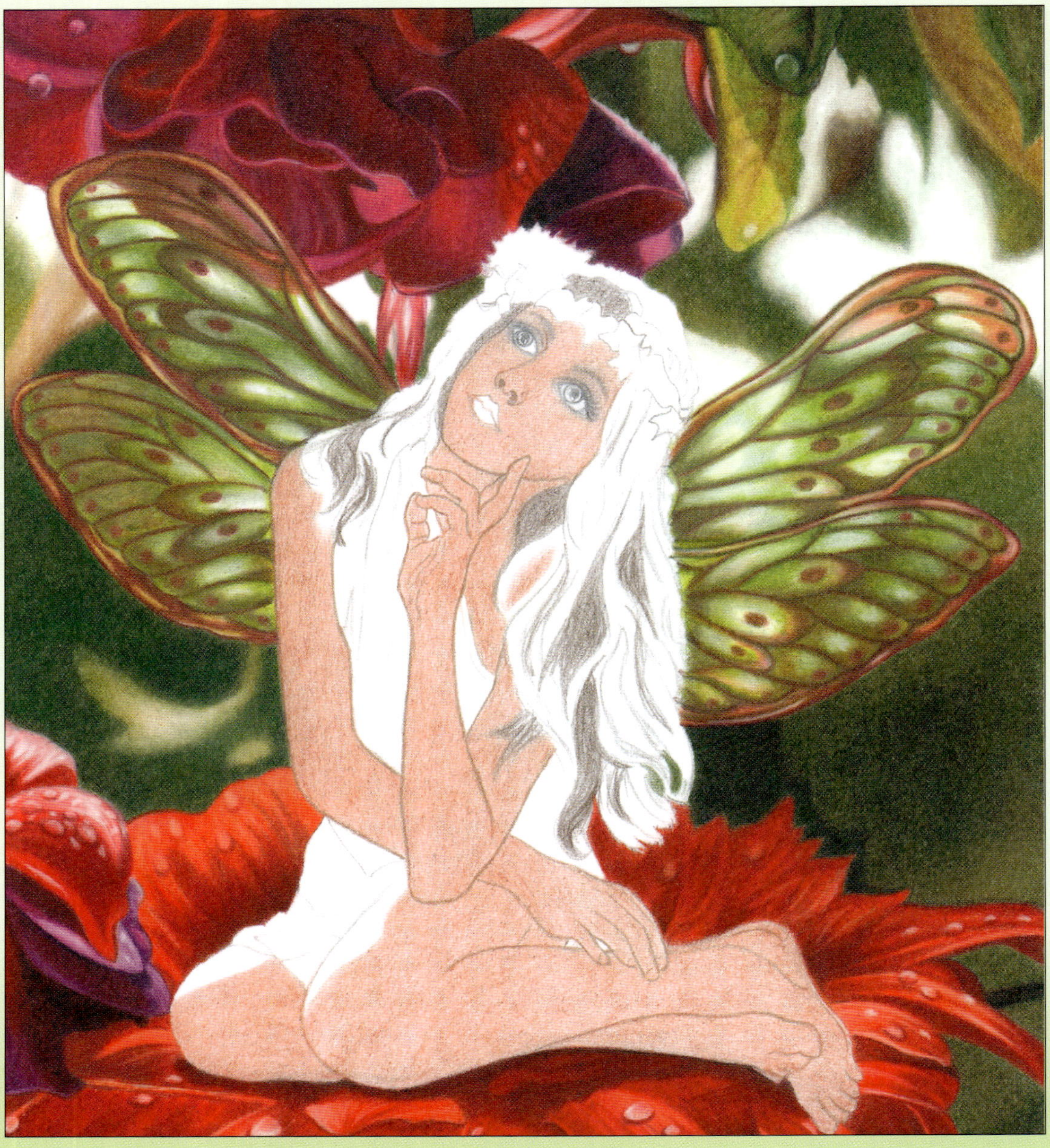

Step 7 Return to the wings and layer marine green and chartreuse for depth, darkening with dark umber and burnishing with white. Darken the veins with dark umber followed by Tuscan red, burnishing small white areas to reflect light. Create the rounded markings with Tuscan red, darkening with dark umber and lightening them with yellow ochre. For the wing outlines, use Tuscan red and yellow ochre, lightening and blending with white. To create the area of the wing in front of the flower, use crimson red and magenta blended with white. Redraw the veins with Tuscan red.

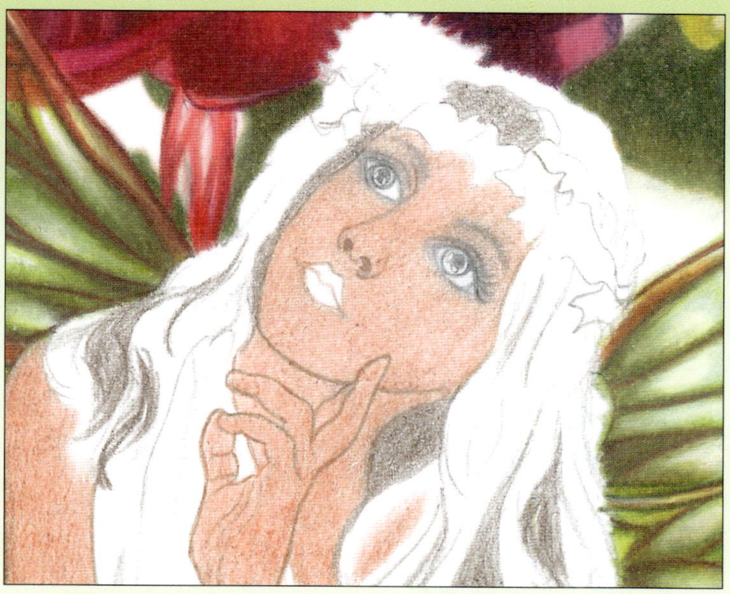

Step 8 For the first layer of the fairy's skin, apply light layers of peach beige and nectar using small, elliptical strokes. Follow this with a coat of burnt ochre. Reclaim any outlines needed with light umber. Then block in the darkest sections of the fairy's hair with dark brown.

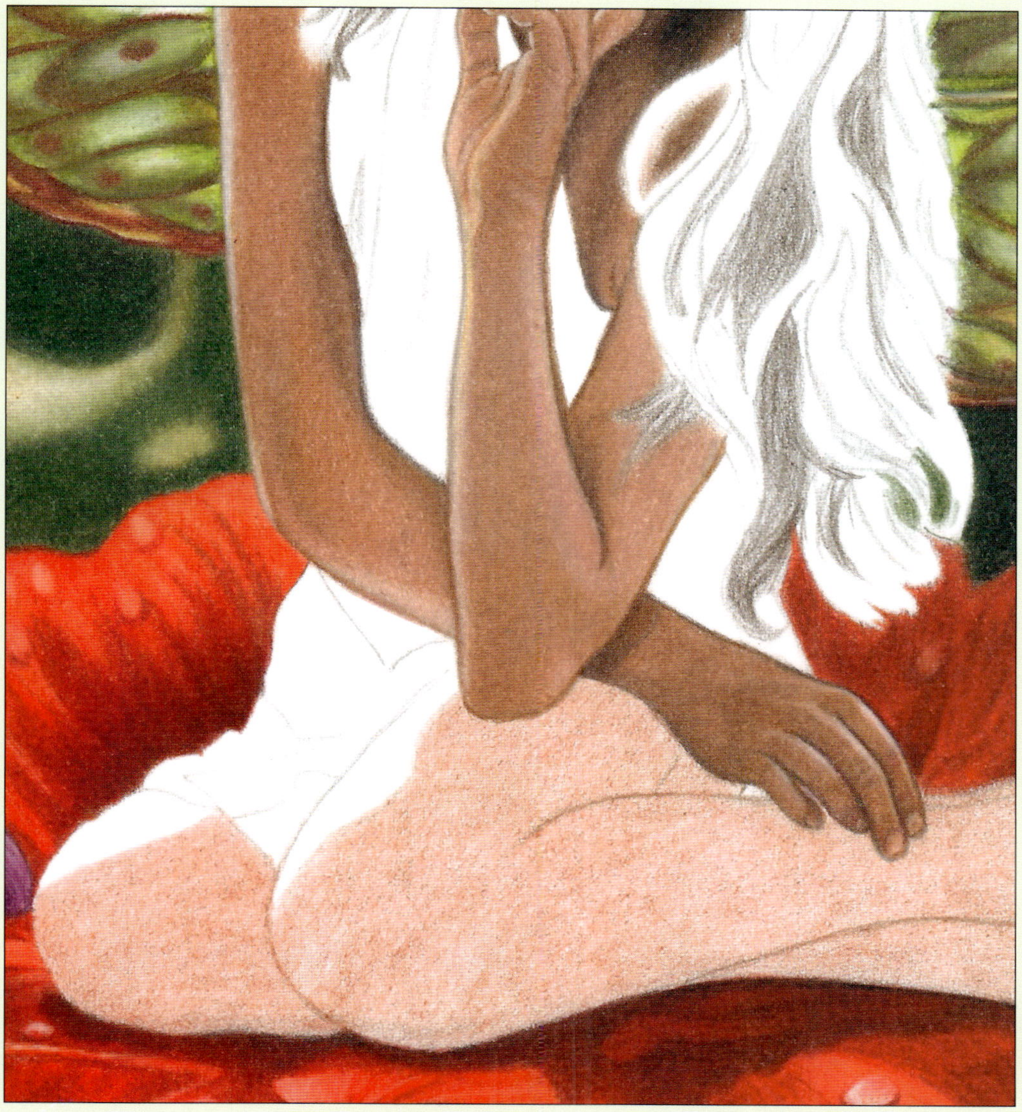

Step 9 Begin the upper body by burnishing with white to establish a sleek surface. Layer over this with sienna brown and dark brown, burnishing with sienna brown and white. Use light umber or chocolate and dark umber for darker areas. Create highlights and light areas of skin using white and nectar. For ruddy areas, bring in some terra cotta; for areas in light, bring in peach or yellow ochre. Burnish and blend frequently with white or sienna brown. Use this same process to build color on the fairy's face.

Tip

To remove "freckles" of wax buildup without compromising the surrounding color, use a sharp white point to nudge the speck off the paper.

Step 10 To create the fairy's eyes, redraw the basic shape with a sharp graphite pencil. Line the rims with black and fill in the pupils, and then color the irises with marine green and cobalt turquoise. Remember to always work around the highlights, bringing them out using a sharp white pencil. Tone down the whites of the eyes with a light layer of cloud blue and use rosy beige for the inside corners. To color the lips, outline them with terra cotta and fill them in using pink. Darken with sienna brown and smooth with white.

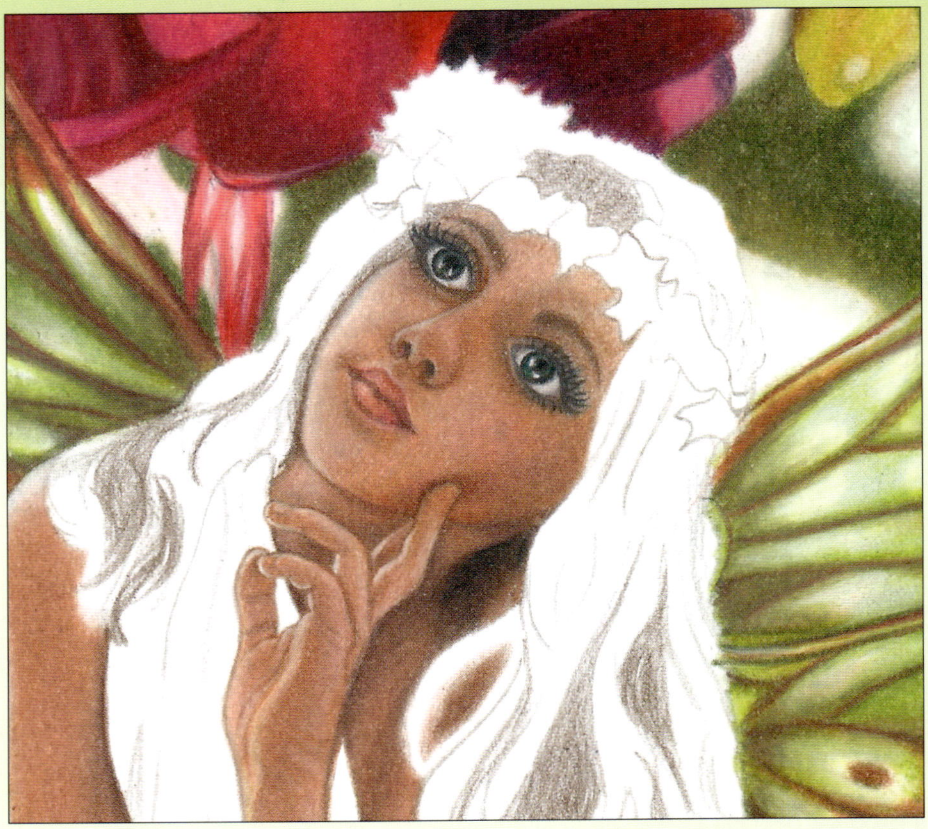

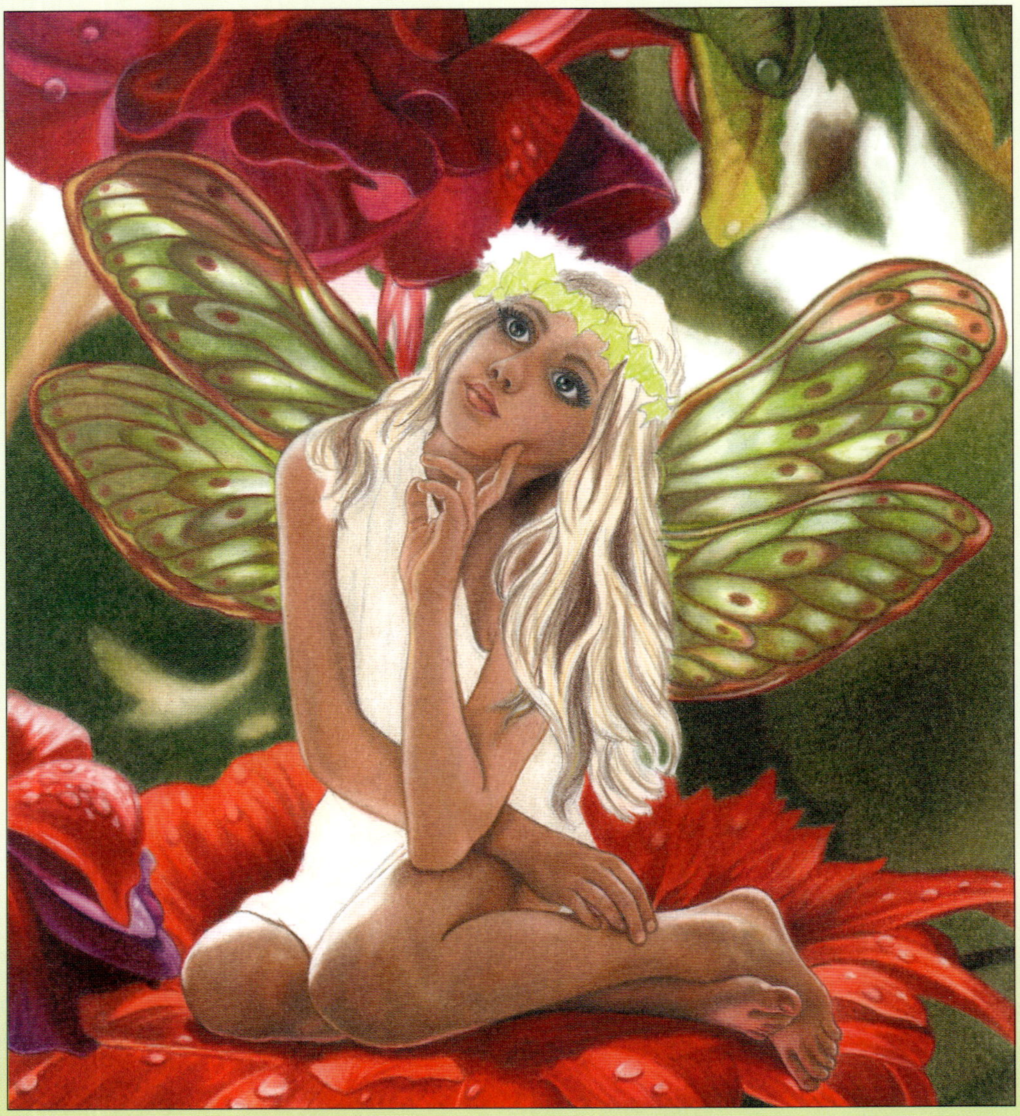

Step 11 Create the fairy's light hair color using beige and cream, adding strokes of burnt ochre, light umber, yellow ochre, and dark umber for dimension. Begin the garland of leaves with chartreuse. For the legs and feet, apply sienna brown, chocolate, and henna, avoiding the lightest areas. Burnish with white for a smooth, blended texture, and then continue to build up the color. For the brownish red areas, use terra cotta; for the shadows, use dark umber and a bit of black. Use crimson red and white to create reflected light from the flower. Using medium pressure, layer peach over the fairy's dress, followed by cream over the lower portion.

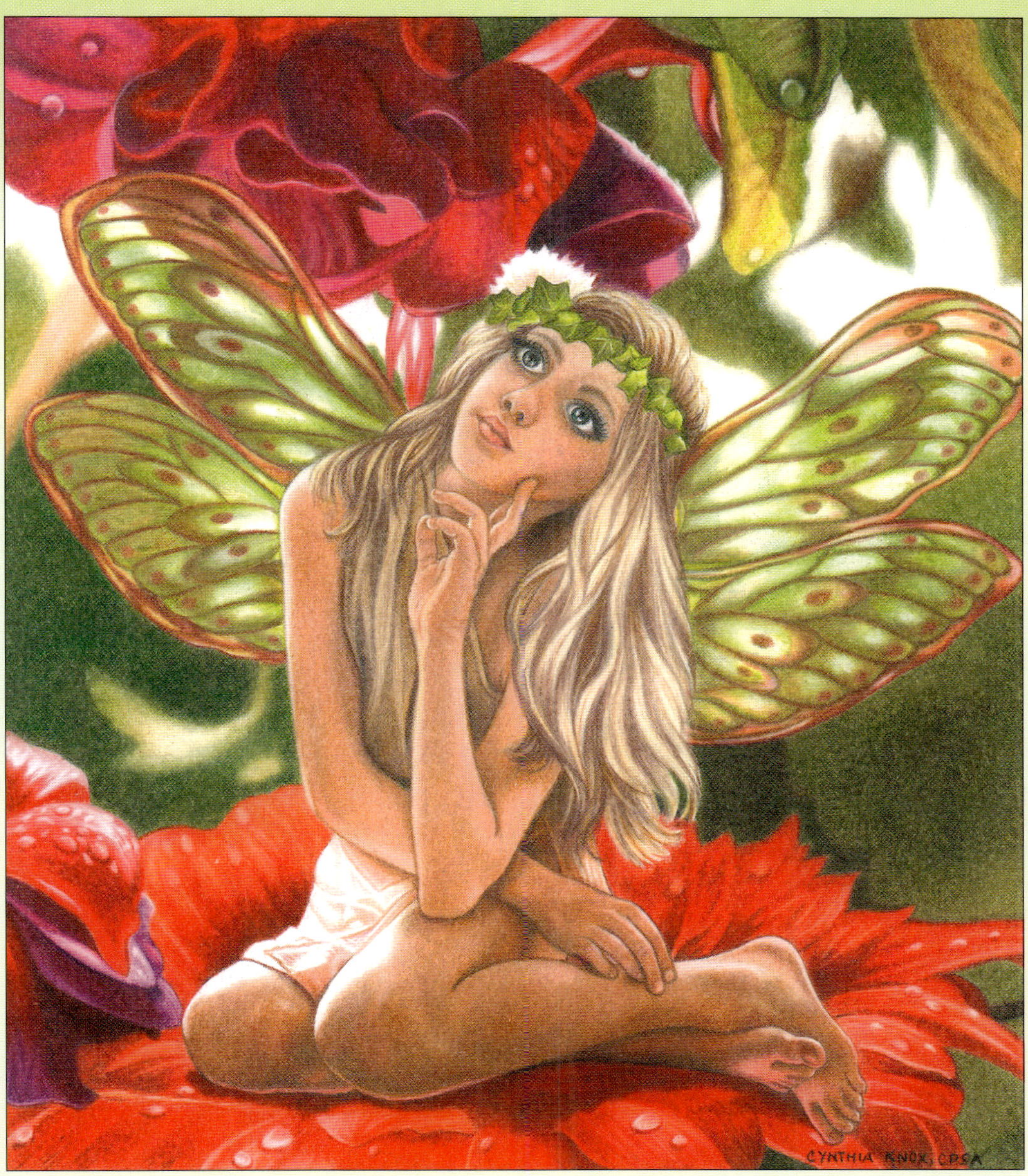

Step 12 Finish the fairy's hair with sweeping strokes of browns and yellows blended with cream. Retrieve the darks using dark umber and dark brown. Apply marine green and black over the garland of leaves for depth, followed by marine green and chartreuse to bring out the brightest areas. Use a sharp chartreuse point for the veins on the dark leaves and marine green on the light leaves. For the dress, use a similar process as you did to complete the hair. Block in the darks with dark umber and the lights with peach beige and chocolate. Blend often for a soft, silky look. Map out the skirt with peach and build color using burnt ochre, yellow ochre, and Tuscan red. Burnish hard with white to capture the light.

Tip

To finish your drawings, wipe away any wax bloom with a soft cloth and spray your work with workable fixative.

Water Fairy

with Cynthia Knox

WATER FAIRIES ARE CONSIDERED "ELEMENTAL" FAIRIES, which are associated with earth, fire, air, or water. This project involves a lovely water fairy in a misty, ethereal lake environment. In this monochromatic composition, the challenge is in creating background depth and a misty, sparkly glow. In addition to the pencils below, you'll need Chinese white watercolor paint, a small brush, and a cup of water.

50% cool gray	Black	Blue violet lake	Blush pink	Cream	Dark brown	Dark umber	Henna	Imperial violet
Light peach	Light umber	Nectar	Peach	Sienna brown	Ultramarine	Violet	Violet blue	White

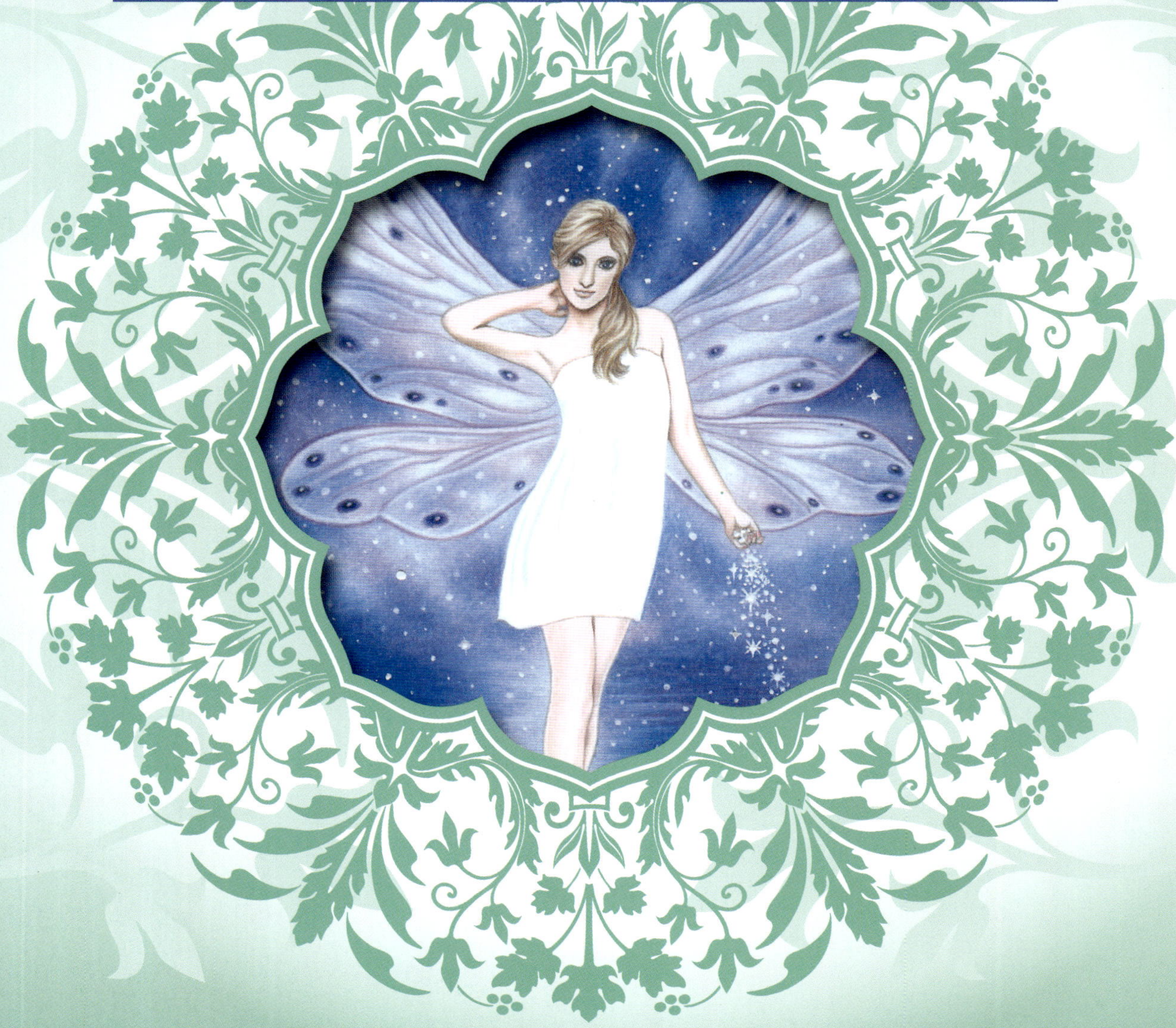

Sketch Outline the fairy, wings, and rock with a soft graphite pencil such as HB or B. These leads erase well and are less likely to leave indented, hard lines on the paper. Sketch with a light hand so you can erase or diminish the lines before adding color. (To transfer the template for this project, see page 121.)

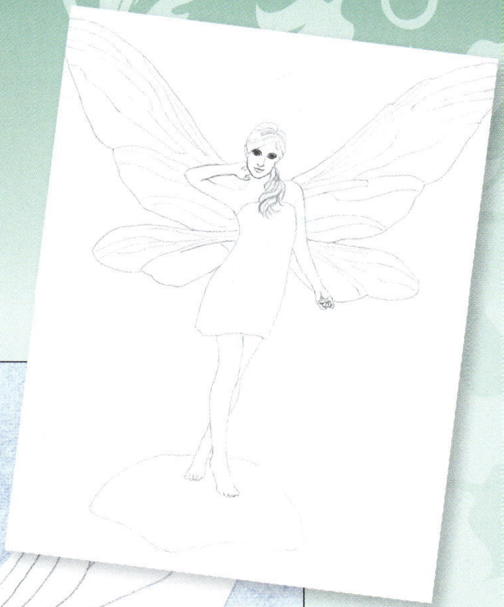

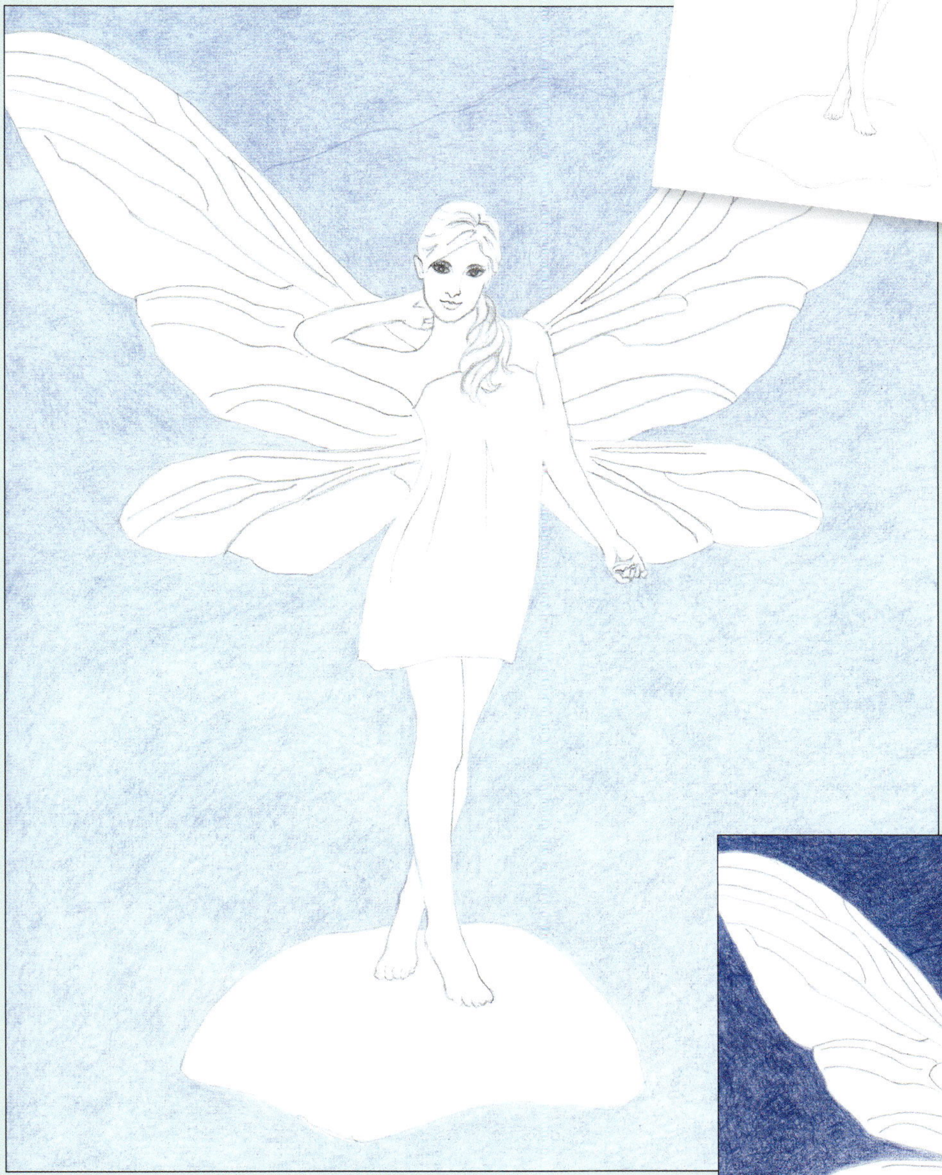

Step 1 This dominant, richly colored background will require much of your attention. Begin by shading the background with blue violet lake using moderate pressure and small, elliptical strokes, which will establish a foundation for lights and darks in later steps. The elliptical strokes will create a smooth background without any obvious lines.

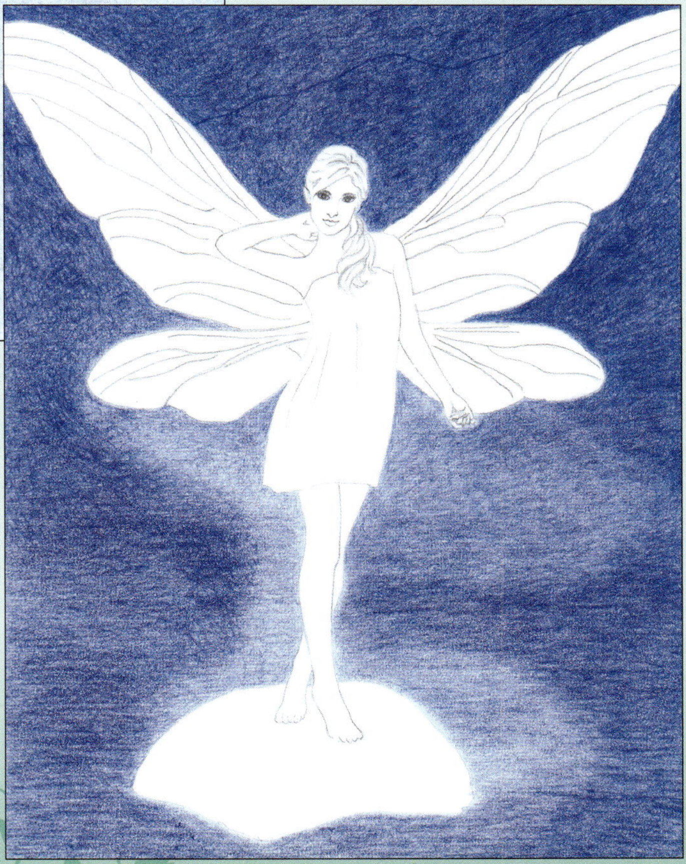

Step 2 Continue shading the background with a layer of ultramarine, followed by a second layer over the darker sections. Stroke horizontally over the lower half to suggest rippling of water. Then layer violet blue over the entire background, using a softer touch in the lighter areas.

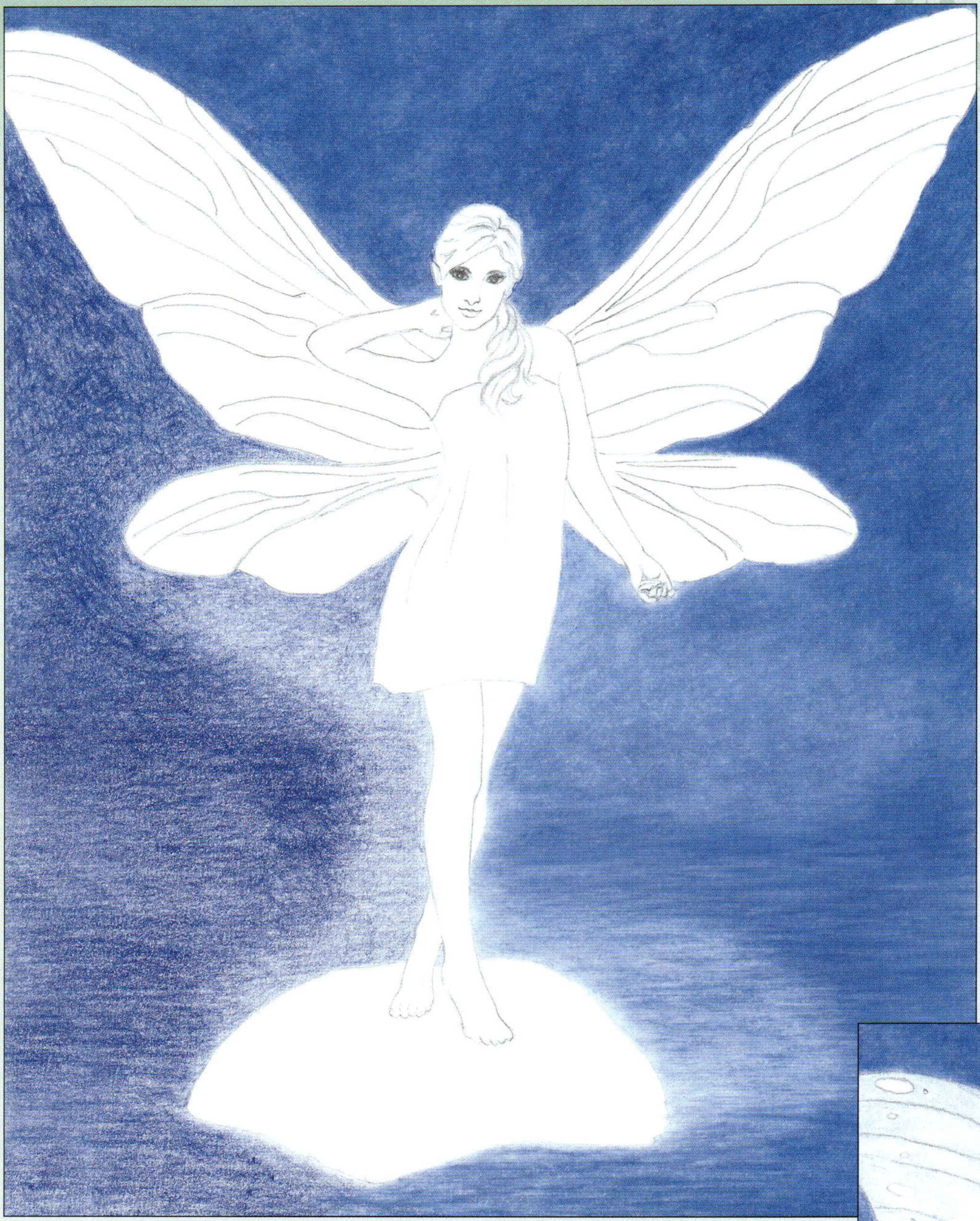

Step 3 Burnish the background with white, using firm pressure and small, elliptical strokes for the upper half and horizontal strokes for the lower half. This process "melts" the underlying colors together as it flattens the paper tooth, yielding a polished, sleek surface. Remember: Using a dull, angled point for burnishing is less likely to break or leave behind harsh lines than using a sharp point.

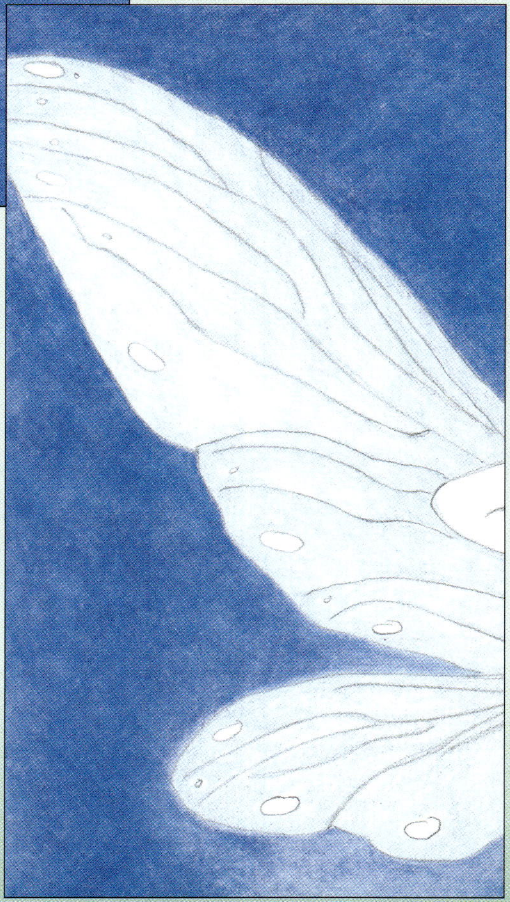

Detail Add round and elliptical shapes near the edges of the wings with a B or HB graphite pencil. Lightly color the wings with a layer of blue violet lake, using a sharp point and gentle pressure. Angle the strokes diagonally to follow the direction of the shapes. Apply color directly over the graphite lines, leaving elliptical shapes white for now.

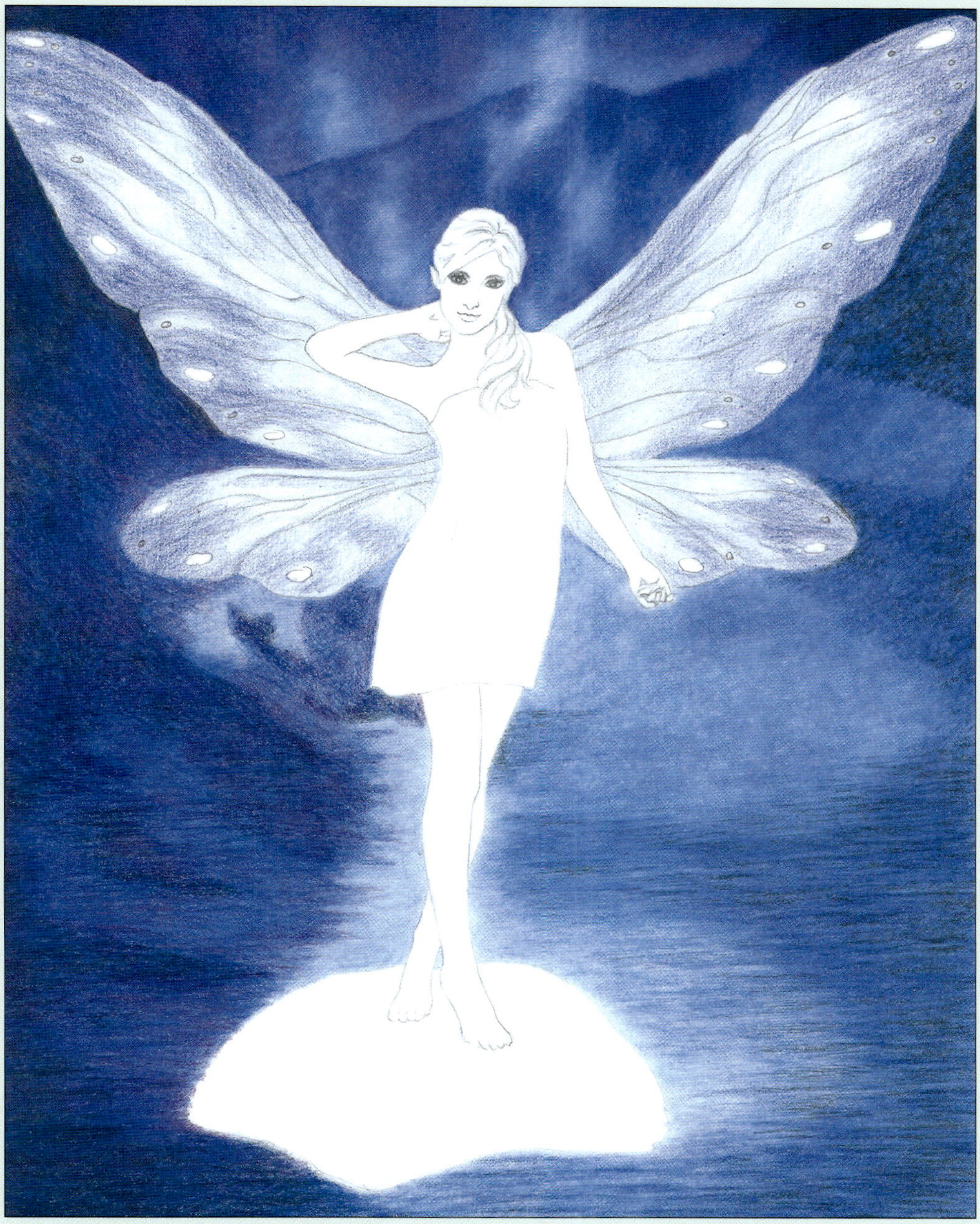

Step 4 Apply a layer of black over the deepest values, using moderate pressure and small, elliptical strokes for the top half and horizontal strokes for the bottom half. Now, over the black, apply coats of violet, violet blue, and ultramarine. (Shown here is the black layer alone (right) followed by the violets and blues (left) so you can see the progress.) Now develop the mountain and mist in the upper section. Using black and purple pencils, add the mountain range and sky. Blend the light sections with a white pencil and firm pressure. On the wings, block in darker sections using ultramarine and moderate pressure.

Tip

Keep the fairy as clean and white as possible. Brush away all pencil debris frequently, and keep a white sheet of paper underneath your drawing hand. Use a ball of adhesive mounting putty to lift embedded crumbs, and use an artist's eraser to remove colored pencil smudges.

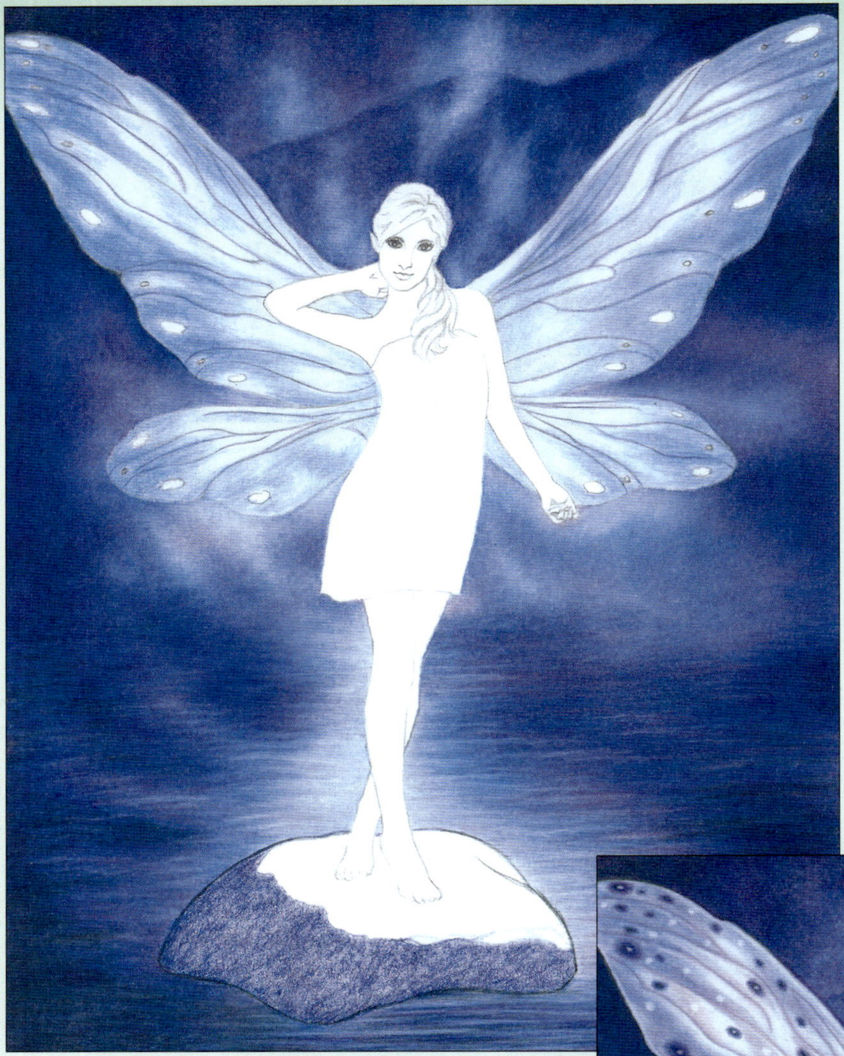

Step 5 Develop the background with violet, violet blue, and ultramarine. Build the color so that the background is darkest near the edges of the composition and lightest toward the center, drawing the viewer's eyes to the fairy. Beginning at the top and working your way down, blend white over the lighter sections with an angled, dull point. To create water ripples, draw thin lines with a sharp white point and blend lightly into the surrounding colors. Then use a sharp black point and light pressure to darken and add dimension to the edges. Burnish the color on the wings with white, lightly adding imperial violet over the graphite lines. Outlines the rock with black, and color the darkest portion with violet blue followed by ultramarine.

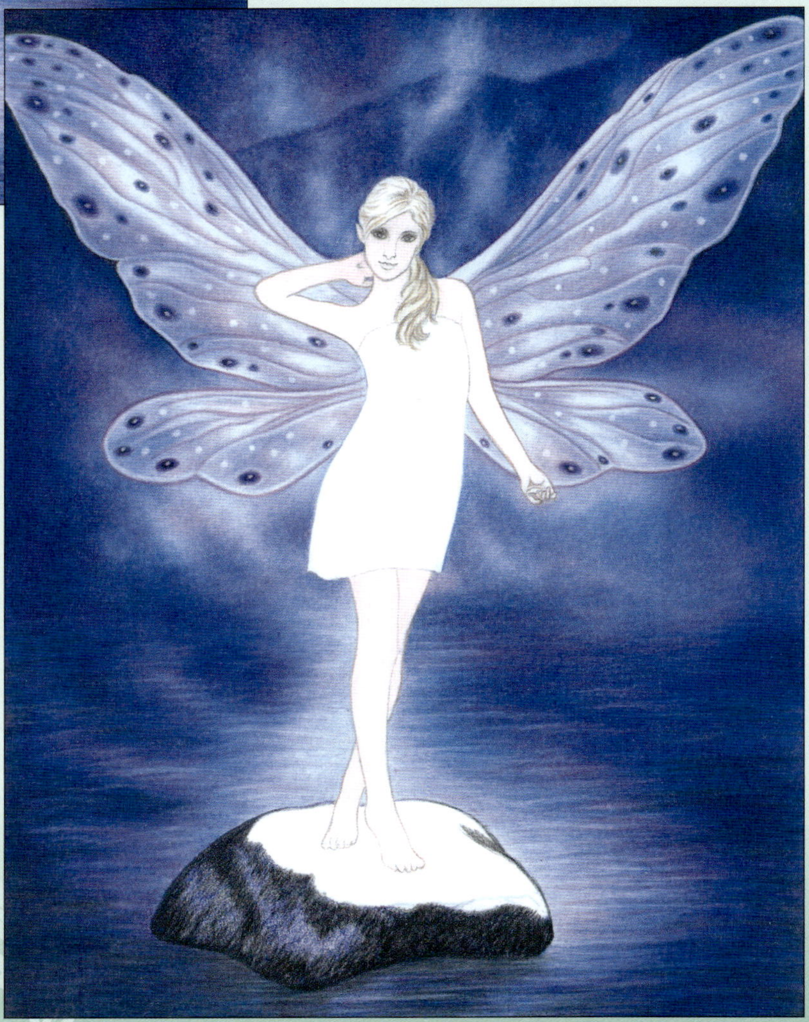

Step 6 Apply violet over the blue sections of the wings, burnishing with white to blend. Fill in the wing spots with violet followed by ultramarine and white, adding a few more spots where desired. In the larger markings, add a soft touch of black in the centers, followed by a tiny dot of white. Line the interior of the wings using a sharp white point for dimension, and outline them with violet or black. Cover the graphite lines with violet and blend with white. Finish the wings by adding dots of white. Then add black to the rock and to the water below it, suggesting a reflection.

Detail Lightly outline her arms and legs with nectar. Fill in her skin with light peach followed by blush pink, using extremely light pressure. Then lightly layer her hair with cream, and block in dark strands with light umber. Cover the dress with an initial layer of white, using firm pressure and small, elliptical strokes.

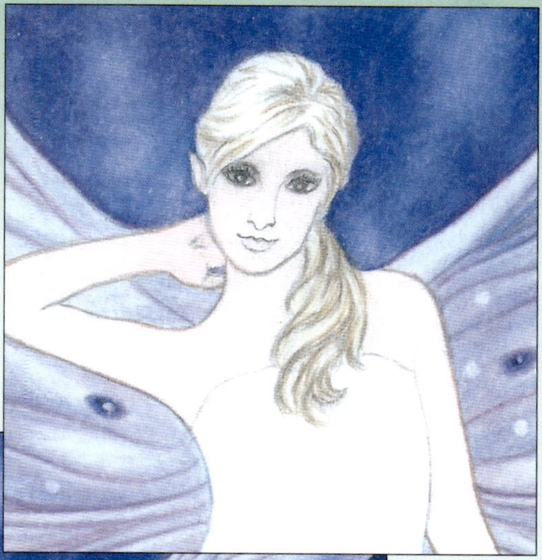

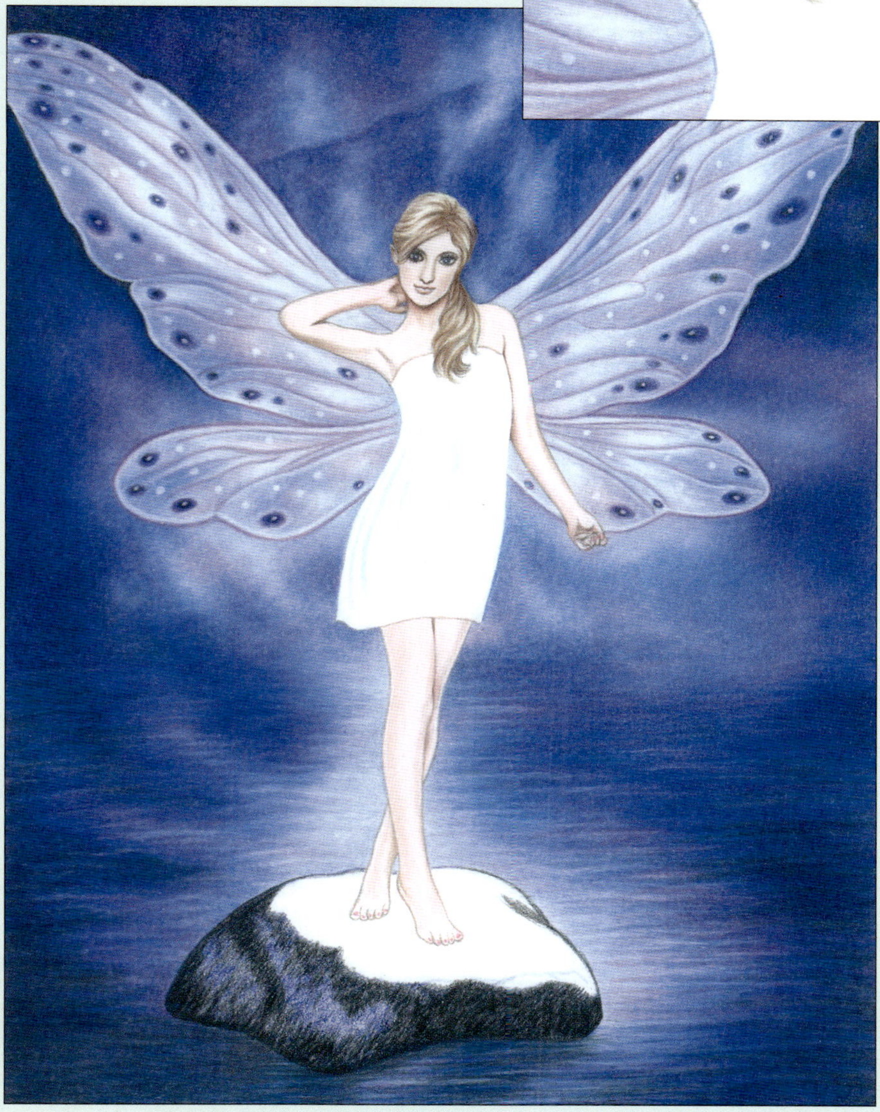

Step 7 Bring out the fairy's skin using light peach in the lightest areas, peach in the darkest areas, and nectar and henna for the reddish-pink areas. Add shadows using light umber and dark brown, and blend with white or light peach. For the fairy's face, begin with a coat of light peach, and use light umber, nectar, and henna to form the cheeks. Develop the lips with henna and dark brown, and sculpt the nose with light umber and nectar. Blend and transition with light peach. Use dark umber to accent the darks of her eyebrows and eyes. Develop the hair with sienna brown, cream, and dark umber, blending with cream for smooth transitions. Now outline the dress with nectar. Then add folds with 50% cool gray followed by blue violet lake, burnishing with white to blend and blur.

Tip

Use sharp pencils while working on the fairy's face, as this involves very small areas!

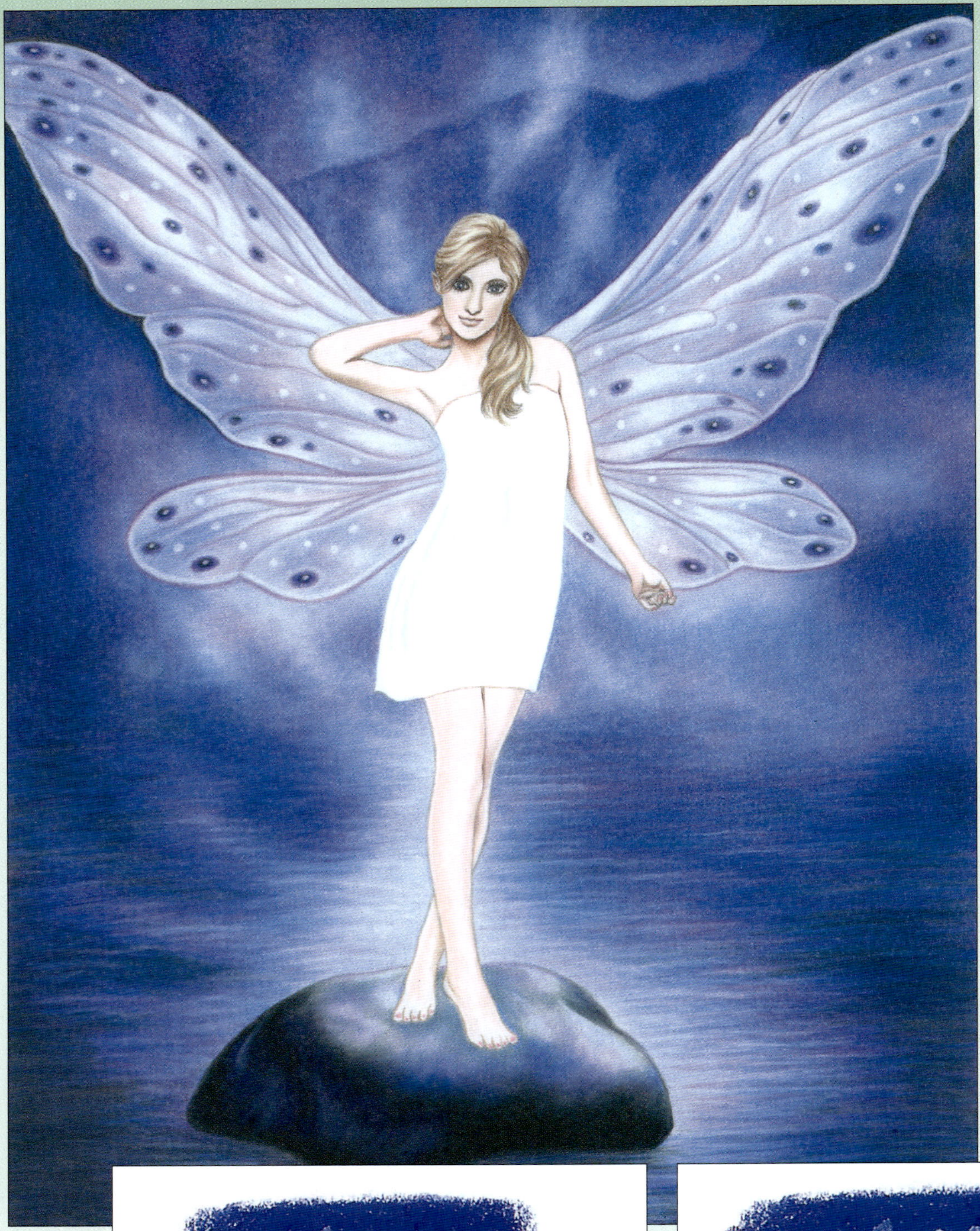

Step 8 Finish the rock with a very light layer of black on top, leaving a few areas white. Then coat the rock's top with violet blue. Follow this with a layer of violet over the entire rock, using less pressure for light areas and more for dark areas. Burnish the darkest areas with black, and burnish the top of the rock with white, blending for a smooth finish. When working near the feet, use sharp points and gentle pressure to give yourself greater control. To tone down overly white areas, use blue violet lake.

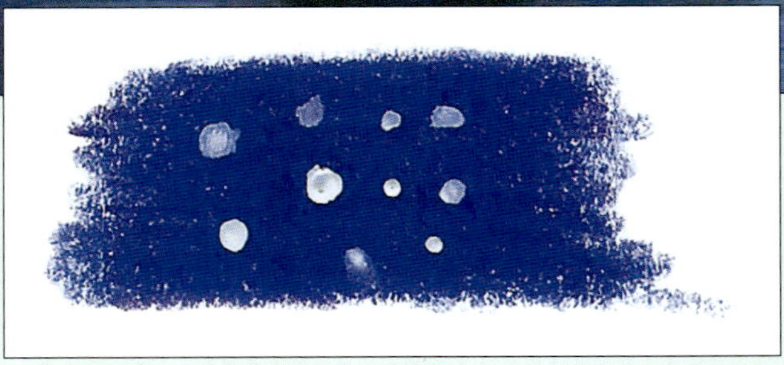

To create fairy dust, use the tip of a fine-pointed brush to dot on diluted Chinese white watercolor. Create randomly sized dots, and vary the brightness of your dots for dimension, fading some into the background. For brighter dots, apply a second dot of paint to the centers.

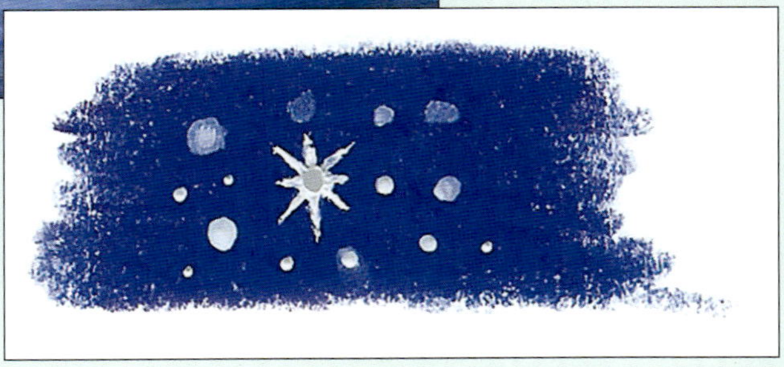

To create a starred effect, use your brush to slowly pull out vertical and horizontal lines. If necessary, you can diminish some of the dots, simply wait for them to dry and stroke over them with ultramarine.

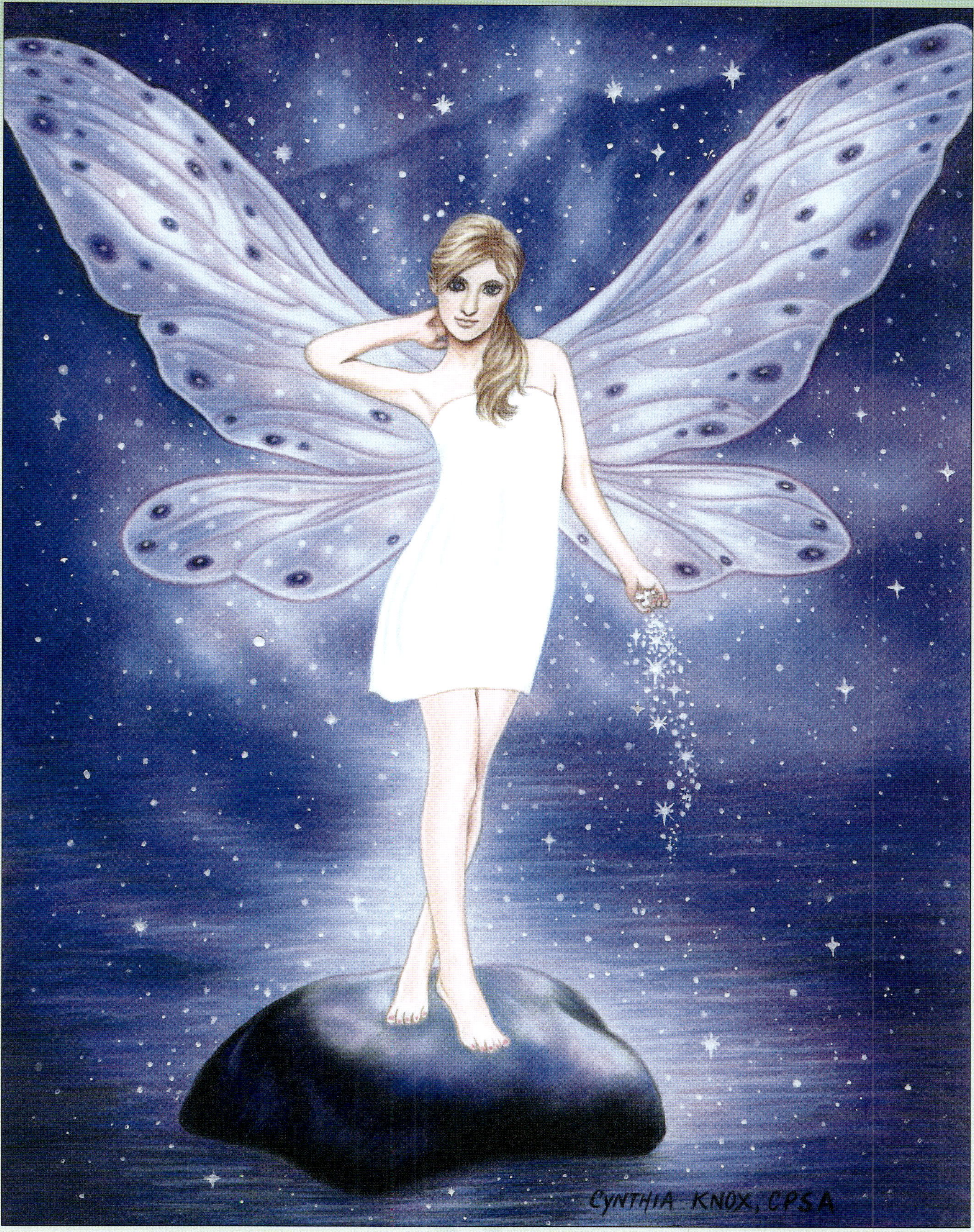

Step 9 To finish, check your composition for any edges that need to be defined or cleaned up, sign your name, and spray with workable fixative.

Fire Fairy

with Cynthia Knox

FIRE FAIRIES ARE COLORFUL, EXOTIC, AND MYSTERIOUS. This project involves bright reds and yellows that highlight the fairy's translucent wings and glowing gown. The flames against the black backdrop create dramatic contrast and a striking composition. In addition to the pencils below, you'll need Chinese white and Naples yellow watercolor paints, along with a small brush and a cup of water.

Black	Canary yellow	Chocolate	Dark brown	Dark umber	Deco yellow	Goldenrod	Henna	Jasmine	Light peach
Light umber	Mineral orange	Nectar	Peach	Sienna brown	Terra cotta	Tuscan red	White	Yellow ochre	Yellowed orange

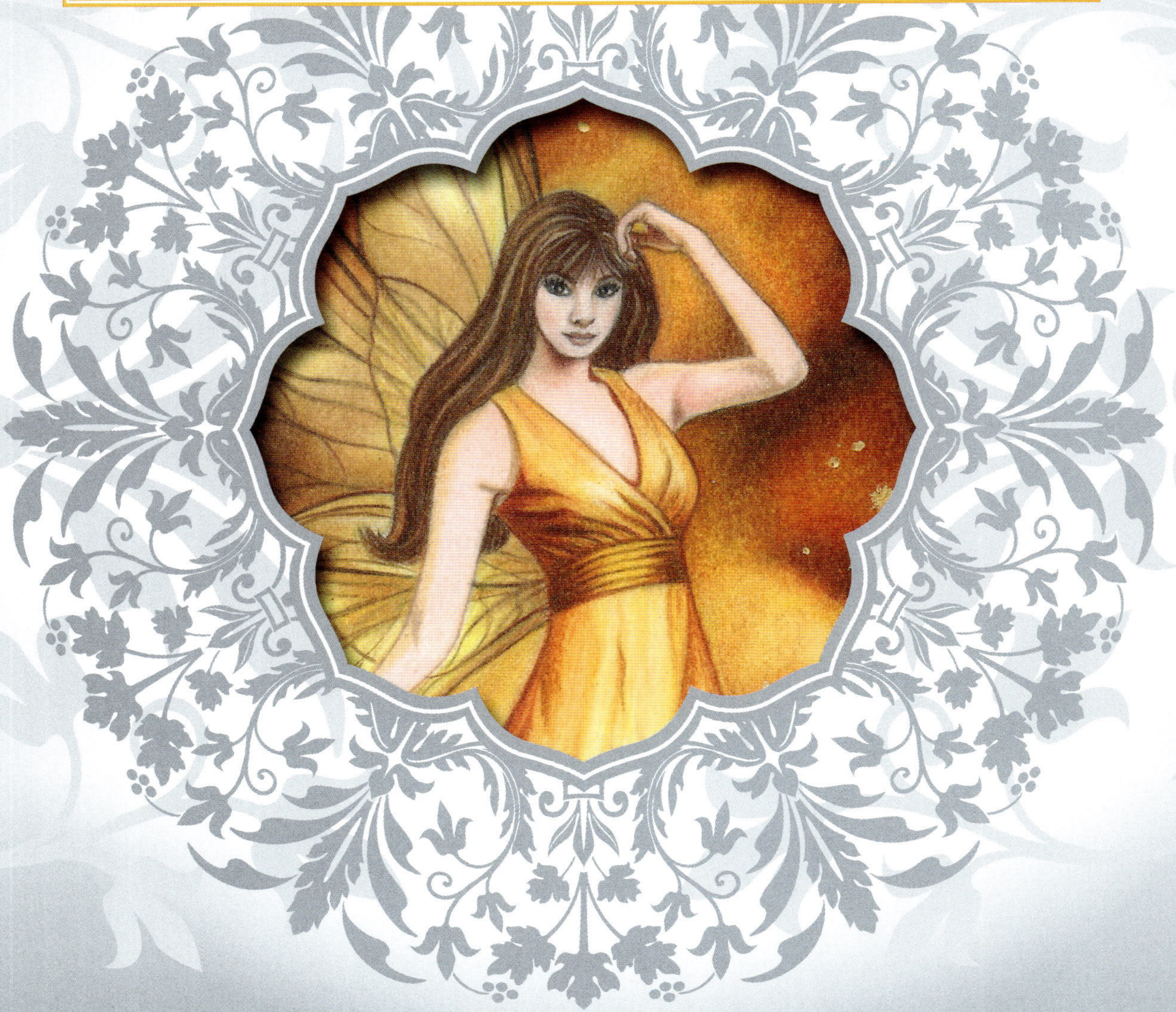

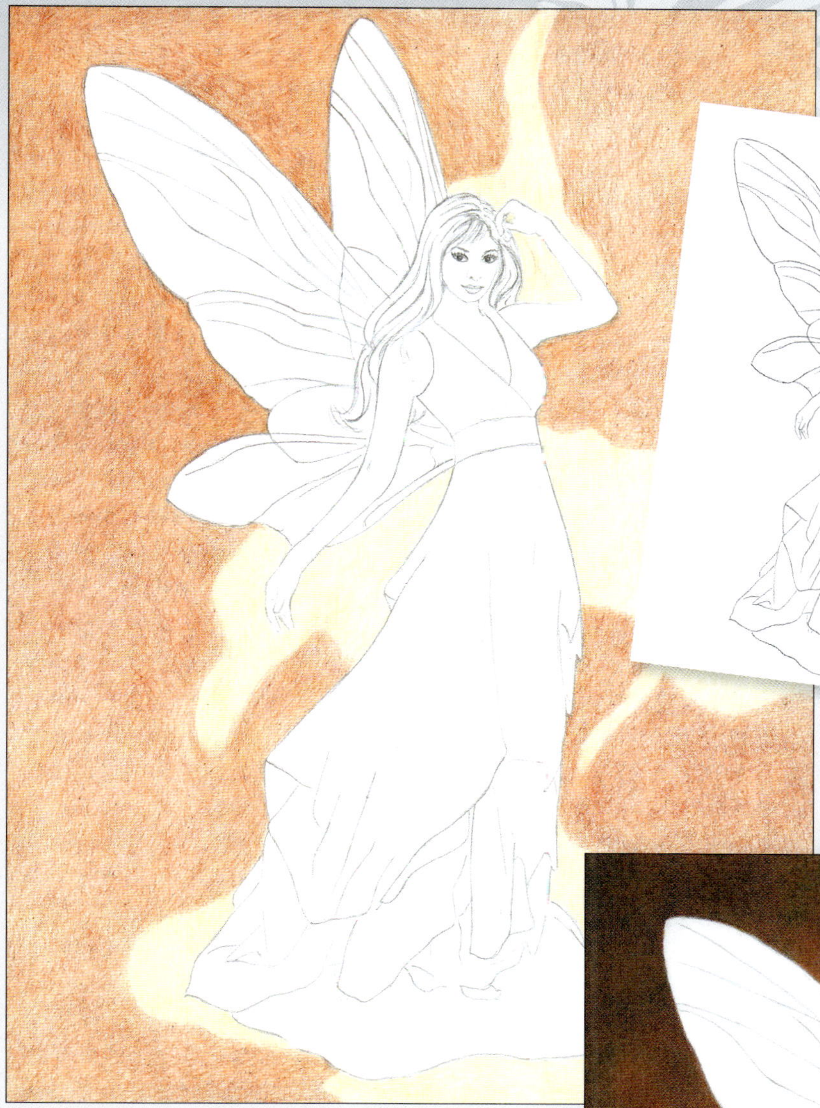

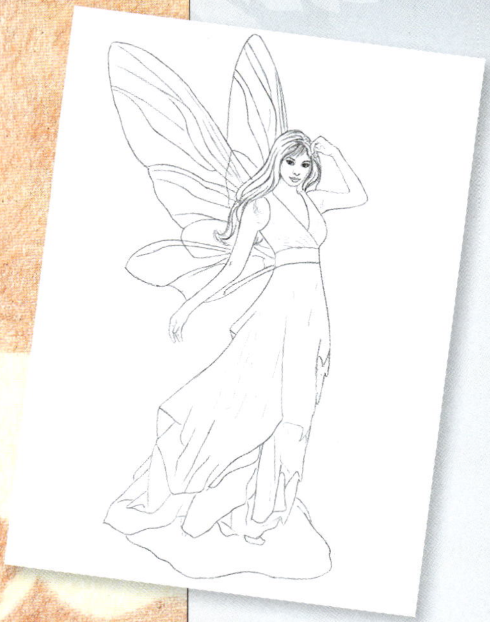

SKETCH Lightly sketch this fairy with a medium-soft graphite pencil (B or HB lead). These lines will easily erase as you add color. (To transfer the template for this project, see page 122.)

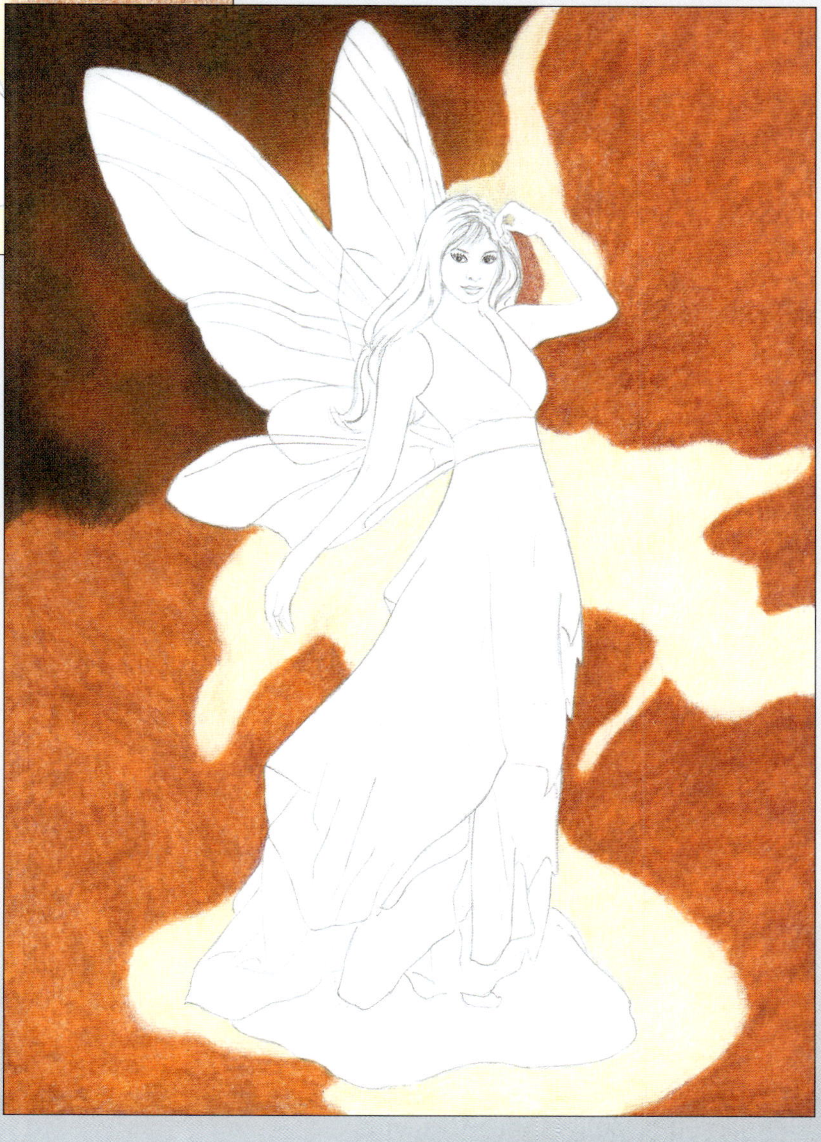

STEP 1 Apply a basecoat of jasmine to the entire background using moderate pressure and small, elliptical strokes. Follow this with a layer of terra cotta over most of the jasmine, leaving the three curved shapes alone for now.

STEP 2 Add Tuscan red and terra cotta, using firm pressure and small, elliptical strokes. This completes three layers of color—the number of layers preferred before burnishing for a painterly surface. Burnish with yellowed orange using an angled, dull point. Beginning in the upper left corner, complete the background section by section. Use black for the borders, dark umber for the dark brown areas, sienna brown to transition the darks into the oranges, and canary yellow to lighten. Blend and blur the colors together.

Tip

Small, waxy blips may emerge while blending and burnishing. To eliminate them, use the sharp point of a similarly colored pencil to apply horizontal or vertical strokes. This both blends and lifts the excess wax.

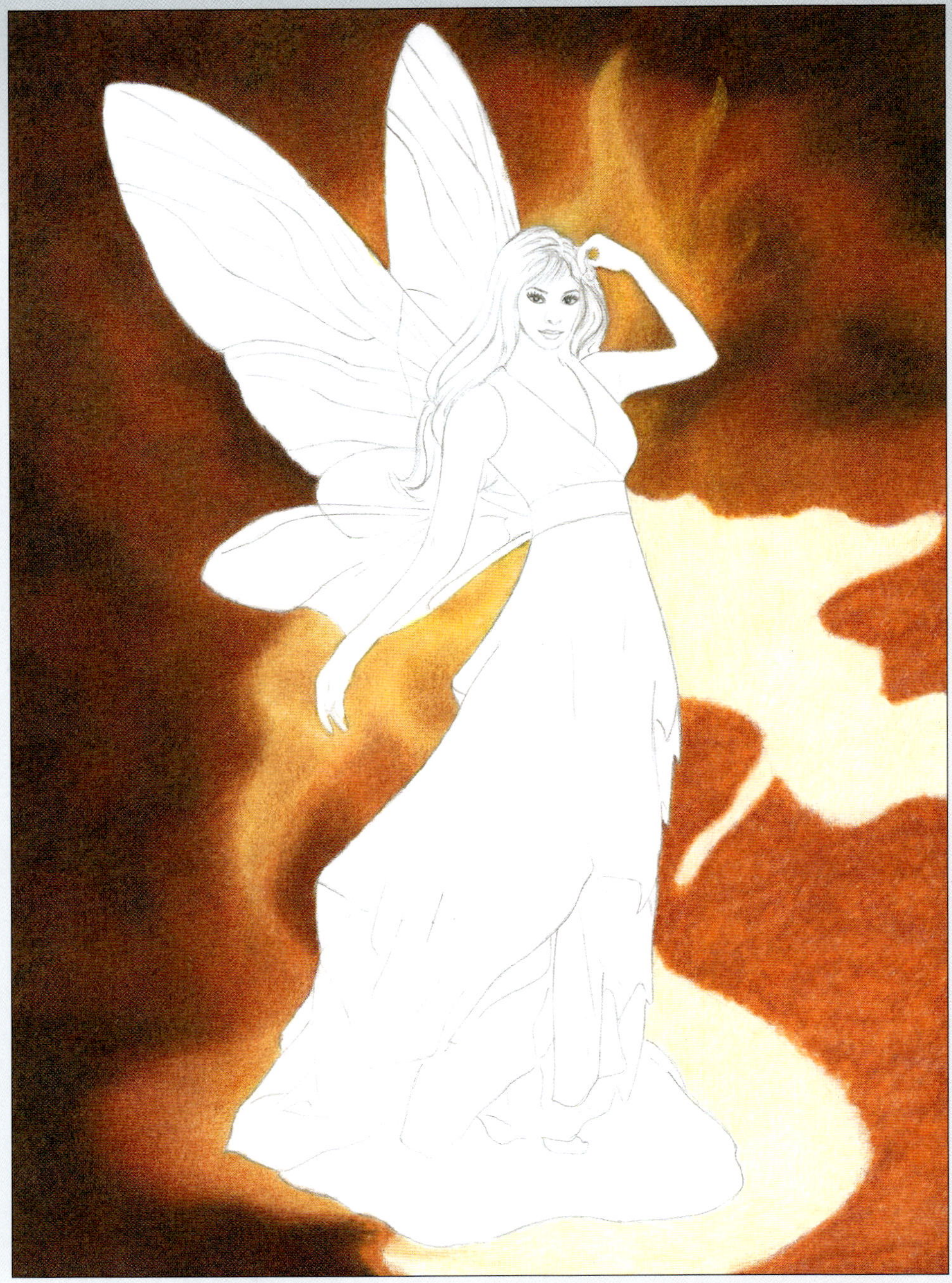

Step 3 Continue rendering the background at left. Lightly block in the darkest sections with black and color with medium pressure, followed by a layer of dark umber. Then use sienna brown to blend and blur the browns into the blacks. Also add Tuscan red and terra cotta to develop the red hues. Reduce the size of the top flame and fill it in with terra cotta, Tuscan red, and yellowed orange. Add black over the dark background. Begin to cover the pale yellow sections with yellow ochre and lightly add areas of sienna brown for depth. Blend down your strokes with canary yellow, extending into the surrounding areas. Begin developing the background on the right in the same manner.

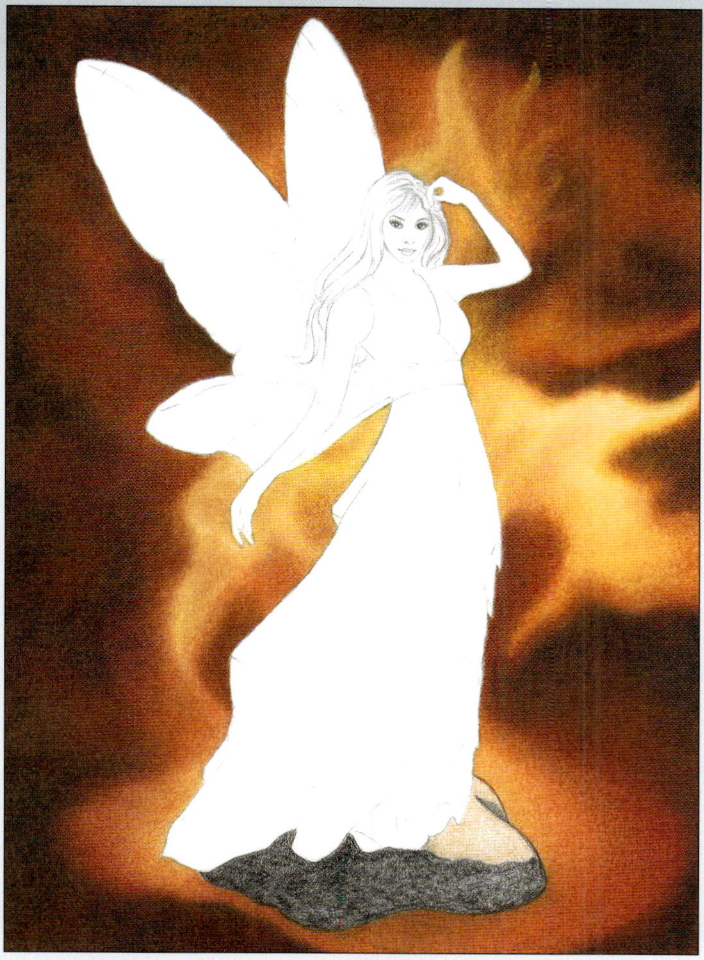

Step 4 In this step, perform a lot of back-and-forth blending within the background. Layer dark umber and black for the darks, along with sienna brown and dark umber for the midtones. Bring out the reds with terra cotta and Tuscan red. Then layer canary yellow and terra cotta over the yellow sections, burnishing the flame at right with white. Begin the rock by applying a coat of black, avoiding the top right. Use mineral orange to glaze an initial coat of color over this highlight. Now erase most of the graphite outlining the fairy.

Tip

If color isn't adhering well to a sleek surface, change the direction of your pencil strokes and use less pressure.

Step 5 Begin layering the fairy's gown with a coat of jasmine, followed by goldenrod and canary yellow. Block in the folds and shadows with terra cotta. Moving on to the wings, apply two layers of deco yellow with small, elliptical strokes and moderate pressure. Use chocolate and dark umber to block in the dark sections of the wings. Use black to outline the borders of the wings. To complete the rock, apply another layer of black, burnishing with chocolate. For the light area, apply chocolate and burnishes of white and yellow ochre.

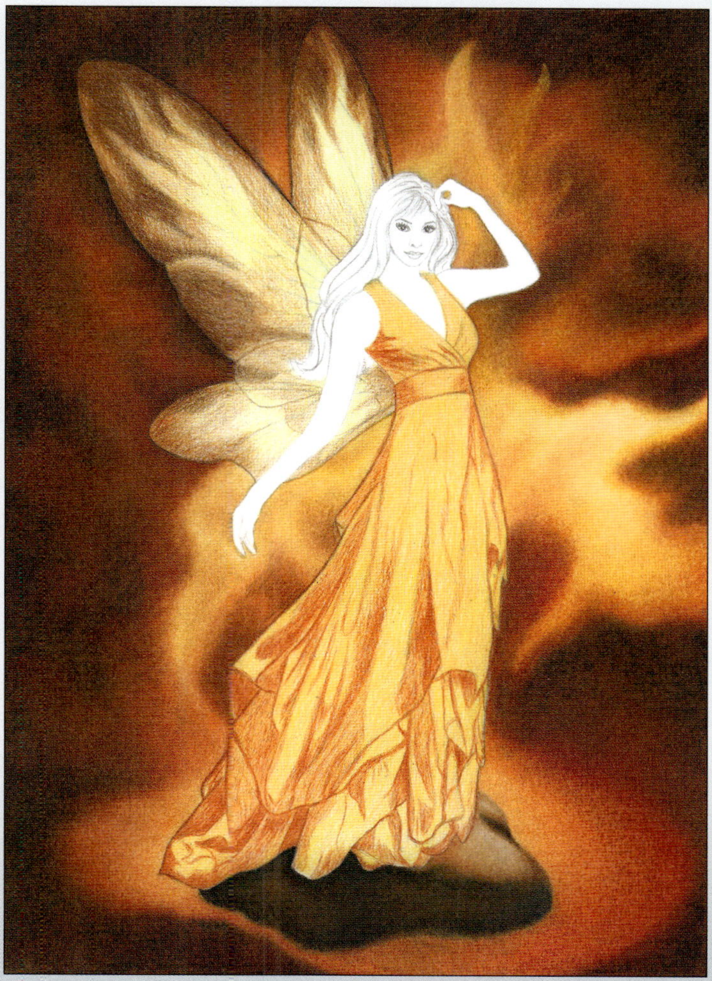

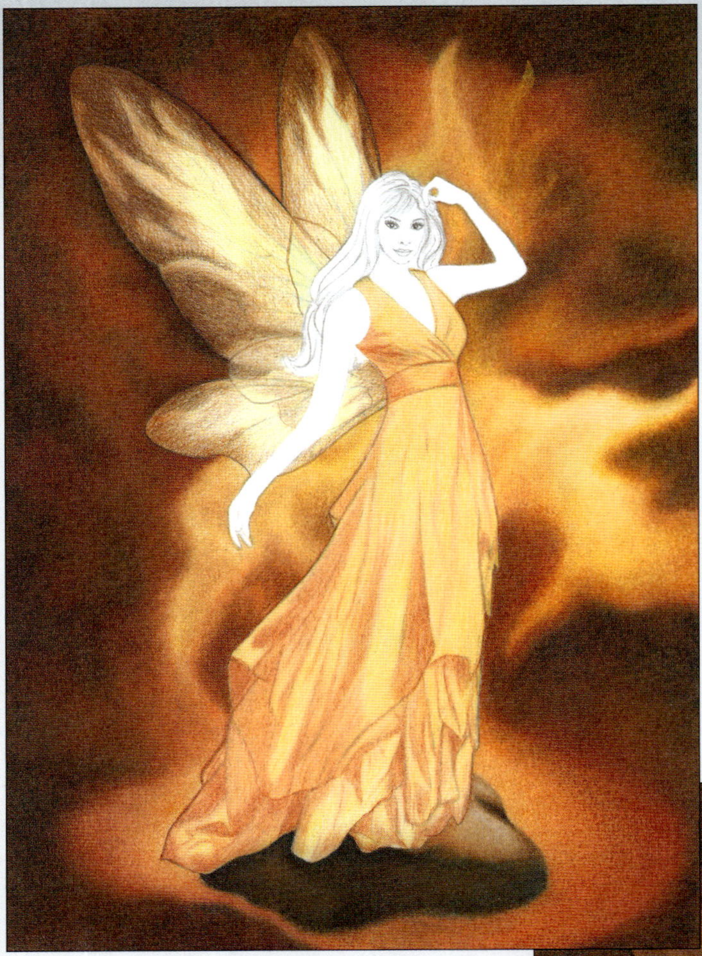

Step 6 Next, burnish the entire gown with white, using firm pressure and small strokes. Blend the reddish brown folds and shadows into the yellow of the dress. While this may appear to overly lighten the gown, it is establishing a sleek, polished surface upon which you can restore color.

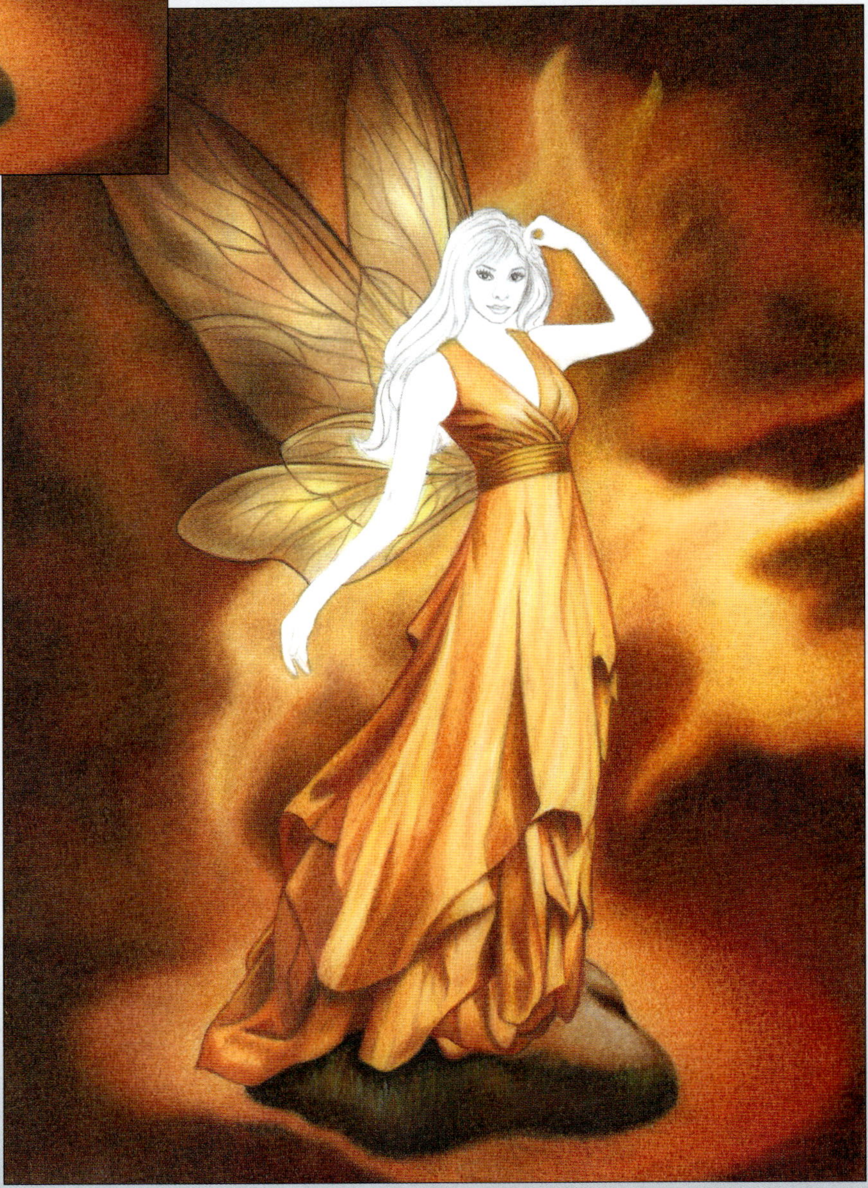

Step 7 Over the newly burnished gown, return some color and apply details using terra cotta, dark umber, and Tuscan red. Use black only in the darkest shadows. For the brightest areas, use yellowed orange and canary yellow. Use white to "erase" mistakes and highlight a few strips of yellow. Next, further develop the wings with a layer of deco yellow and follow up with a burnish of white. Apply black in the dark upper section using a sharp point, moderate pressure, and small, elliptical strokes. Block in the darks with black, Tuscan red, and dark umber. Then layer yellow ochre over everything else, blending with deco yellow or white. For the reddish brown hues, use terra cotta and chocolate. Also lightly apply dark vein lines using sharp dark umber and sienna brown points, followed by touches of black and Tuscan red. Then scribble vertical lines of canary yellow and terra cotta over the rock for a vague highlight.

STEP 8 Use a small eraser to clean up all the smudges from the fairy's skin and hair, lightly erasing most of her jawline. Apply a light layer of light peach, followed by peach over her skin and lips. Apply more pressure with the peach over the armpit, elbow, and jawline, preparing them for darker shading. Begin the fairy's hair with a layer of jasmine to establish warm highlights within her brown hair. Block in the dark sections with dark brown, using moderate pressure and small strokes.

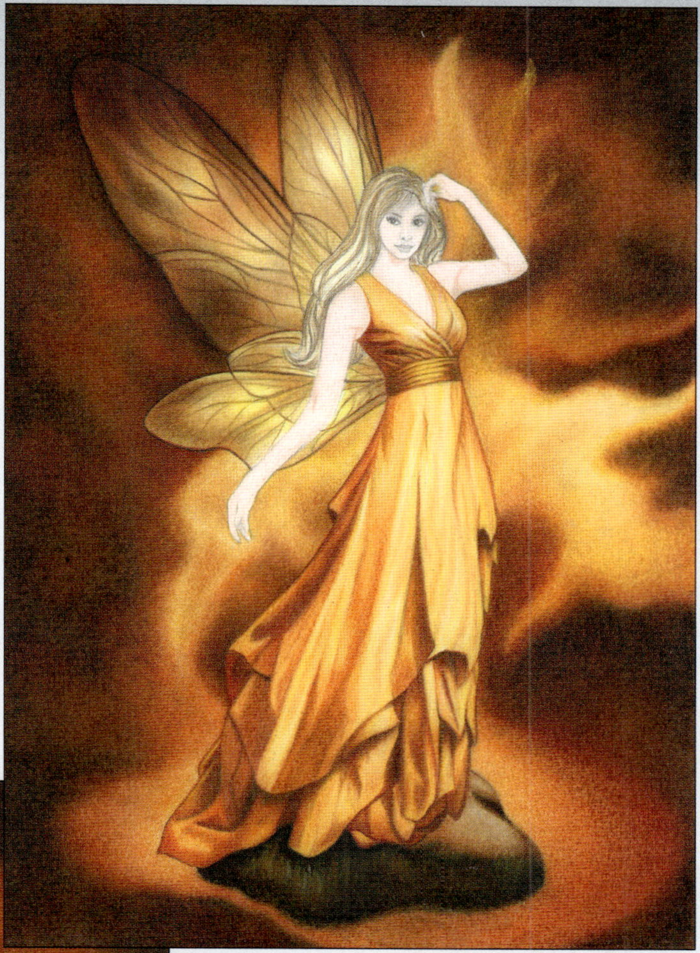

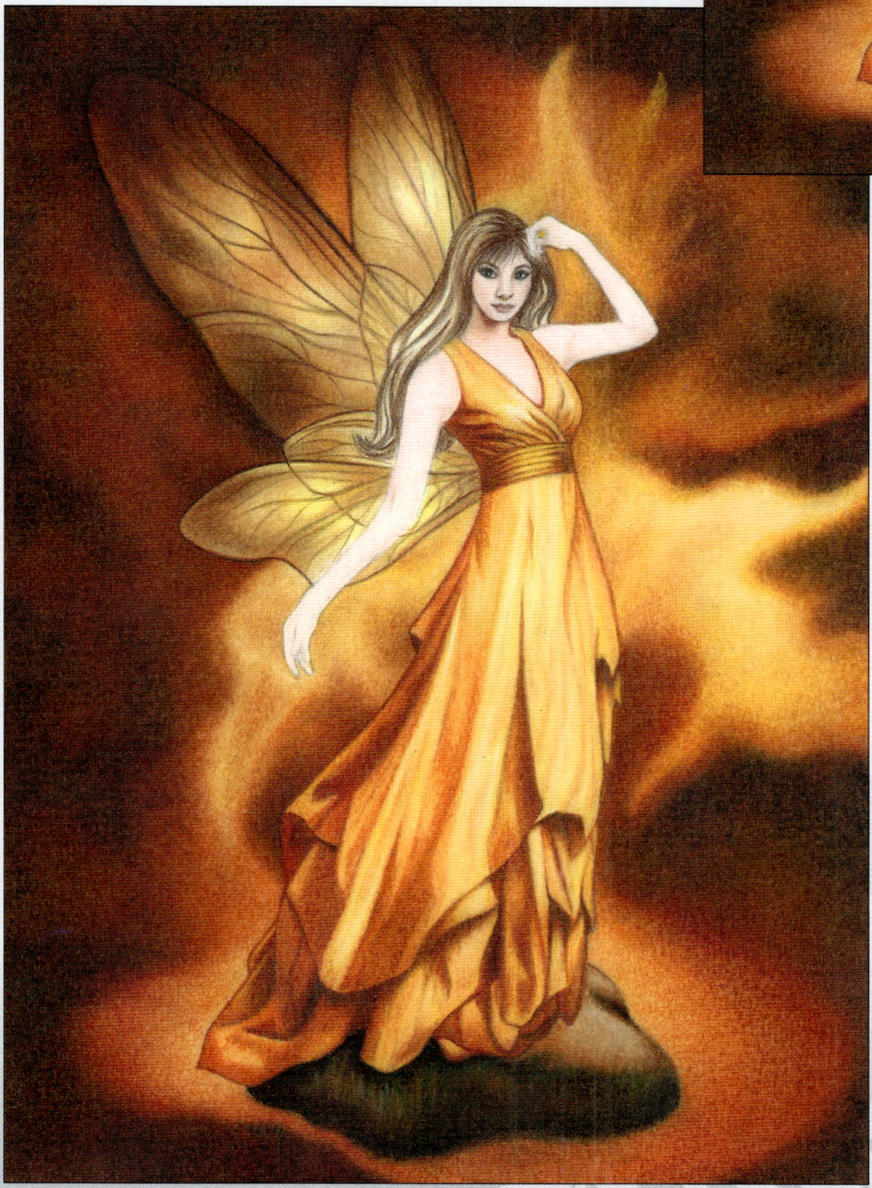

STEP 9 Blend the two skin colors using a sharp white pencil. Then render the fairy's face, adding a shadow under the chin with sienna brown. Build color density with dark umber and Tuscan red, blending outward and adding jasmine to reflect the yellow wings. Line the neck, collarbone, and neck of the gown with terra cotta. Accent with Tuscan red and blend everything into the chest with peach. Using a sharp black point, carefully line the eyelids and add nostrils. Use dark umber for the eyebrows, with a touch of sienna brown underneath. Shape the nose with sienna brown. Detail the mouth with dark umber and henna. Then contour the face with nectar and dark umber, blending it all down with light peach or white. Darken strands of hair with dark umber.

Tip

Layers of colored pencil wax can result in a film that rises to the surface. Called "wax bloom," this substance is not a threat to the image and can be wiped away with a soft cloth and moderate pressure. Wipe with small, circular strokes to replace the dull appearance with a soft shine.

Step 10 Develop the fairy's hair with sienna brown for the lights and black for the darks, blending with dark umber. Highlight thin streaks with white and add jasmine. To finish the arms, add peach and blend down with white for a smooth finish. Next, use sienna brown, light umber, and dark umber for the underarm and elbow shadows, adding henna for color and blending down with peach. Use the same process to complete the hands and fingers.

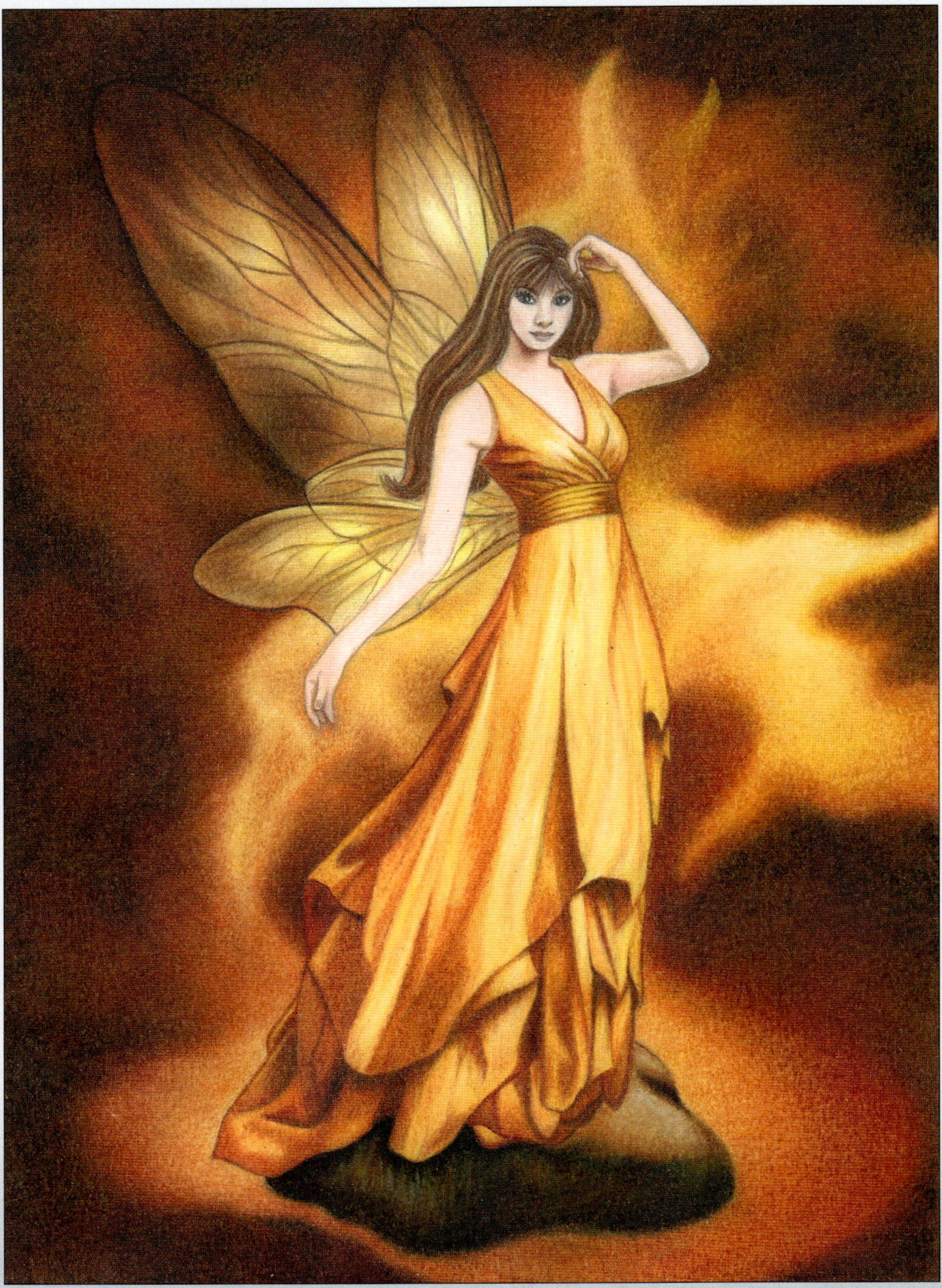

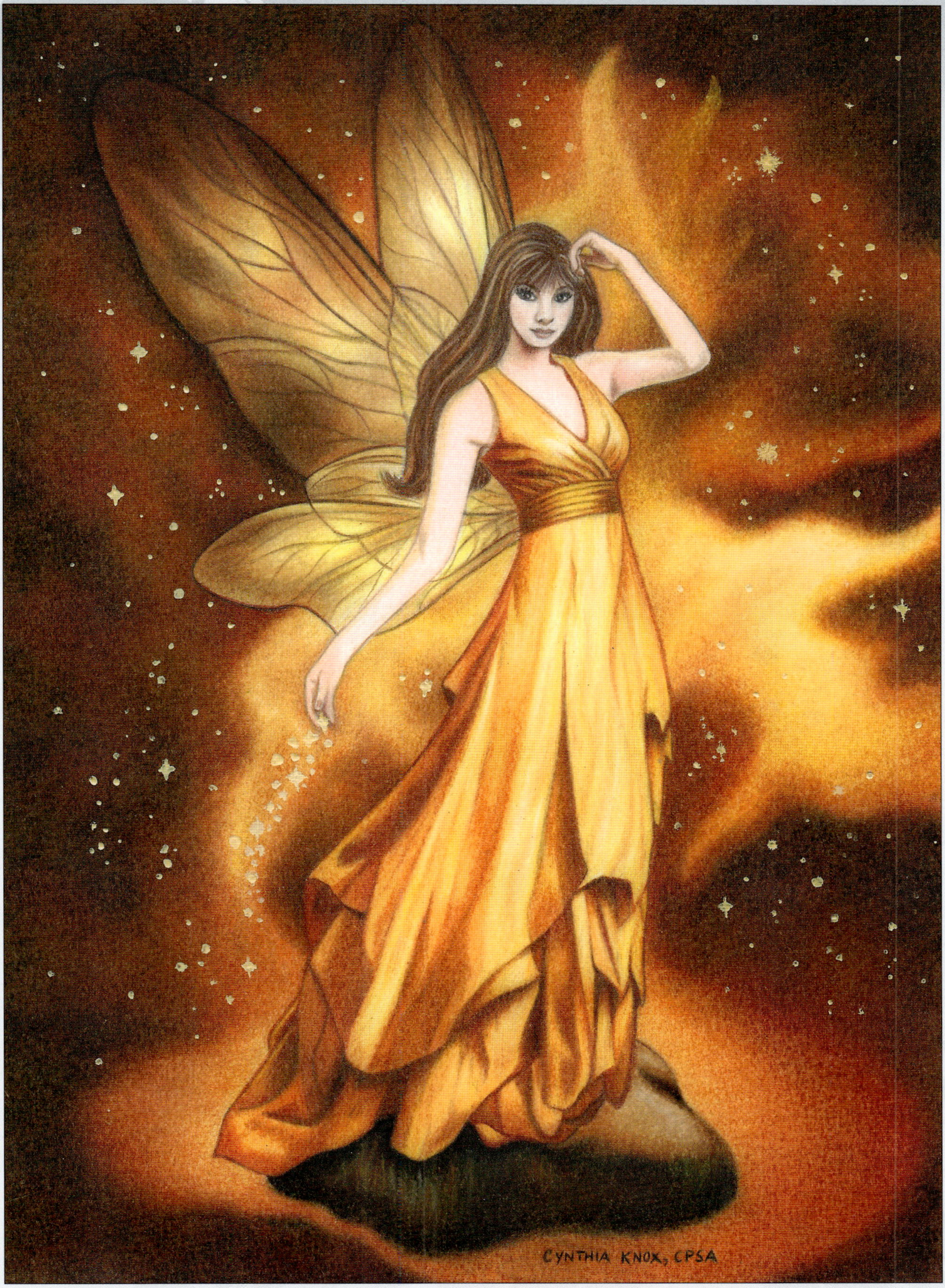

Step 11 To finish the piece, add some fairy magic by creating sparkle with light watercolor paint. Create a mix of Chinese white and Naples yellow, which has a warm, luminous hue. Then use a very fine, damp round brush to apply random dots over the artwork. To give some dots a starry look, pull the paint outward using the tip of the brush. Allow the project to dry, sign, and then spray with workable fixative.

Celestial Fairy

with Cynthia Knox

THIS PROJECT INVOLVES A LOVELY CELESTIAL FAIRY sprinkling moon dust into the night. The color palette of pinks and yellows is fairly simple, and the dark background helps the subject "pop." Learn how to create rich depth in the background, blur the moon to suggest distance, and render the fairy's delicate fabric and wings. In addition to the pencils below, you'll need Chinese white and Naples yellow watercolor paints, along with a small brush and a cup of water.

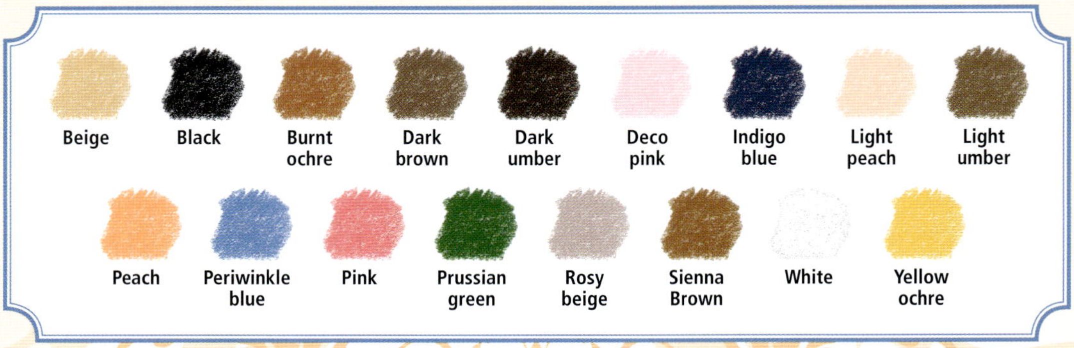

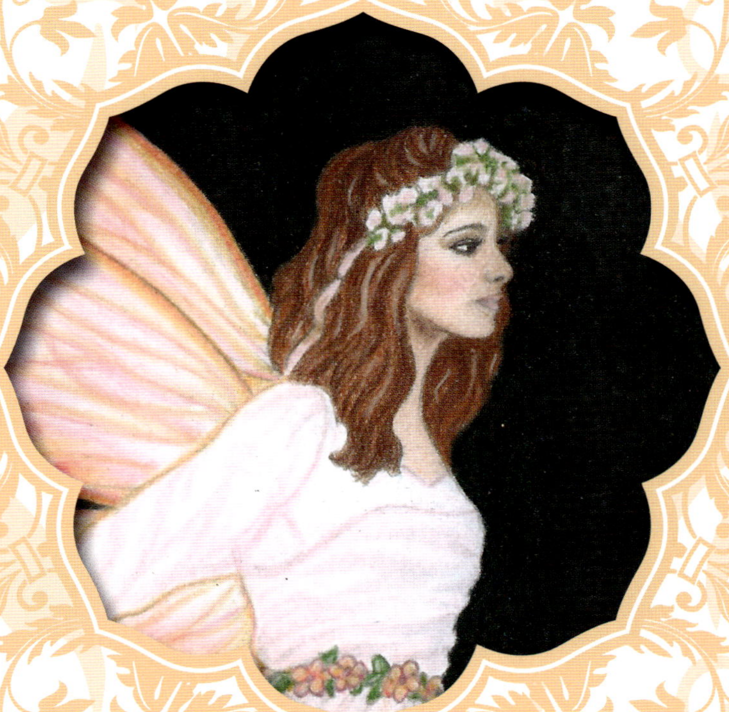

Sketch Use a B or HB pencil to outline the fairy and her wings. Delineate the folds of her dress with peach to avoid harsh lines. Lightly erase all the lines before coloring. (To transfer the template for this project, see page 123.)

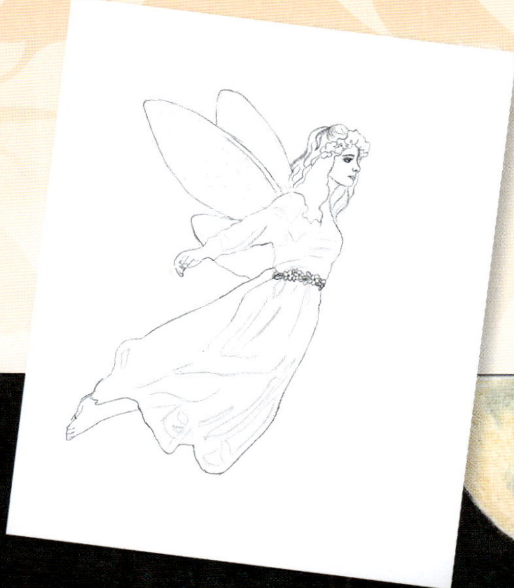

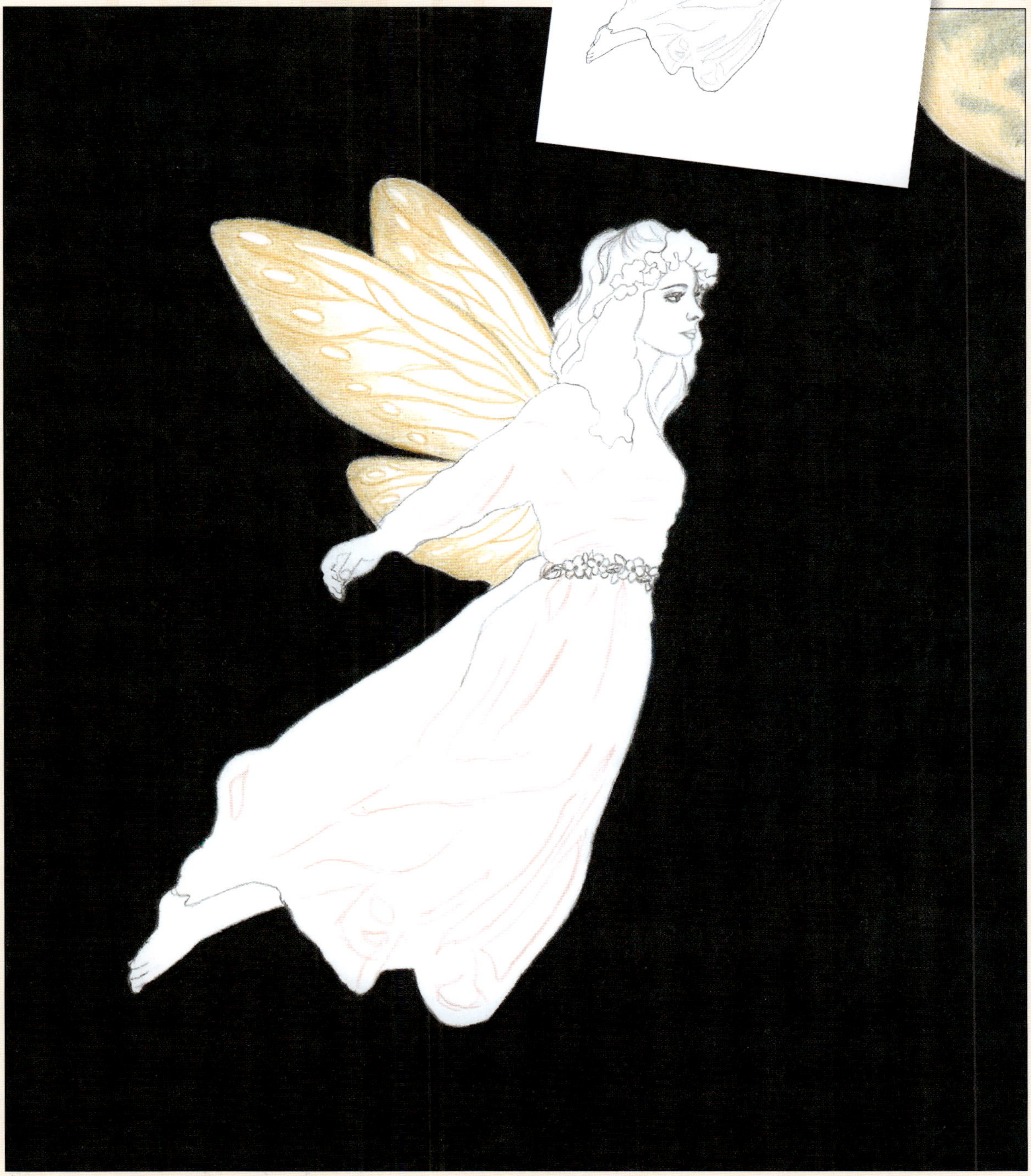

Step 1 Sketch a partial moon and color it with beige. Cover the remaining background with a layer of black, followed by indigo blue. Apply both colors with medium pressure and small, rounded strokes to avoid the appearance of directional lines. Layer the background again with black using small, rounded strokes and firm pressure. Add yellow ochre over the entire moon and then periwinkle blue in random areas over the moon.

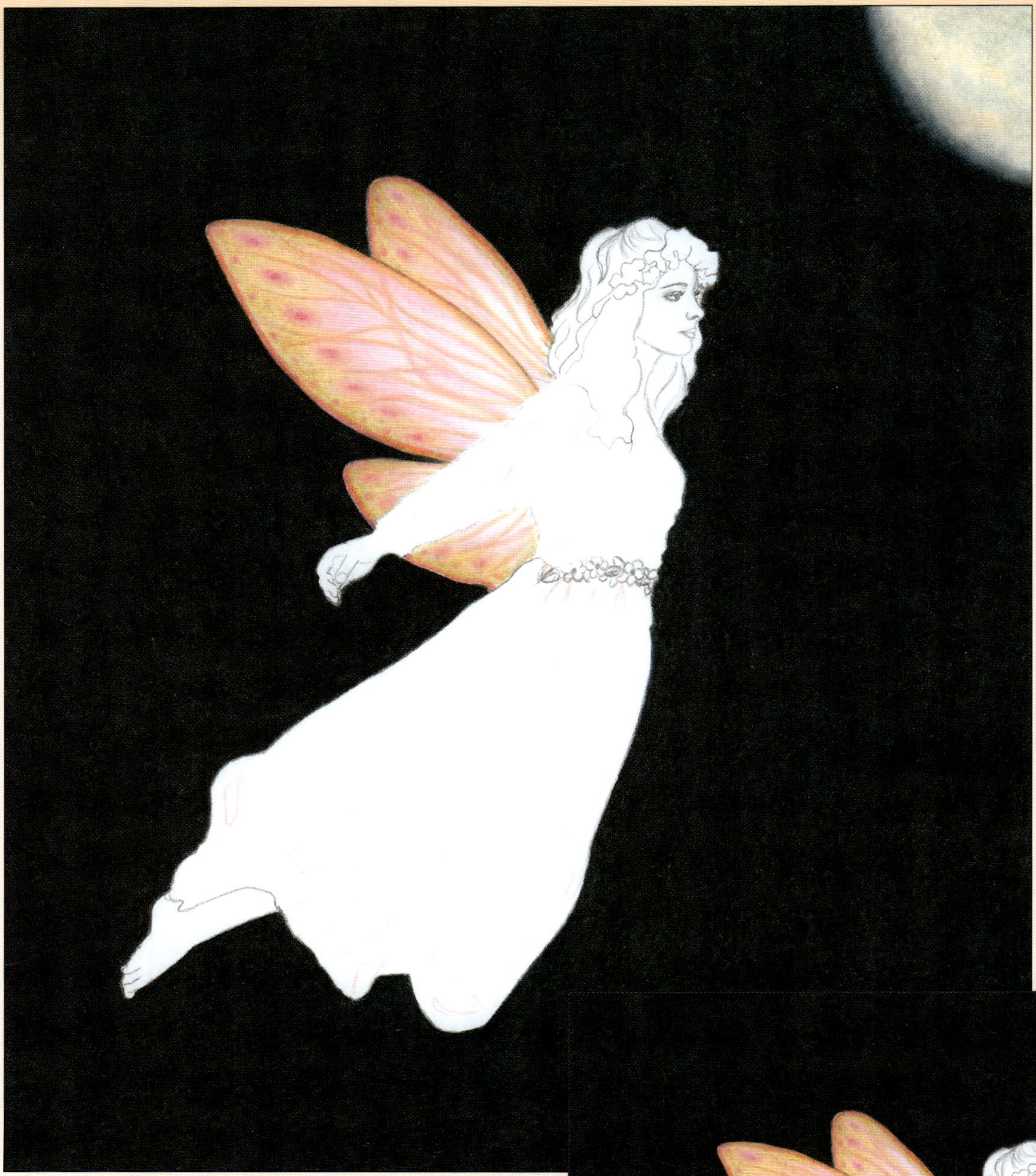

Step 2 Add pink and yellow ochre to the wings and blend them down with white. Line the rims and add vein lines with pink followed by yellow ochre. Blend the inside of the moon with white using firm pressure. Using a white pencil with a flat point and hard pressure, blur a glow around the moon and then cover the outer area with beige. Erase the graphite lines of the fairy's arm and torso and then lighten the peach lines within her dress.

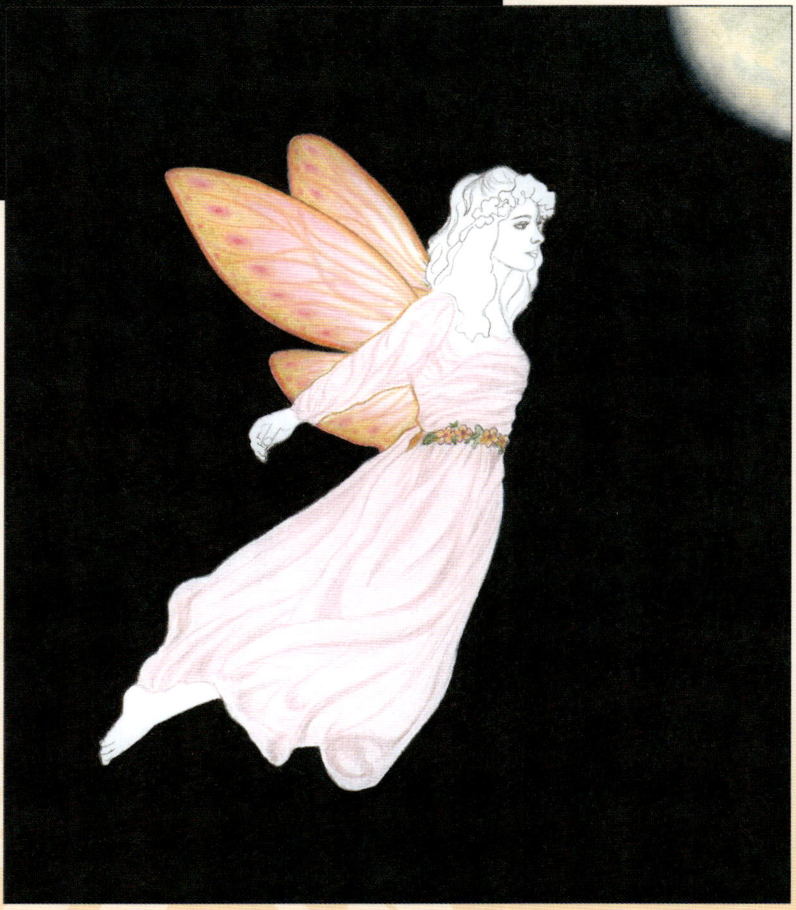

Step 3 Lighten the fairy's dress hemline and flower belt with an eraser. Line her arm and torso with yellow ochre followed by pink. Using light pressure, cover the dress with two layers of deco pink and block in the folds with rosy beige. Color the flowers of her belt with yellow ochre and pink, as well as the leaves with Prussian green.

Step 4 Using medium pressure, blend the dress colors with white, which lightens the overall hue and transitions the shadows and folds into the dress. Restore color as needed with deco pink and rosy beige. Add more color to the flower belt with yellow ochre, pink, and Prussian green. Then blend it all down with white.

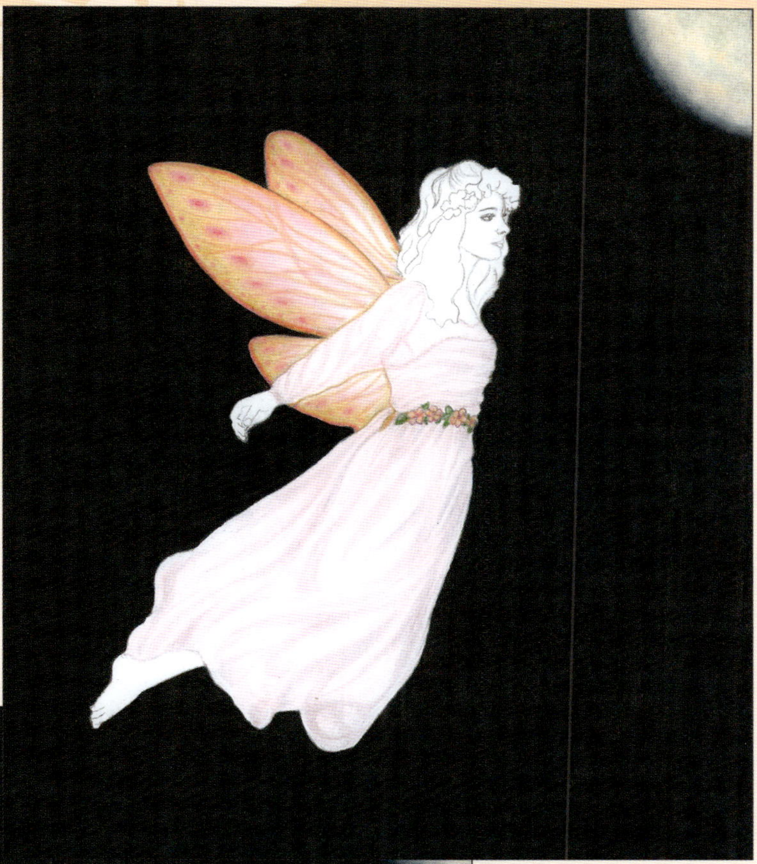

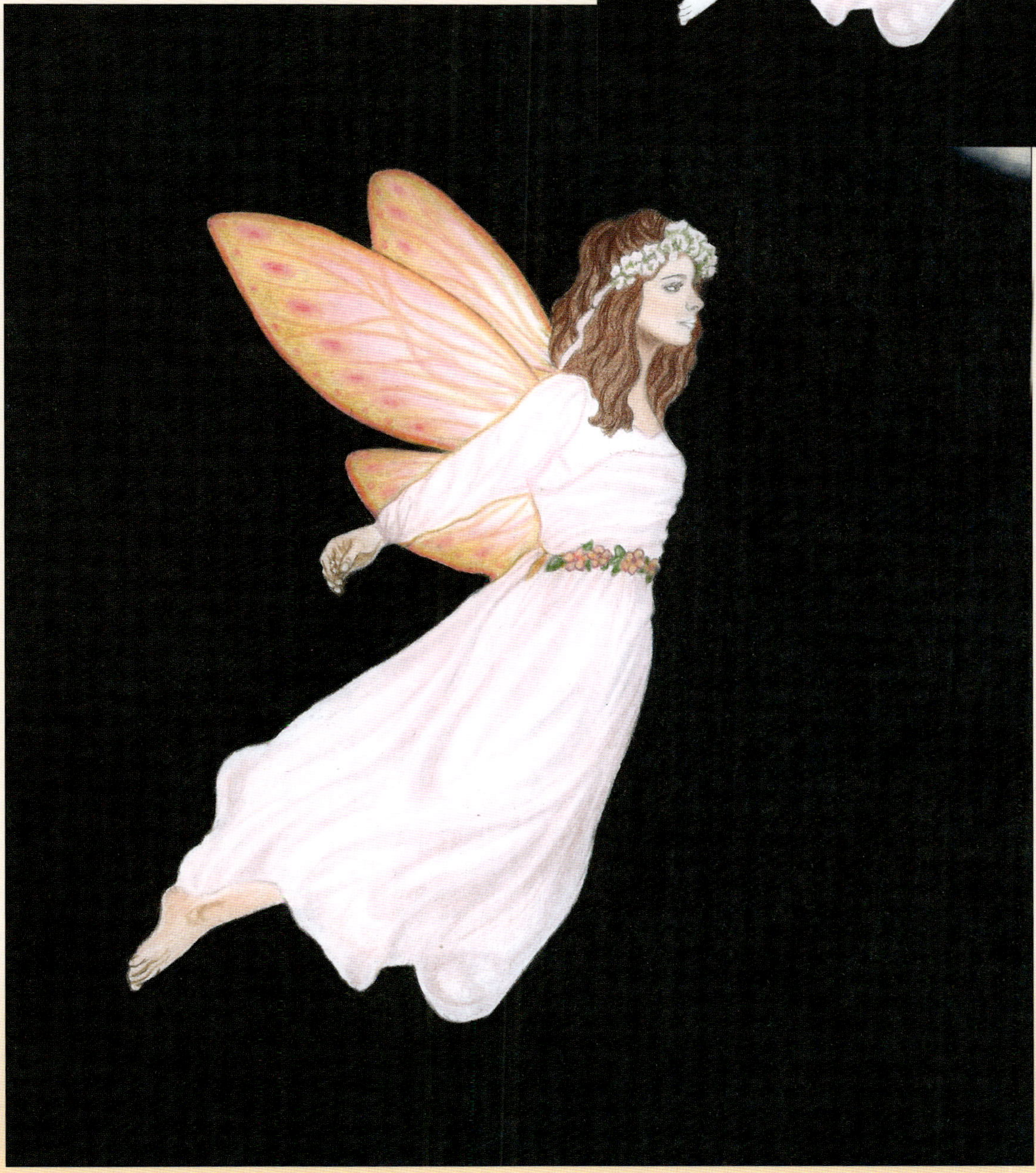

Step 5 Begin the fairy's hair with a layer of burnt ochre followed by dark brown, using moderate pressure. Block in the darkest sections with dark umber. Begin the garland headband with light layers of deco pink and Prussian green. Over the skin of her face, neck, hand, and foot, apply two coats of light peach and one coat of peach with light pressure, blending the layers with white. Develop her jawline and shadow with dark brown, and then block in the dark sections of her hand, ankle, and foot with light umber and dark brown.

Step 6 Finish the fairy's hair with an overall coat of sienna brown and another layer of dark umber over the darkest sections. Add highlights with random streaks of white. To finish the garland, add touches of pink, Prussian green, and light umber, shadowing the forehead with light umber. Define the fairy's cheeks with light umber and pink. Using a sharp dark umber point, darken the eyebrows and eyelids, switching to light umber for eye shadow. Use black to draw a few eyelashes and lightly color the nostril with dark brown. Touch the lips with pink and lighten the facial features with white. For the fairy's hand and foot, use peach, light umber, and dark umber, blending and smoothing with white.

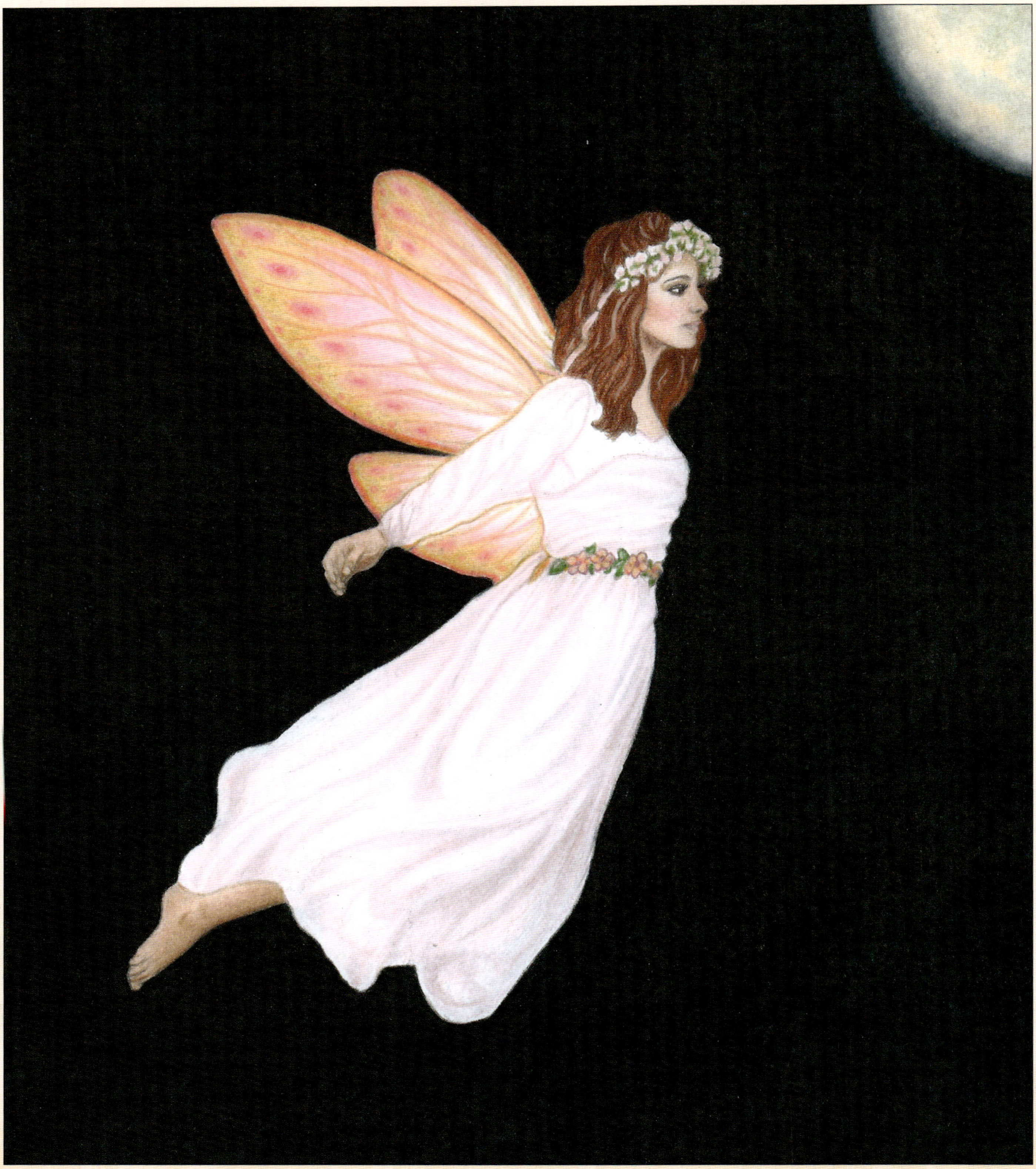

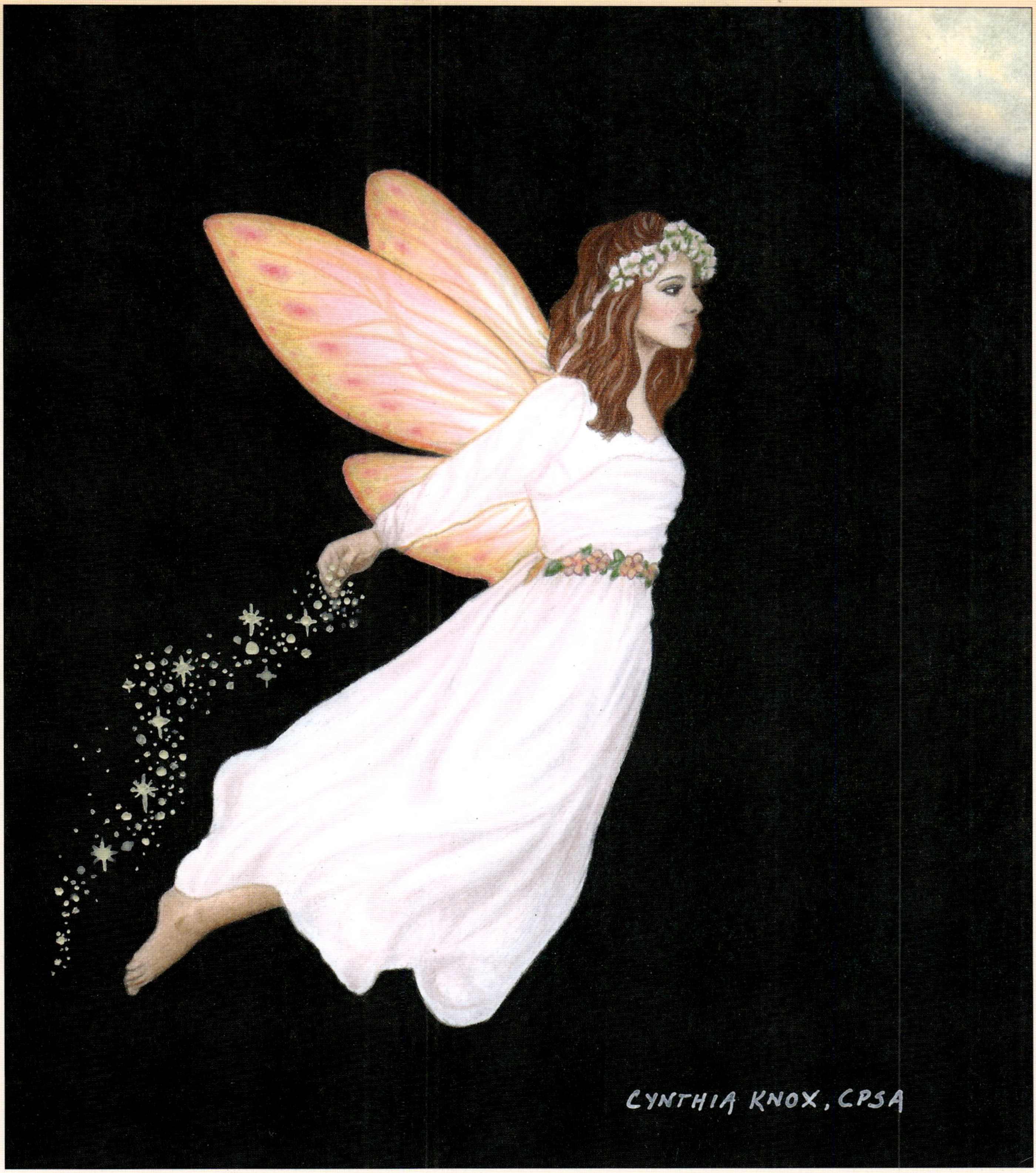

STEP 7 Using a very small round brush, add the fairy dust with Naples yellow and Chinese white watercolor, blended with water. Apply dots in a curved pattern extending above the dress, and pull streaks out of some of the dots with slightly more paint added to the brush tip. Reapply paint to the centers of some dots to add brilliance. Let the artwork dry and spray it with workable fixative.

Snow Fairy

with Cynthia Knox

FANTASY ART ALLOWS US TO INDULGE OUR IMAGINATION. For example, large snowflakes with dark blue borders are quite acceptable when rendering a snow fairy's environment. You are free to design the fairy's wings however you'd like—pointy, curly, compact, or long and slender—and you can build the most unusual settings. Experiment and create a fairy world that is unique to your ideas and artistic sensibilities.

50% cool gray	Black grape	Blue violet lake	Dark brown	Dark umber	Henna	Light peach
Light umber	Peach	Powder blue	Sienna brown	Sky blue light	Ultramarine	White

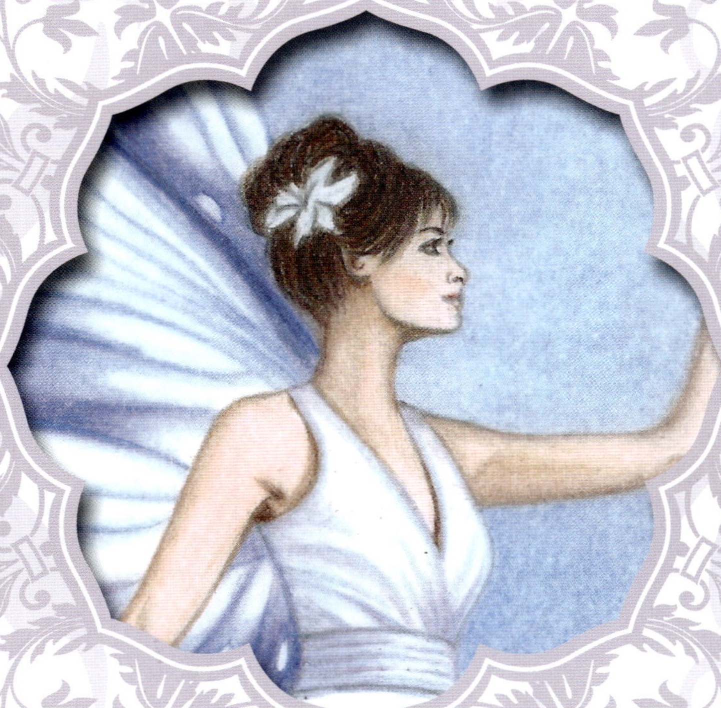

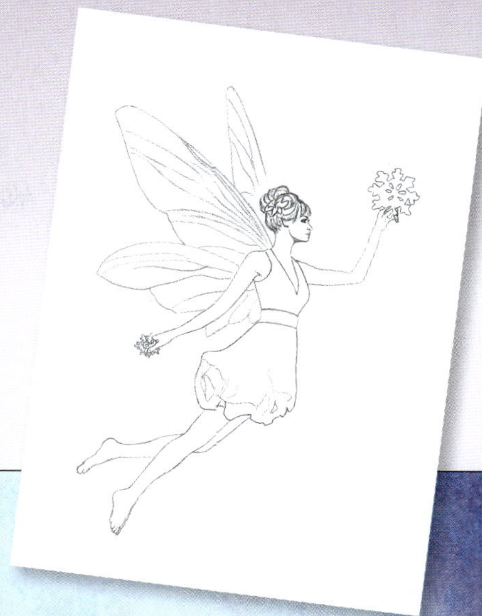

Sketch Use a B or HB pencil to sketch the fairy and two snowflakes she is holding. At this point, the facial features, fingers, and snowflakes are approximations. You will work out the details once the background and wings are in place.

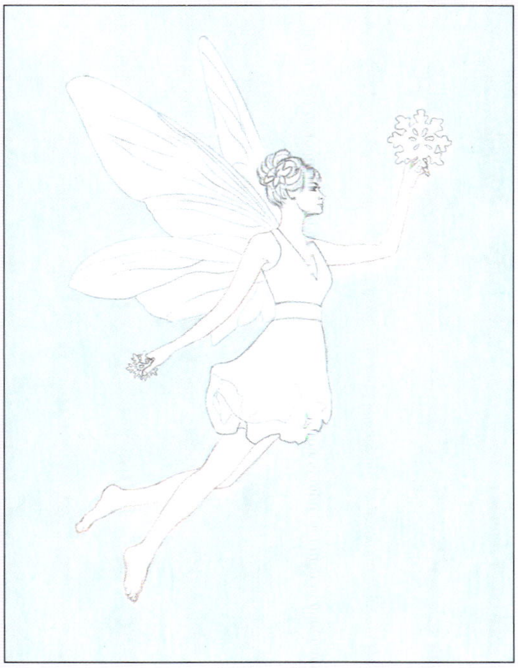

Step 1 Apply a layer of sky blue light over the entire background, using light pressure and short, vertical strokes. Follow this with a layer of powder blue, using moderate pressure.

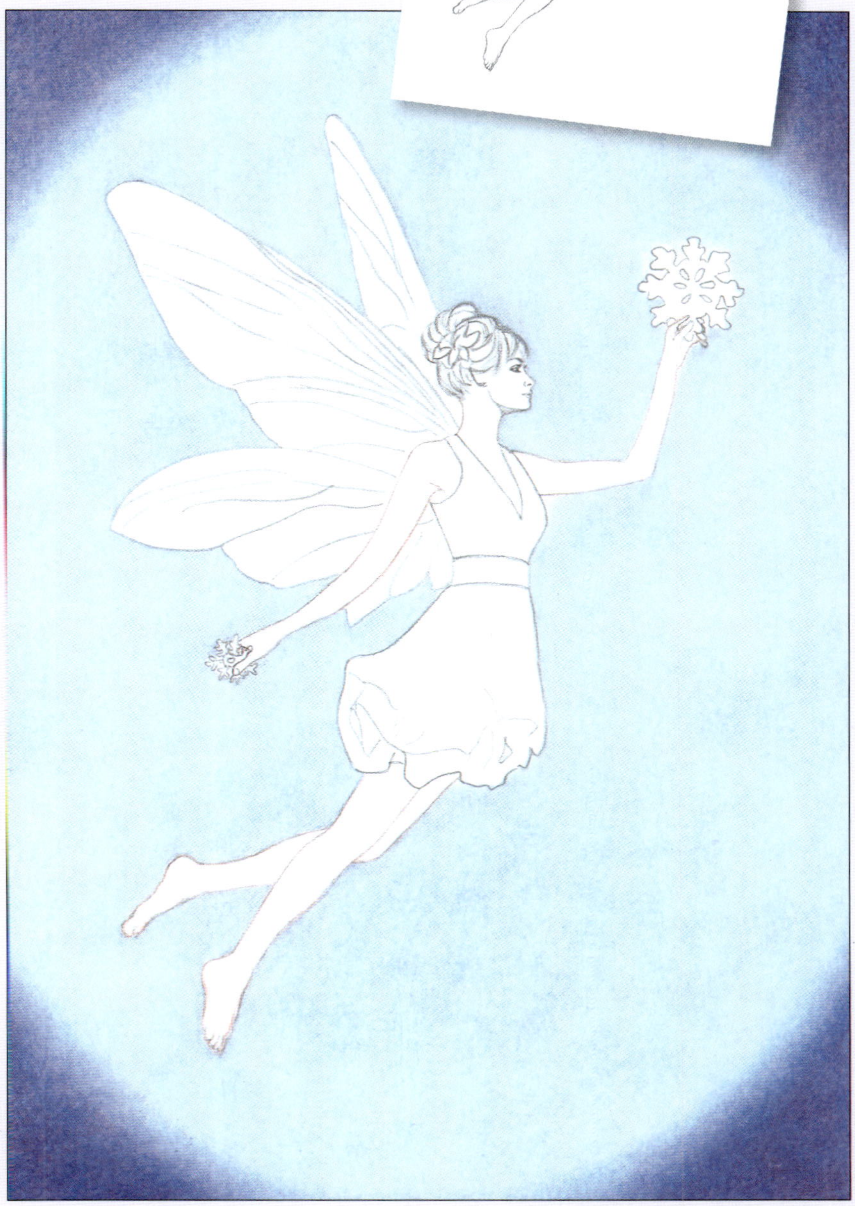

Step 2 Cover the background with a layer of blue violet lake and then burnish with white for a consistent, soft blue appearance. To create the vignette look, layer the corners with two coats of ultramarine, and add black grape over most of it; then burnish and blend it with white to create a smooth transition to the light blue interior.

STEP 3 Erase much of the wing lines to make them only lightly visible. Outline the exterior wing borders and the interior vein lines with ultramarine. Create elliptical shapes at the end of the wings with ultramarine. Over much of the wings, apply two layers of blue violet lake, leaving the inner elliptical spaces white. Then block in the dress folds and shadows with 50% cool gray, using light pressure.

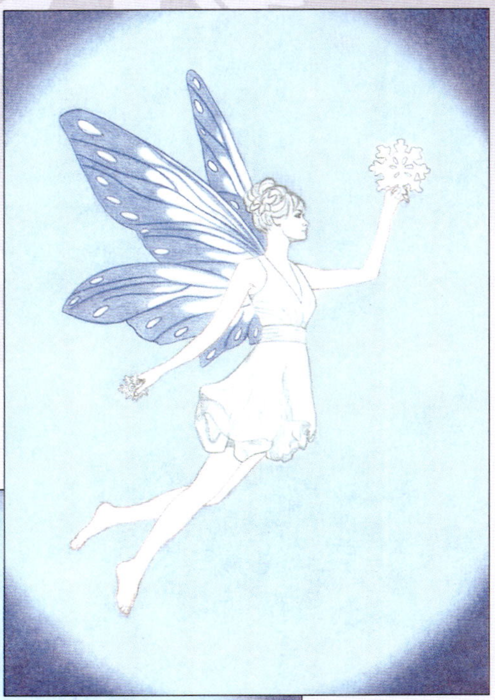

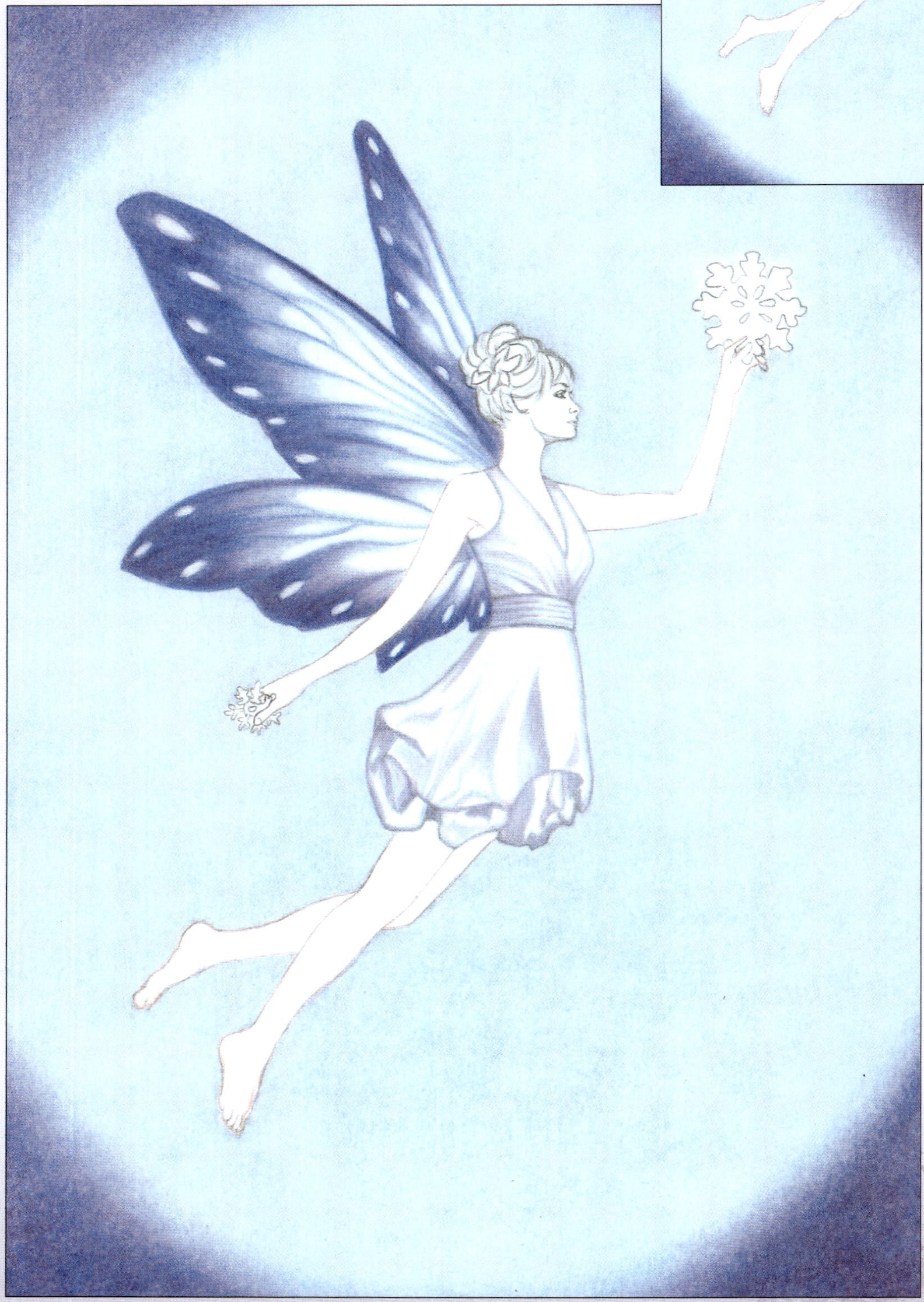

STEP 4 Add black grape to the outer portion of the wings. Follow this with a layer of ultramarine over the black grape, burnishing with white to blend. Pull color over the white sections of the wings with white, adding ultramarine and black grape where desired. Over the gray folds and shadows in the dress, apply a light layer of blue violet lake. Outline the dress with blue violet lake as well. To blend and blur the colors into the dress, burnish with white. Repeat this process with a light layer of black grape and blend it down with white. Bring back some blue violet lake where desired.

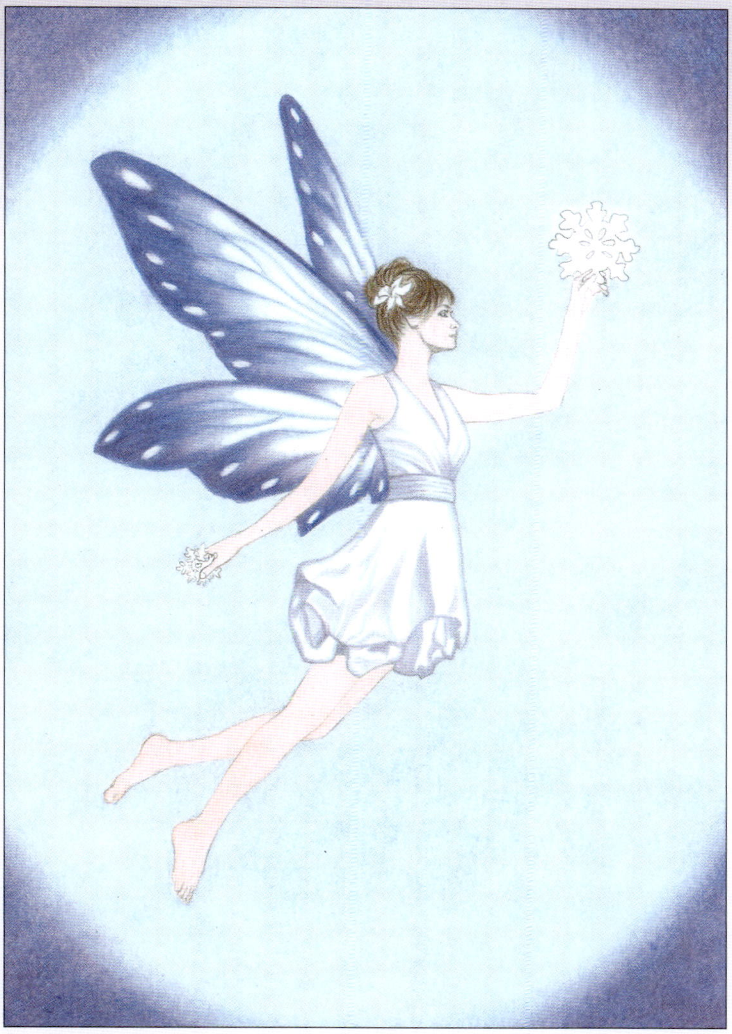

Step 5 Begin the fairy's skin by erasing any smudges. Then layer her face and body with light peach and moderate pressure, followed by a layer of peach. Using firm pressure, burnish with white to lighten and blend the peach tones together. Add light umber over the fairy's hair using light pressure, stroking in the direction of hair growth. Draw individual strands with dark umber for depth.

Step 6 Complete the fairy's skin by adding light umber to the shadow areas followed by a light coat of dark brown. With a sharp point and small strokes, blend in light peach or white. Build up shadow color with dark brown and dark umber, blending down with light peach or peach. This includes the hands and feet. Finish the fairy's hair with layers of dark brown and dark umber applied in the direction of hair growth. Over the gray lines, touch blue violet lake into the white flower and burnish with white. For the snowflakes, add powder blue to the holes and blue background bordering the fairy. Make any necessary color adjustments to the fairy's dress.

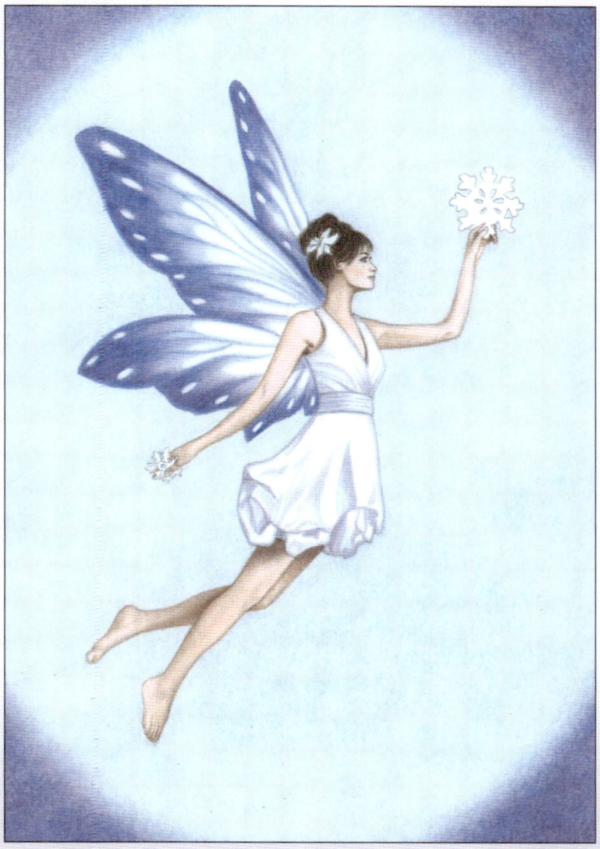

Tip

To achieve smooth color transitions, layer several colors, burnish with white, and then lightly restore the color. Use small, elliptical strokes to avoid the appearance of directional lines.

Step 7 Touch peach into the fairy's face over her cheekbone and neck. Draw the eyebrow, lashes, eye, nostril, and inner ear with dark umber, using a very sharp point. To correct mistakes, "lift" the pigment with a sharp white point and reapply color. Touch henna into the lip lightly. Using sienna brown and dark brown, blend into the neck with peach. Dot the thumbnails with a touch of blue violet lake.

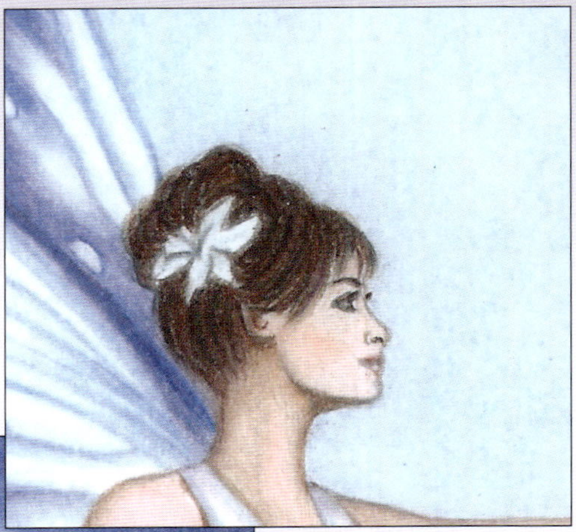

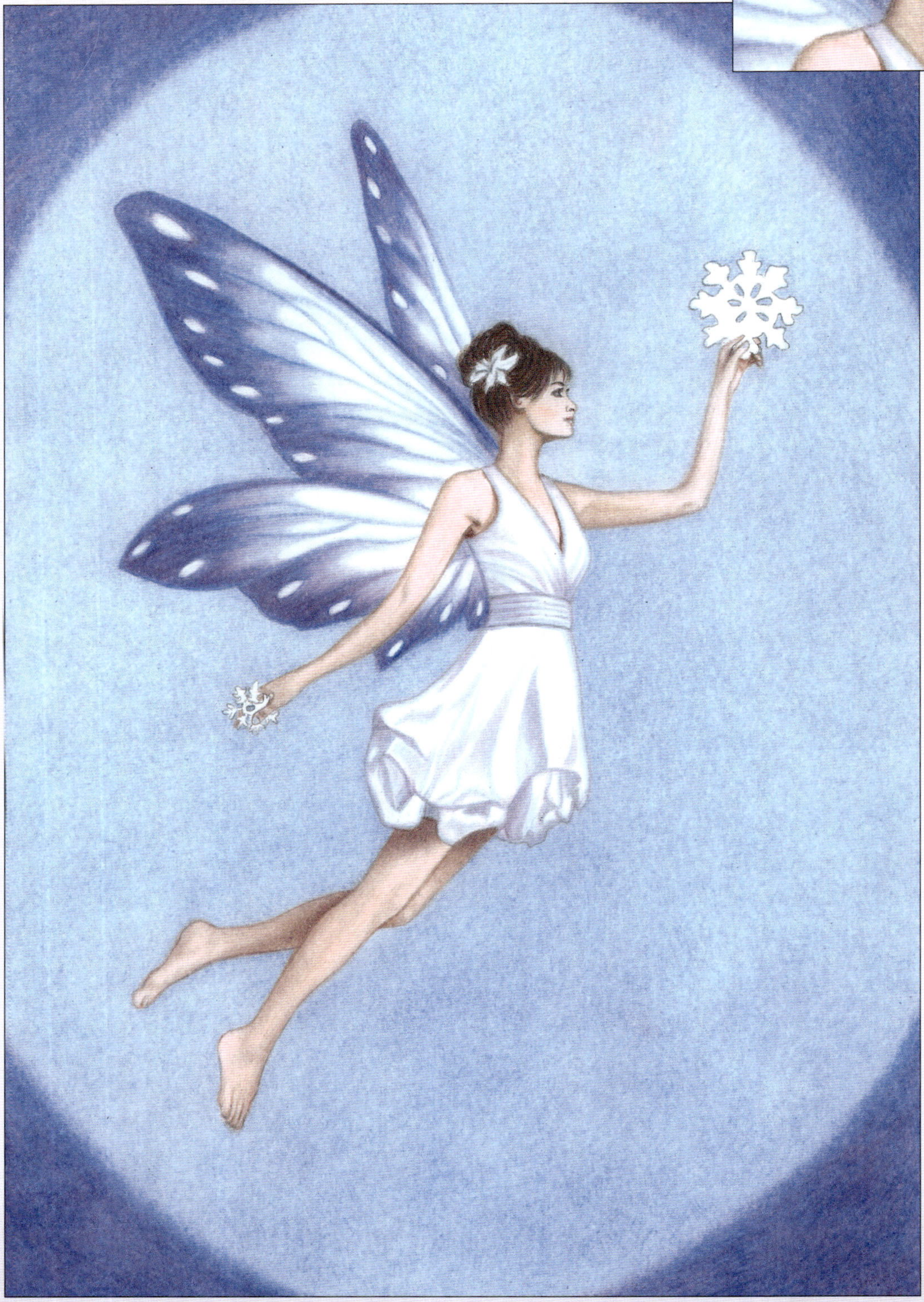

Step 8 Add blue violet lake over the entire background, using medium pressure and small, elliptical strokes with an angled point for good coverage. Enlarge the corner vignettes with black grape. Apply ultramarine over the triangular section of each corner using small, elliptical strokes. Blur the rounded borders into the light blue background with blue violet lake, using circular strokes and pulling the darker color into the light blue background.

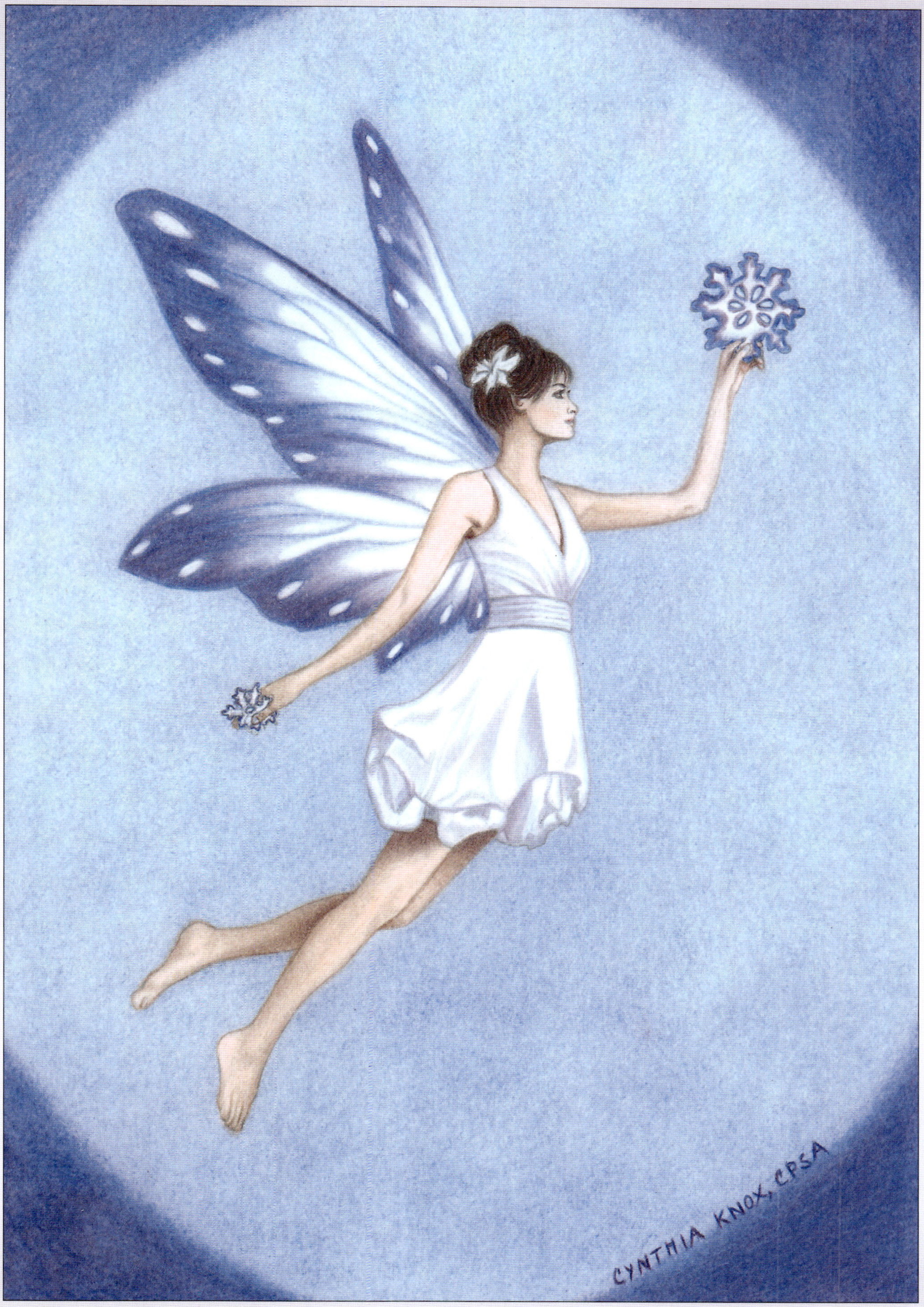

Step 9 Outline the snowflakes first with black grape and ultramarine. Blend with white and burnish the interiors with white to brighten. Clean up the edges, sign, and spray with workable fixative.

Woodland Fairy

with Cynthia Knox

WOODLAND FAIRIES ARE OFTEN WHAT WE THINK OF when we hear the word "fairy." They live in magical forests and leave trails of fairy dust behind them as they travel through lush greenery and dense tree foliage. In this intimate forest scene, we will focus on contrasting a blurred background with a detailed foreground.

- 20% French gray
- Apple green
- Beige
- Black
- Burnt ochre
- Canary yellow
- Chocolate
- Crimson red
- Dark brown
- Dark green
- Dark umber
- Deco yellow
- Ginger root
- Henna
- Kelp green
- Light peach
- Limepeel
- Moss green
- Nectar
- Olive green
- Peach
- Prussian green
- Sap green light
- Sienna brown
- Sunburst yellow
- Terra cotta
- Tuscan red
- Violet
- Violet blue
- White
- Yellow ochre

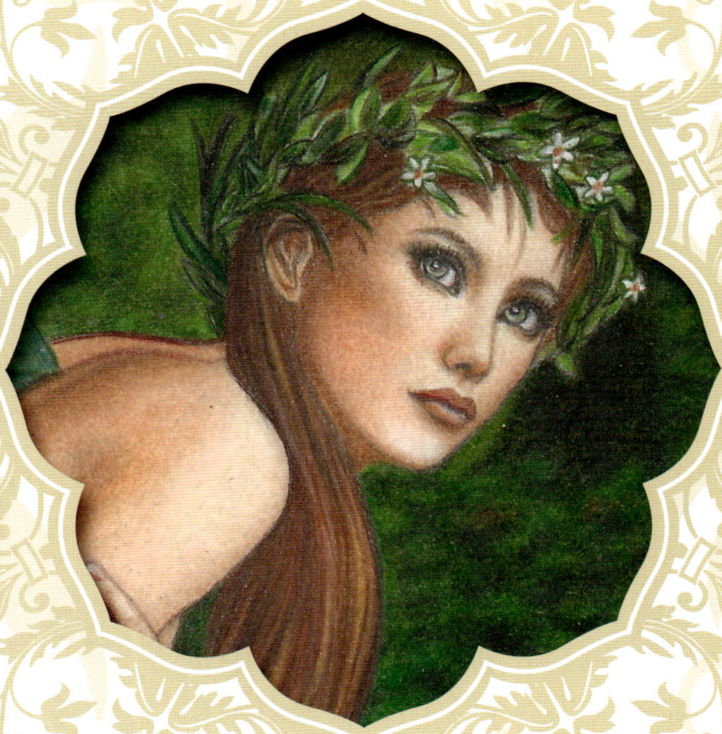

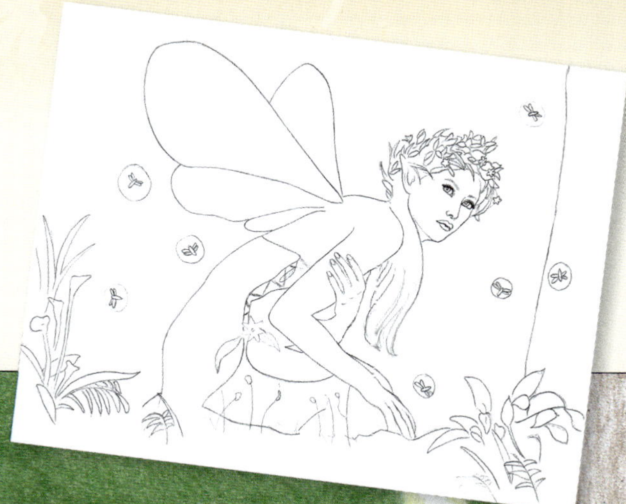

Sketch Use a soft graphite pencil to lightly sketch the fairy and woodland scene. (Be sure to erase these marks just before adding color.) The circles around the fireflies delineate space for a yellow glow that will blend into the background.

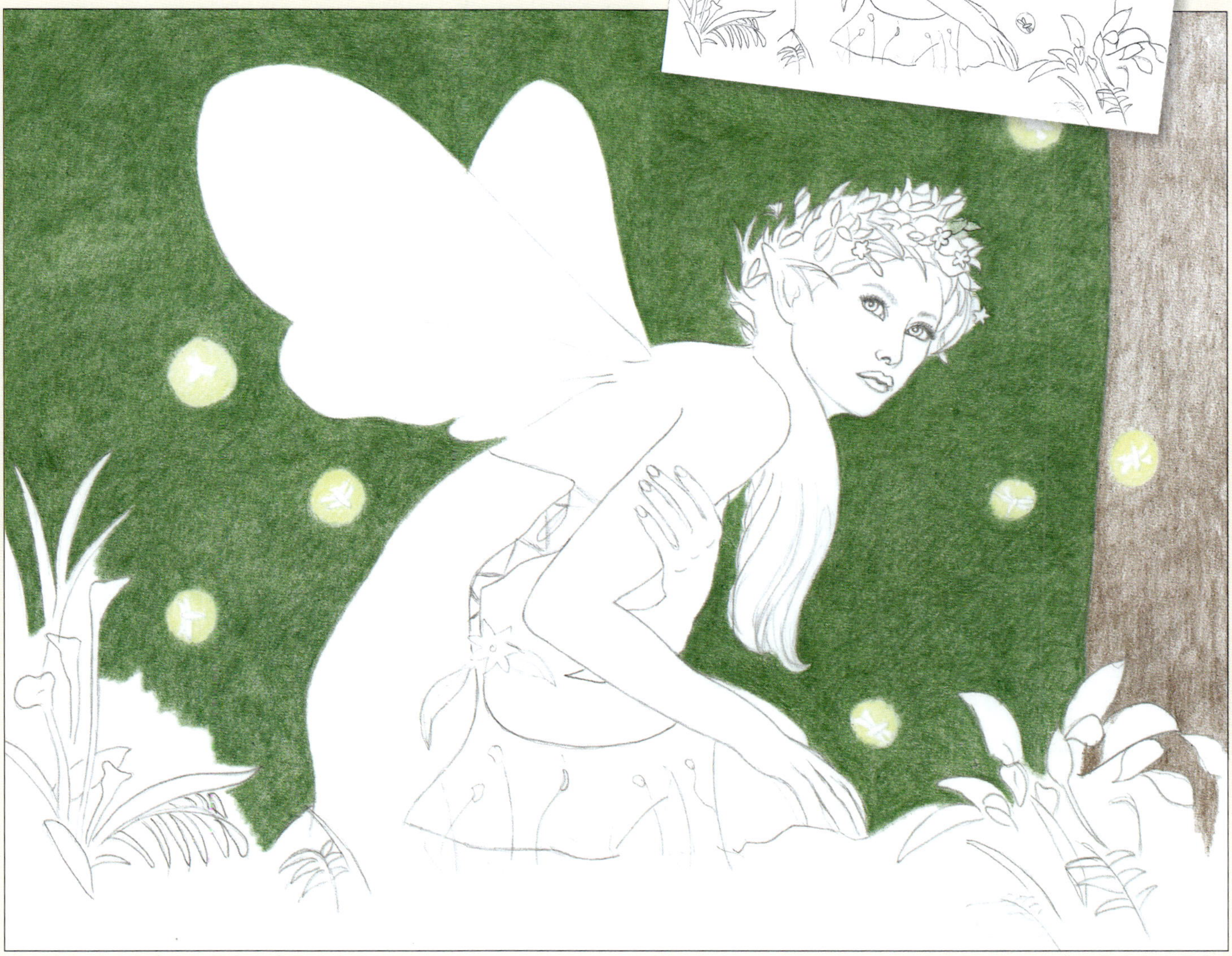

Step 1 Cover the main background with a layer of Prussian green followed by olive green, using medium pressure. Apply dark brown down the tree trunk. Erase the firefly outlines nearly completely, and color in the surrounding circles with deco yellow.

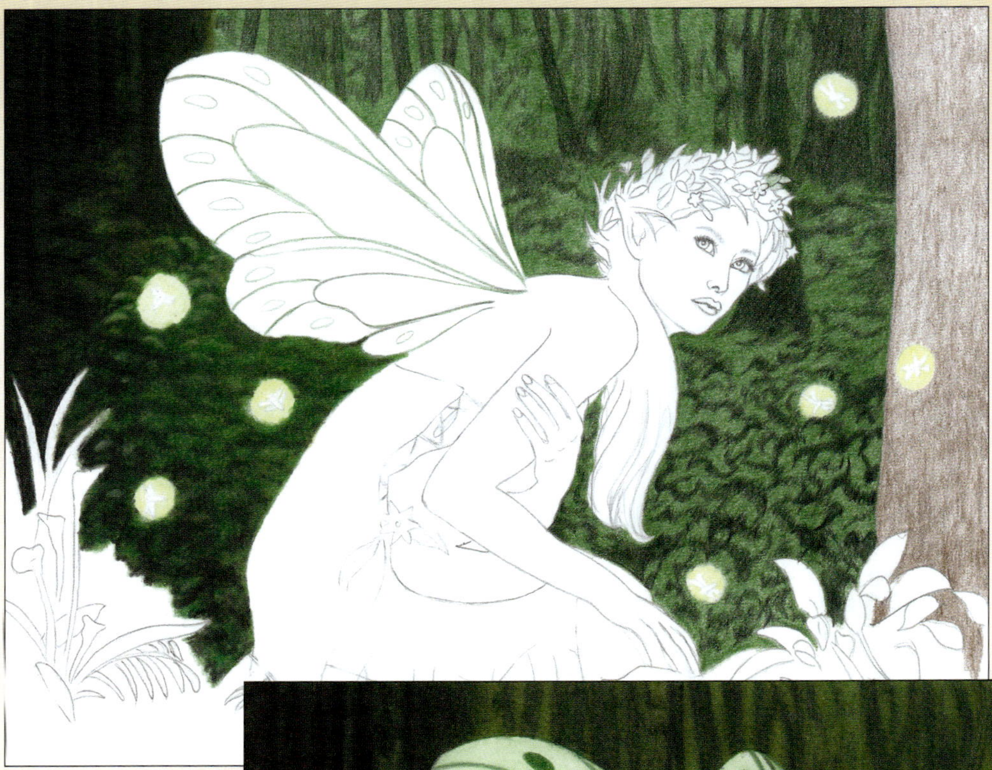

Step 2 Block in the trees and shadowed areas of the foliage with black. Apply moss green over the left side with a dull point and firm pressure. Then reapply black to intensify and add more moss green to blur. Over the foliage beneath the fairy's wings, apply Prussian green and apple green, using a dull point and firm pressure. Use limepeel to create a few leaf shapes next to the top firefly. Lightly line the wing pattern with an HB graphite pencil followed by a darker outline with olive green.

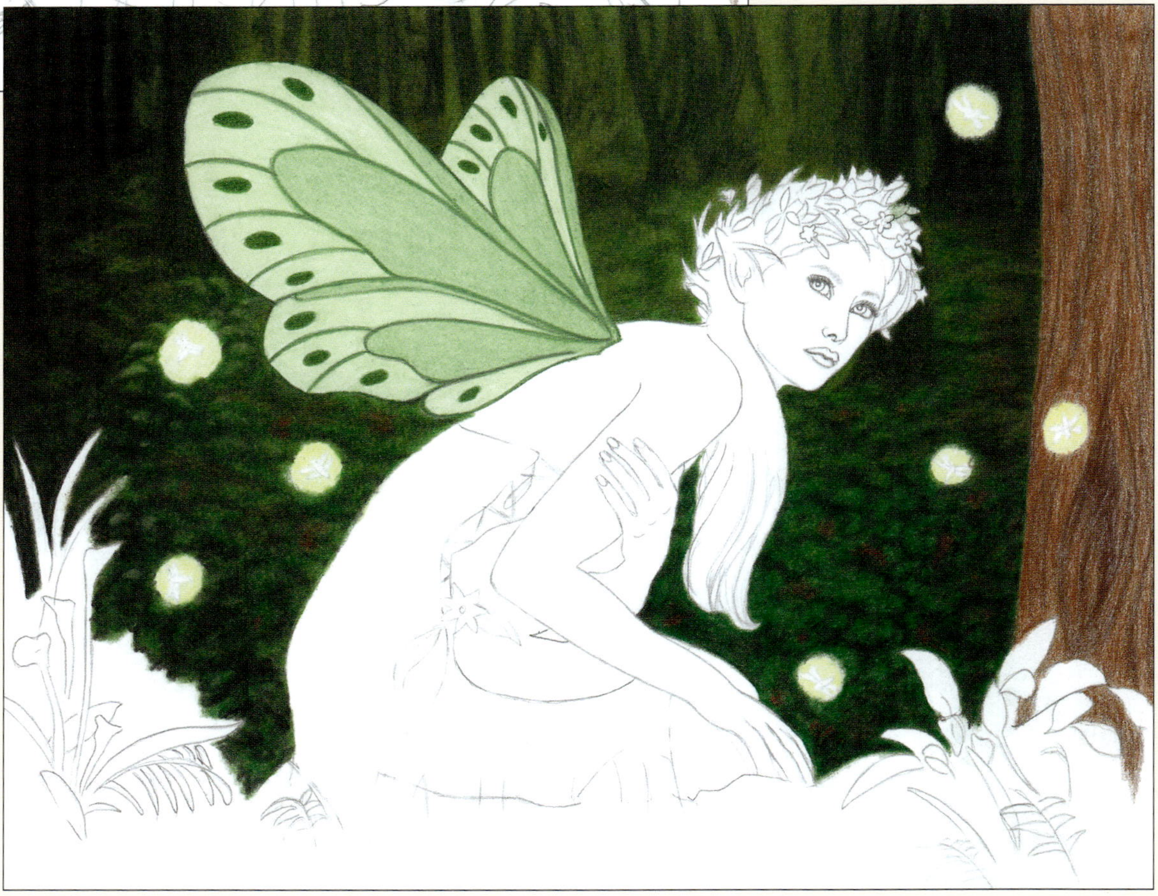

Step 3 Finish the background by darkening the trees and dark areas with more black. Layer moss green over the top section and dark green over the bottom section, using firm pressure and a dull point. Lighten where desired with apple green, and for variety and depth in the background, add touches of dark umber and crimson red throughout. Draw and color the bark striations down the right tree trunk with dark umber layered with chocolate. Outline the wing pattern again and fill in the oval shapes with olive green, using medium pressure. Apply pale sage over all of the background and sap green light over the darker sections.

STEP 4 Develop the wings by adding olive green, Prussian green, and sunburst yellow over the three largest sections. Use white to streak along the base and sap green light to circle the elliptical shapes. Add sap green light over the interior and blend out with white. Apply black over the existing lines of tree bark. Add dark umber and black over the darker areas of the tree, followed by chocolate over the entire tree. Lightly fill in the circles around the fireflies with olive green and dark umber, blending this into the background with deco yellow and white. Use chocolate instead of olive green for the firefly in front of the tree trunk. Reapply colors and blend again for a transparent look. Color the firefly bodies with deco yellow.

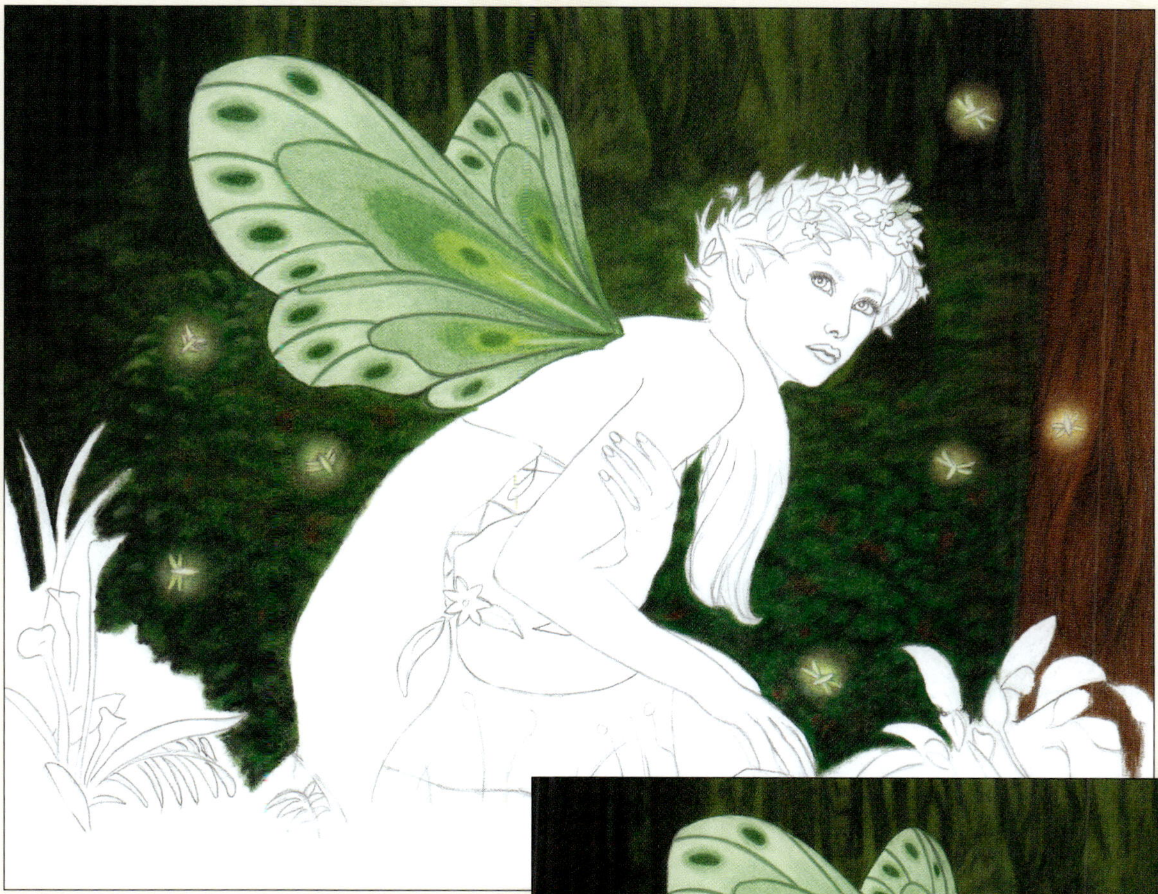

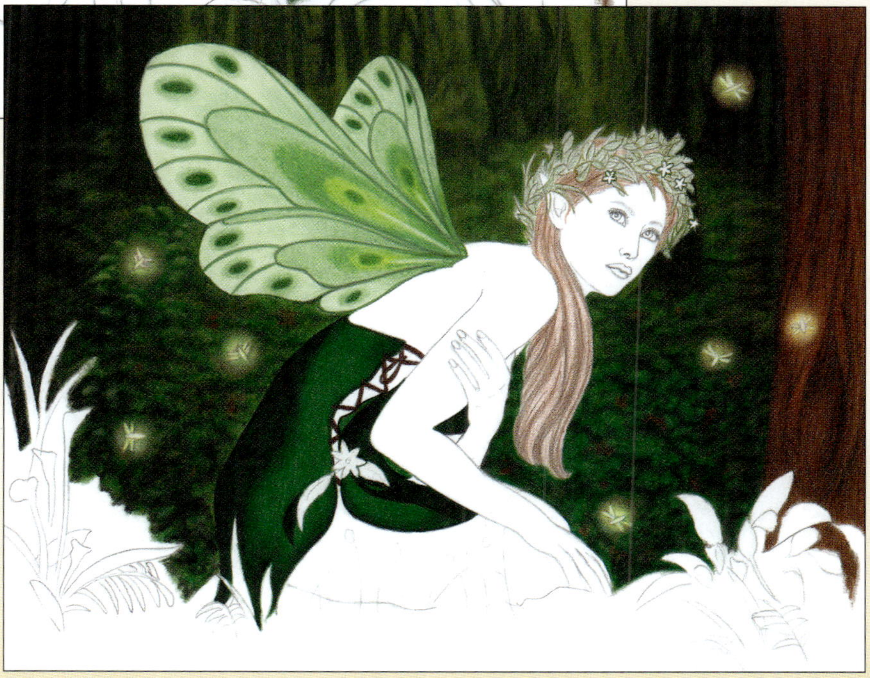

STEP 5 Color the fairy's dress with dark green and then Prussian green, outlining it with black. Fill in the shadowed areas with black and blur it into the green by applying circular strokes with light pressure. Blend dark green into the black areas with the same process. Draw the laces with dark umber and black. For the fairy's hair, layer burnt ochre with light pressure and color in the dark streaks with dark brown. Begin the leafy garland on her head by defining and filling in the shapes with olive green. Use light pressure to color in the leaves.

STEP 6 Create vein lines within the leafy dress using a sharp white point. Lightly shade around the veins with dark umber and blend into the green dress with dark green. Add another layer of burnt ochre to the fairy's hair and add streaks with more dark umber, blending with white. Color the leafy garland with random selections of dark green, olive green, and apple green. Add black and dark umber for depth, blending with white for highlights. For the flower centers, use white and burnt ochre. Erase smudges on the fairy's skin along with any graphite lines. Apply an initial layer of beige followed by peach over her face and body, using small, circular strokes and light pressure.

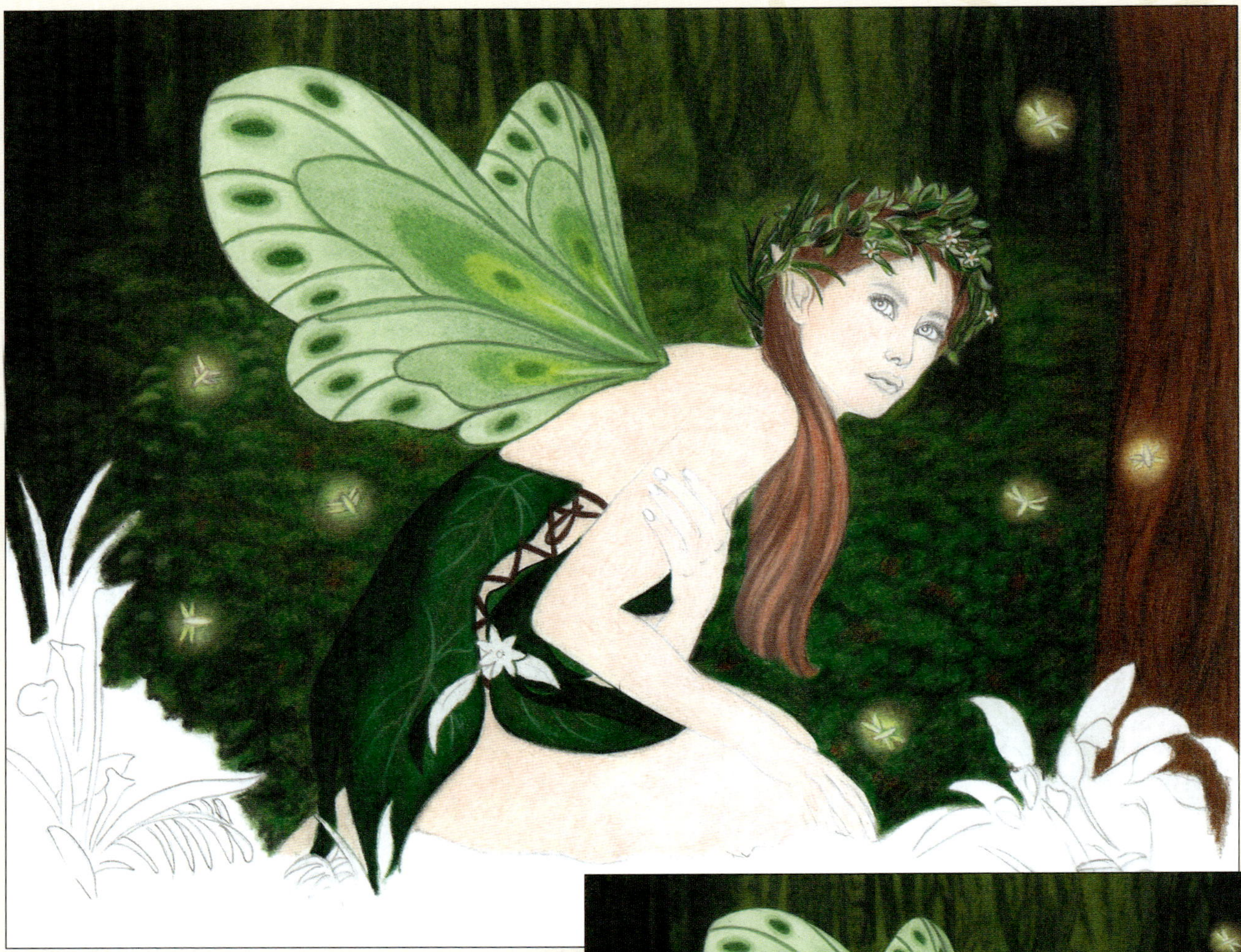

STEP 7 Finish the fairy's hair with strokes of dark umber and black for the darkest sections, burnt ochre and sienna brown for the midtones, and streaks of yellow ochre for the highlights. Burnish her skin with white, using firm pressure and circular strokes to blend the underlying colors together. Add ginger root to warm up the skin tones. Starting near the wings, add burnt ochre and dark brown over the shadows. Intensify with dark umber and soften with burnt ochre and beige.

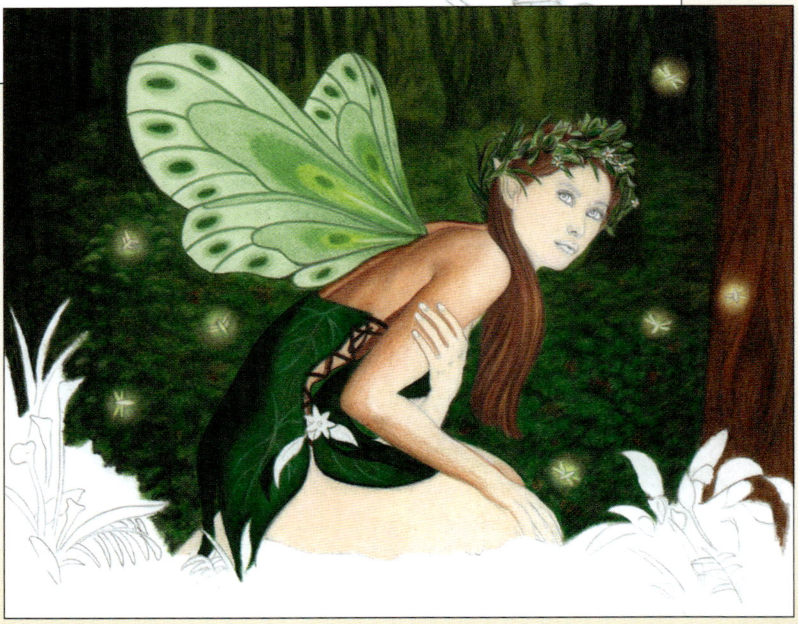

Step 8 Continue this process for the entire body, blending for smooth transitions. Use peach and beige for highlights, dark umber and Tuscan red for the darkest shadows, and terra cotta with yellow ochre for warmth. Use touches of dark brown and nectar for the knuckles, along with nectar and white for the fingernails. Draw random leaves and weeds in the foreground and over the fairy's leg with dark green. Convert the tip of her ear into a green leaf.

Tip

If you mistakenly pull dark color into the fairy's skin, simply "lift" it off or lighten it with a sharp white pencil point.

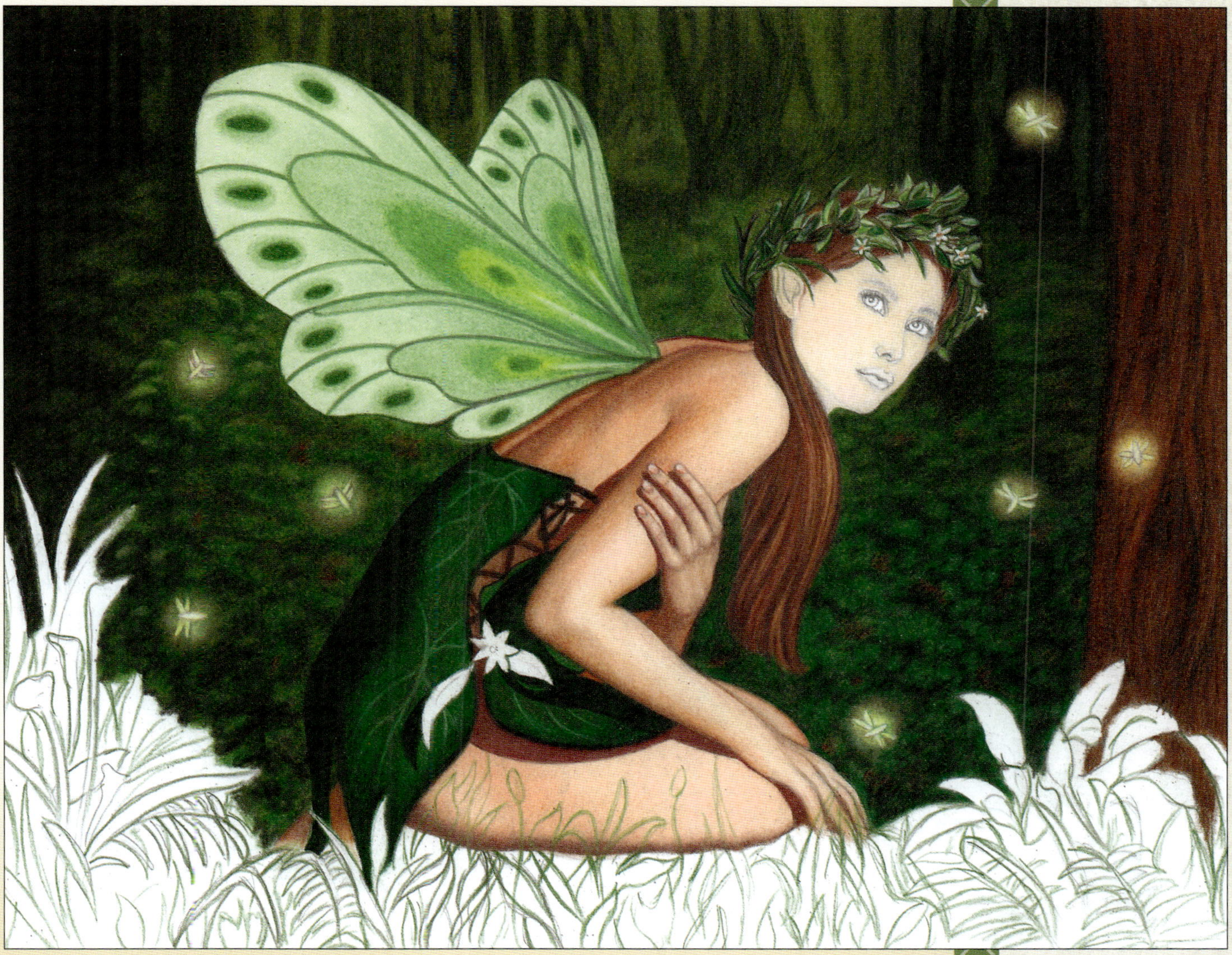

Step 9 Burnish the fairy's face with white to achieve a smooth surface. Add light peach over this and block in the shadowed areas, including the cheek and nose, contouring with burnt ochre, terra cotta, dark brown, and dark umber. Blend down with beige to reclaim a smooth color transition. Add colors back into the face, blending with beige until satisfied. Add nectar to the pink areas and color the lips with burnt ochre, henna, and dark brown. Use dark brown and burnt ochre for the eyebrows and eyelids. Make the pupils, lashes, and eyeliner "pop" with black, and use kelp green for the irises. To dull the whites of the eyes, apply 20% French gray. For the fairy's ear and forehead shadows, use dark brown and burnt ochre.

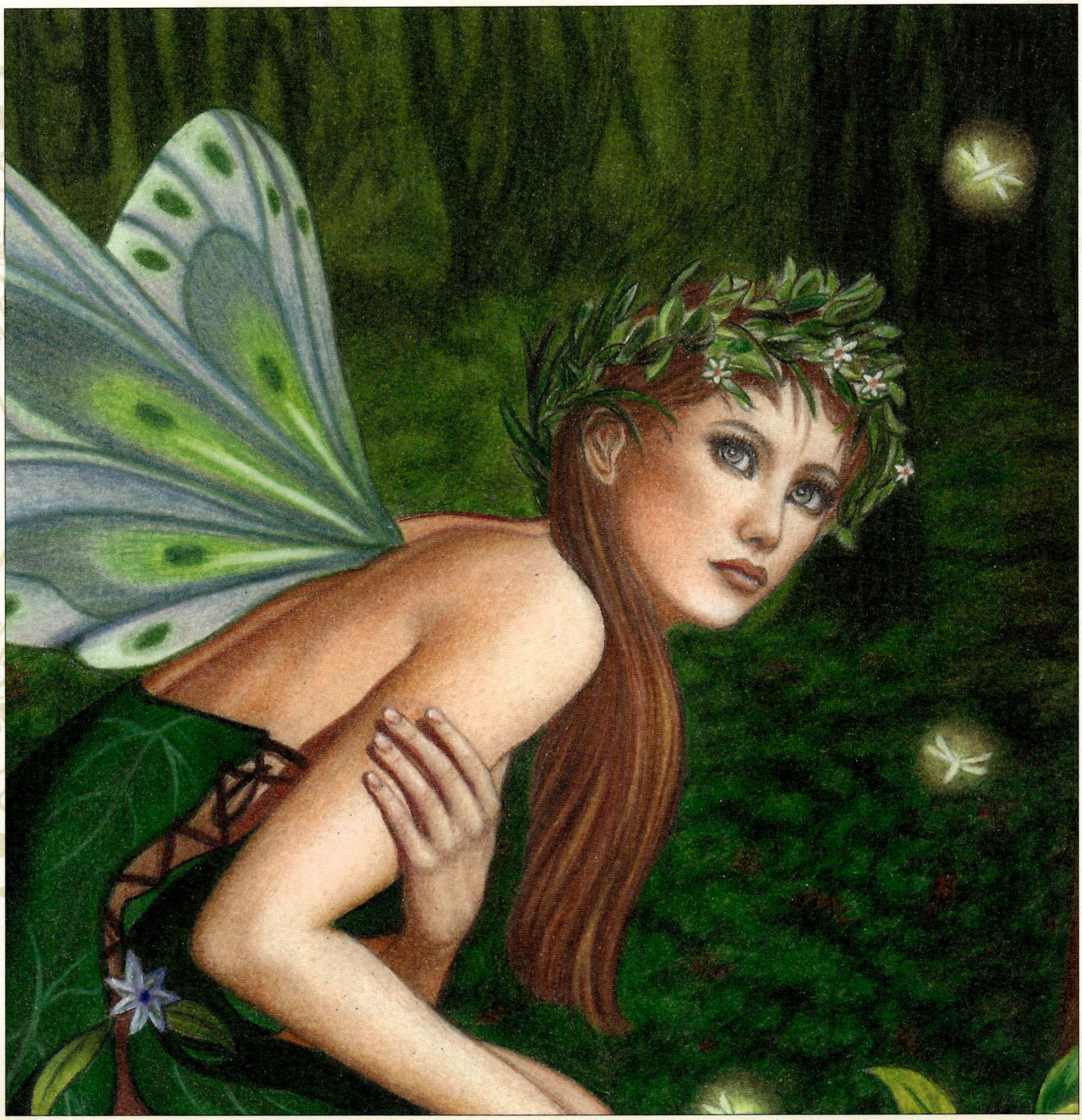

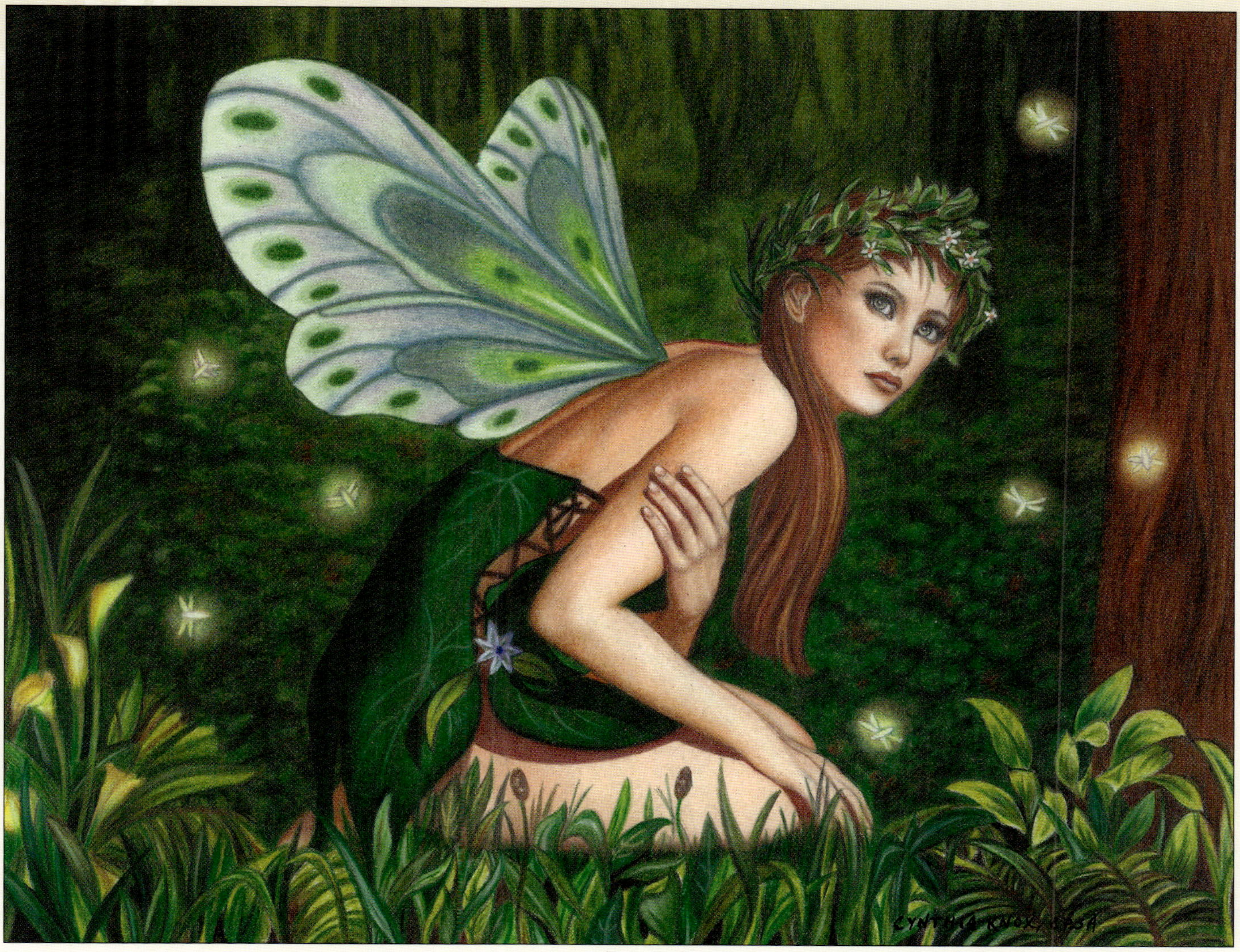

Step 10 Develop the foreground foliage one leaf at a time, creating random leaf shapes as you go and blending with the background colors. Add black for depth and white for highlights, using canary yellow for the yellow flowers. Develop the flower at the fairy's waist with violet and violet blue, blended with white. For more depth in the wings, add violet and violet blue, blending with white until smooth. Now sign and spray the drawing with workable fixative.

Windblown Fairy

with Sara Burrier

IN THIS PROJECT, the long, curling locks of golden hair suggest a windy moment for this fairy and her bumblebee friends. Learn how to use a white gel pen to add sparkle to this scene as a magical finishing touch. In addition to the palette below, you'll need a 6H pencil and a white gel pen to complete this project.

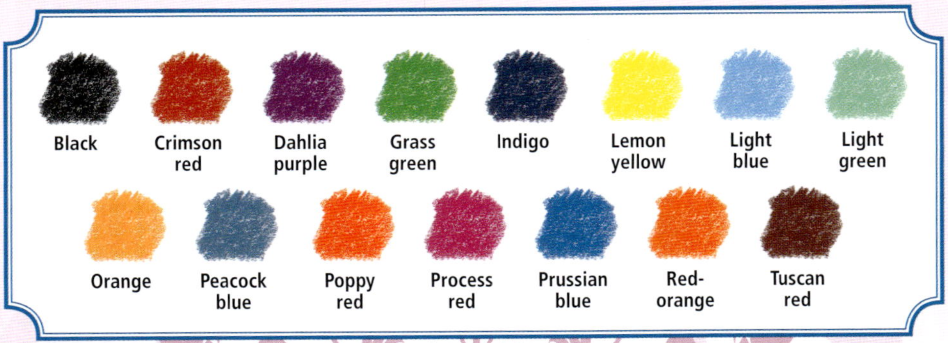

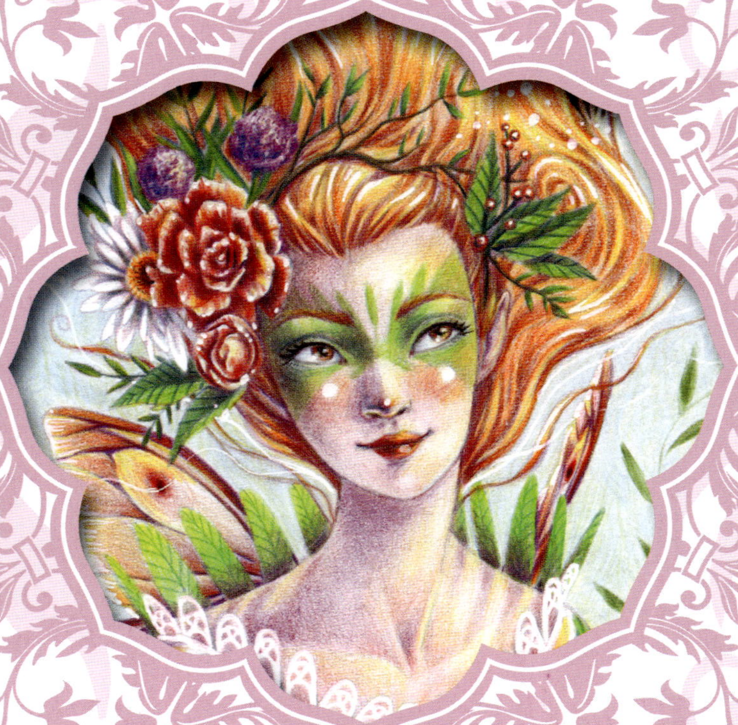

SKETCH Start by lightly sketching the fairy with a 6H pencil. Avoid pressing too hard, as the pencil can indent your paper and leave behind a white streak, even after you color over it. Draw only the most solid structures, focusing on the fairy's face and shoulders. You can leave the hair and flowers to interpretation with colored pencil in the steps that follow. (To transfer the template for this project, see page 124.)

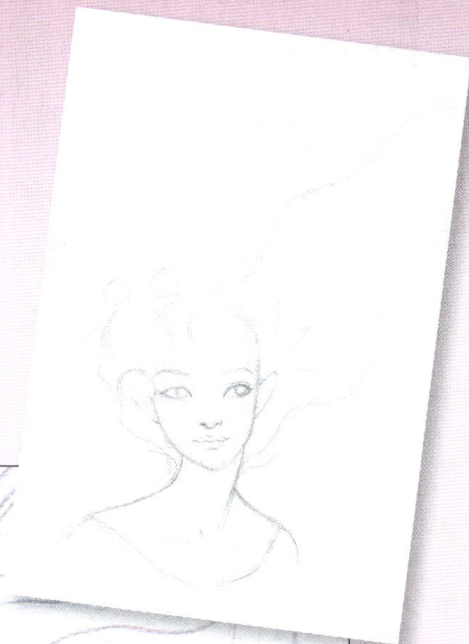

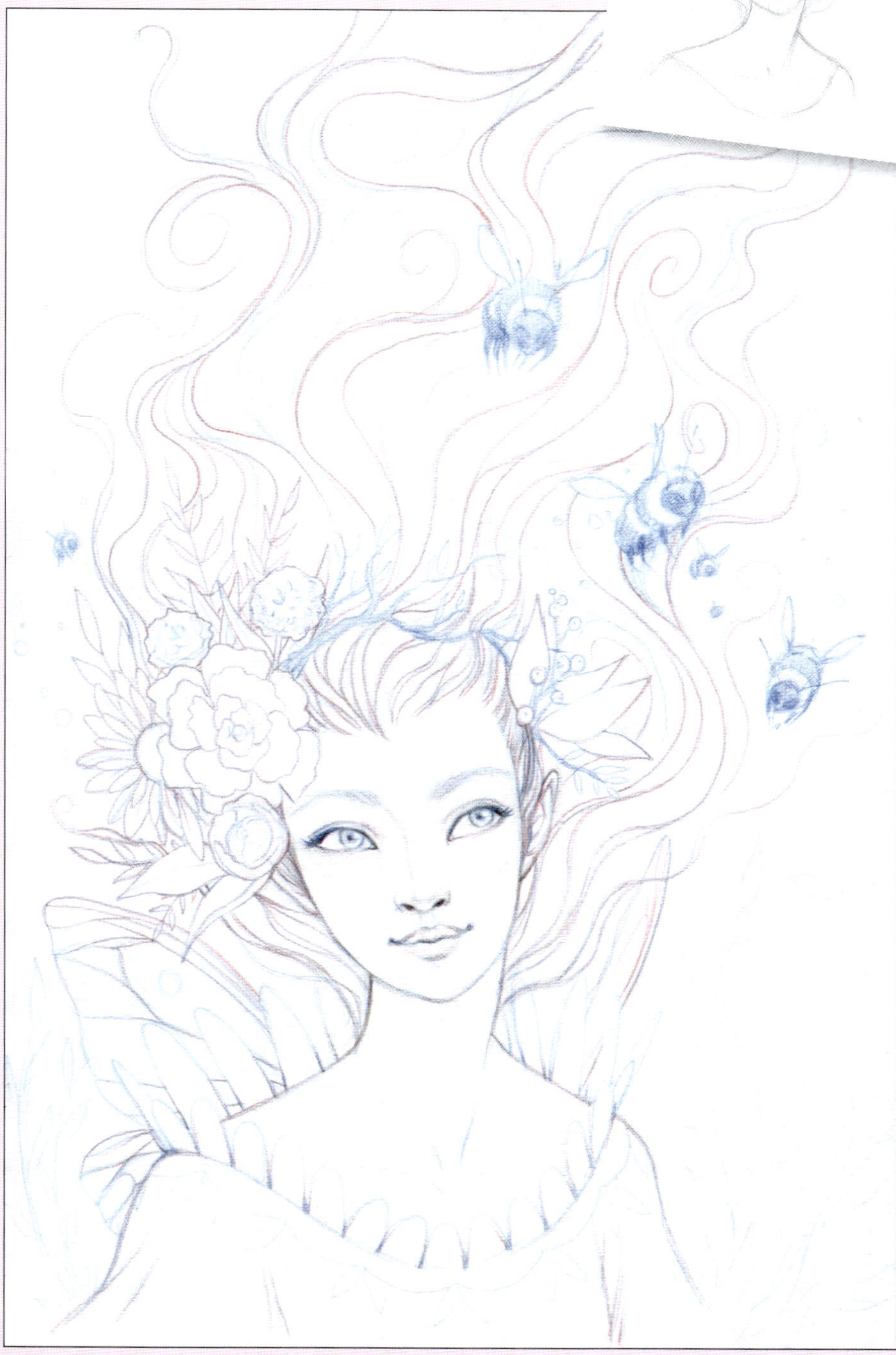

STEP 1 Finish the drawing using indigo and Tuscan red colored pencils. Use oil-based pencils so you can achieve long, fine lines. Use indigo for the darkest and lightest areas, such as the bumblebees and crown of branches, and use Tuscan red to draw the midtone areas, such as the hair and flowers. Erase your initial sketch lines as you go.

Tip

IT'S EASY TO LOSE YOUR PLACE AS YOU WORK WITHIN THE HAIR. BUILD YOUR COLORS AND VALUES SLOWLY, AND TRY TO STAY IN THE MOMENT AS YOU CREATE EACH WAVE AND SWIRL.

STEP 2 Begin laying in reds to define the light source. Alternate using Tuscan red and crimson red for flesh areas, such as the nose and cheeks, and use process red in darker shadow spots. For the skin, use soft, short strokes with very light pressure. To fade out the color, use gentle crosshatching. Fill in the hair using long strokes that follow the waves and swirls. Use light to medium pressure, and feel the waves as you stroke.

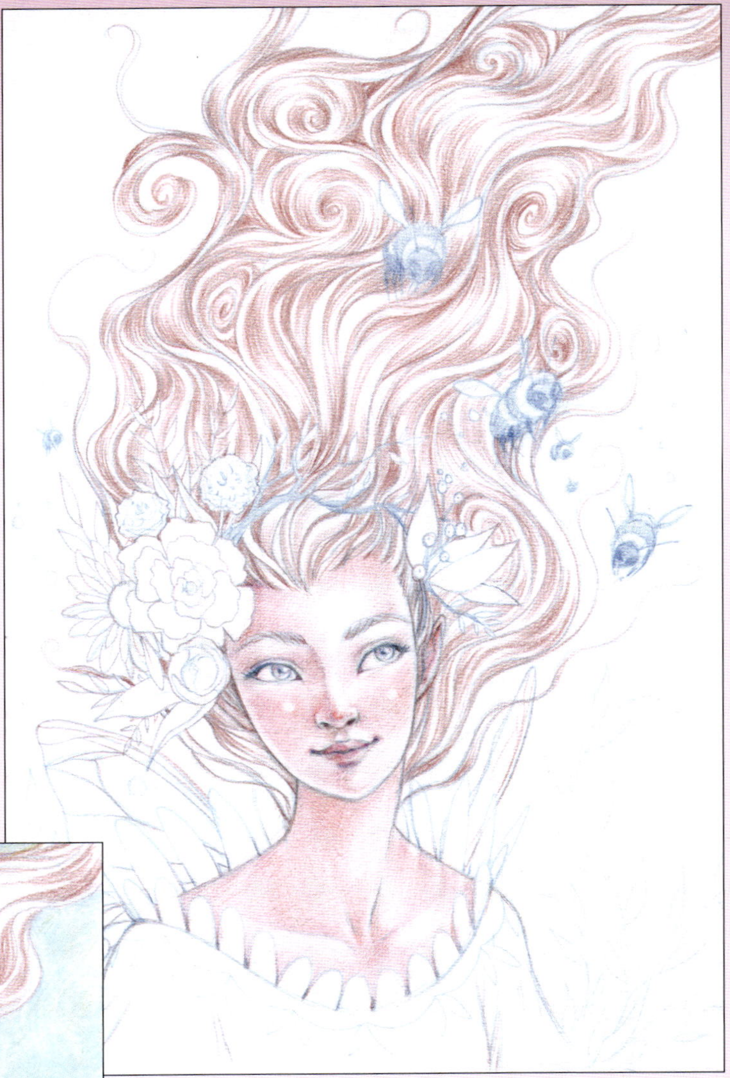

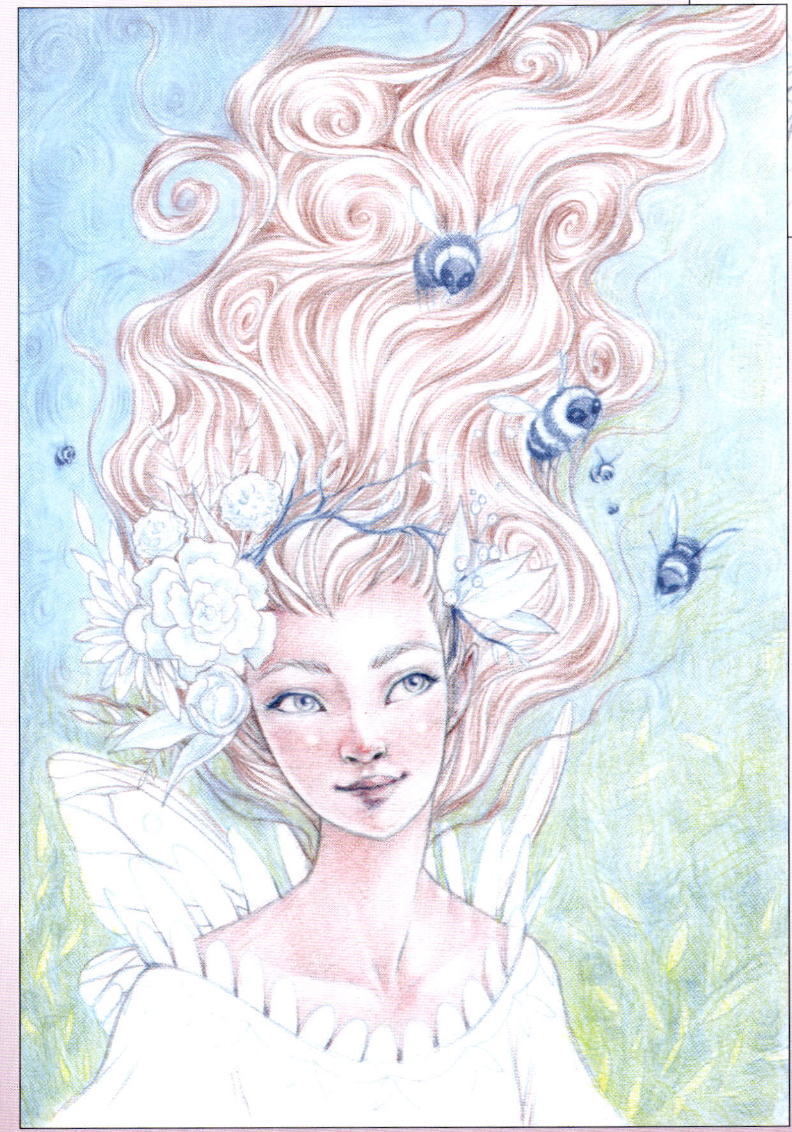

STEP 3 Using light blue, draw swirls and spirals randomly for the sky, keeping them close together for a pattern-like appearance. Then use light blue to shade the flowers. Switch to Prussian blue to fill in the bumblebees' blacks and the crown of branches. Returning to the background, follow the spirals and layer Prussian blue, starting at the top of the drawing and lightening as you approach the fairy. Next, lightly add peacock blue in the upper left corner to intensify the color. Burnish the background with a waxy white pencil and heavy pressure. Lastly, with light pressure and short strokes, add lemon yellow on the left and bottom of the drawing to create atmosphere.

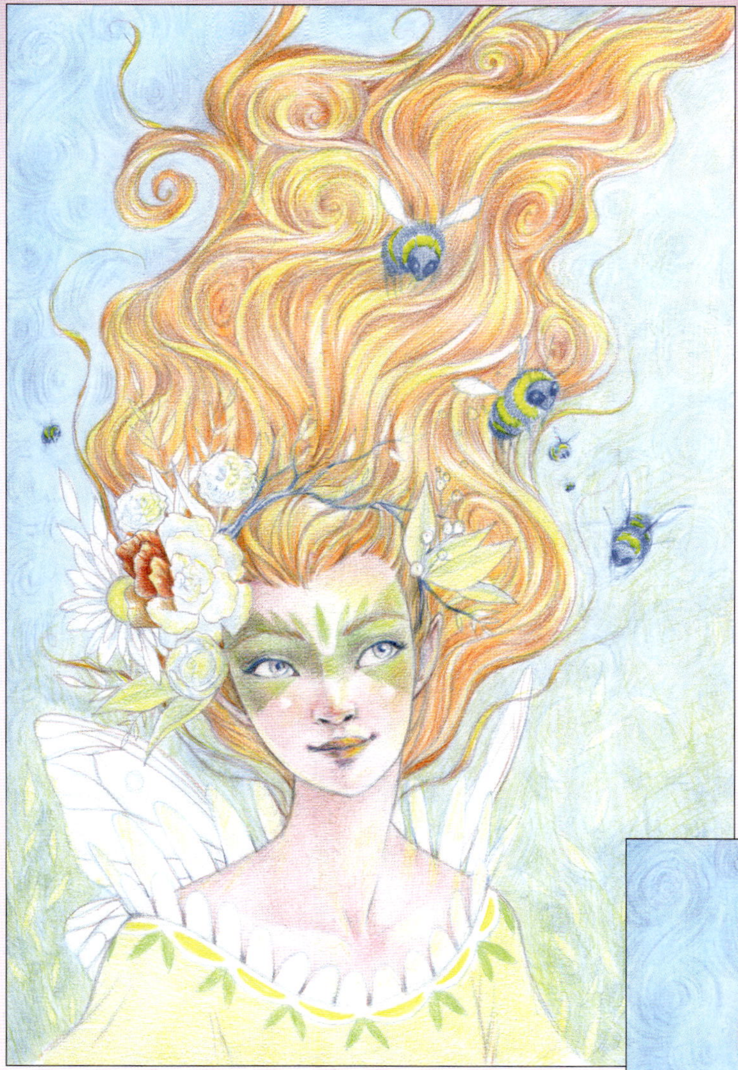

STEP 4 Apply lemon yellow over all areas of light, starting with light pressure in the face and clothes. Switch to medium pressure for the bumblebees, lips, and daisy flower. Add lemon yellow to the tips of the flowers with tiny, light, circular movements. In the hair, use medium pressure, again following the waves and spirals using long strokes. Lastly, return to the hair with orange, going over the darkest strokes and blending out into the yellow. Then use light pressure to add light green to the face mask and leaves on the clothes.

STEP 5 Using heavy to light pressure, fill in the peony flowers with poppy red followed by crimson red. Use process red in small, circular marks for the pompom flowers, building the shadows using dahlia purple and heavy stippling. For the branches, leaves, and berries, use peacock blue, Prussian blue, and grass green. Add dahlia purple to the wings, starting with medium pressure and lightening as you move outward in small strokes. Darken the veins using heavy pressure.

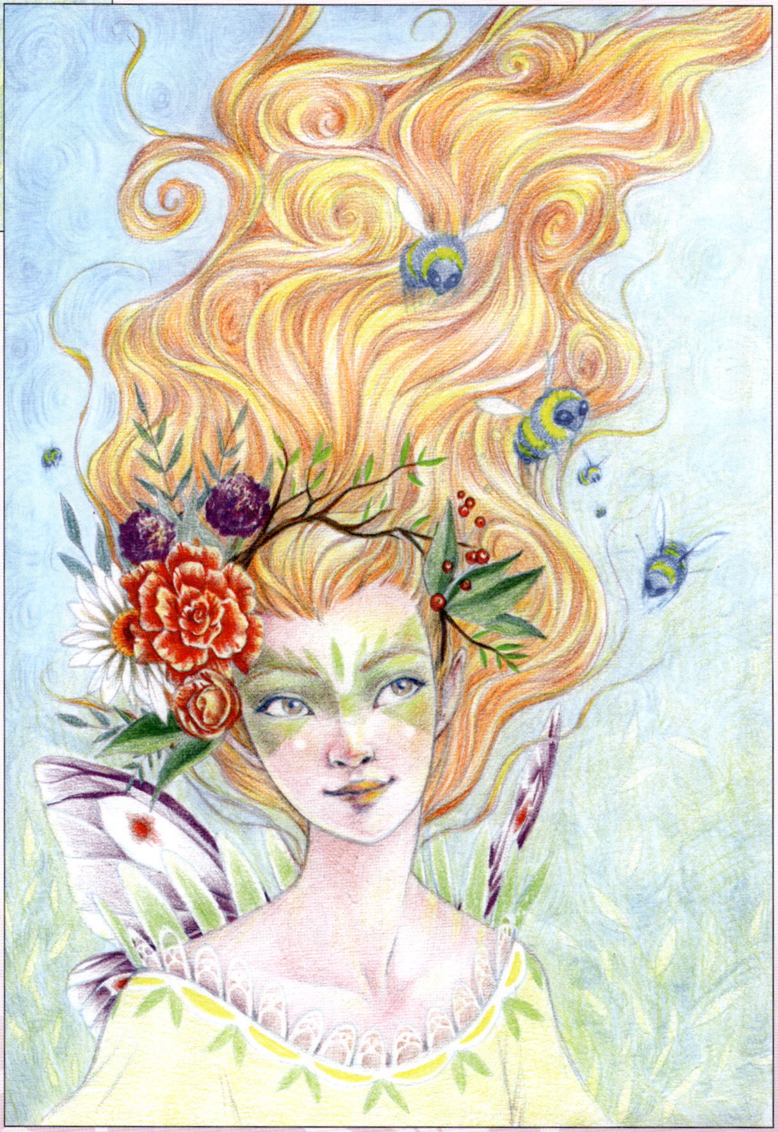

STEP 6 Using dahlia purple and black, begin to intensify shadows while keeping your strokes short at medium to heavy pressure. In the clothes, keep the shadows a little lighter. Return to the hair, applying red-orange and dahlia purple to intensify the shadows. Keep your strokes short, following the movement of the waves and working with medium to heavy pressure.

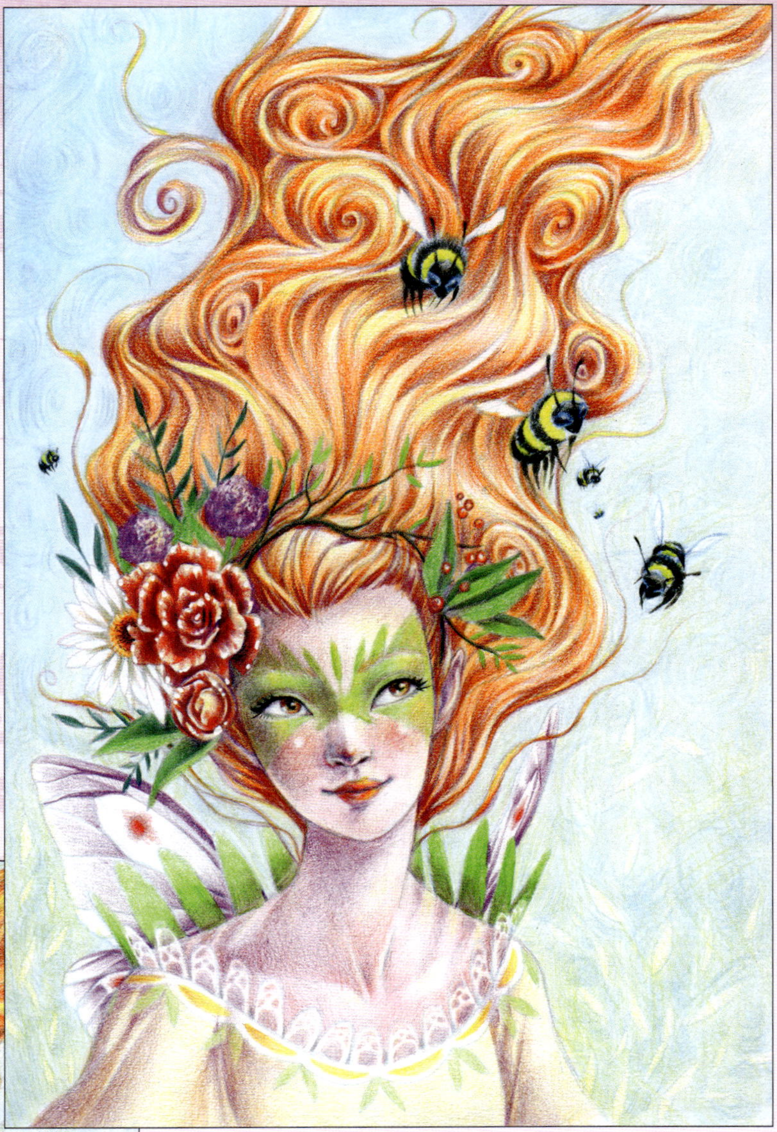

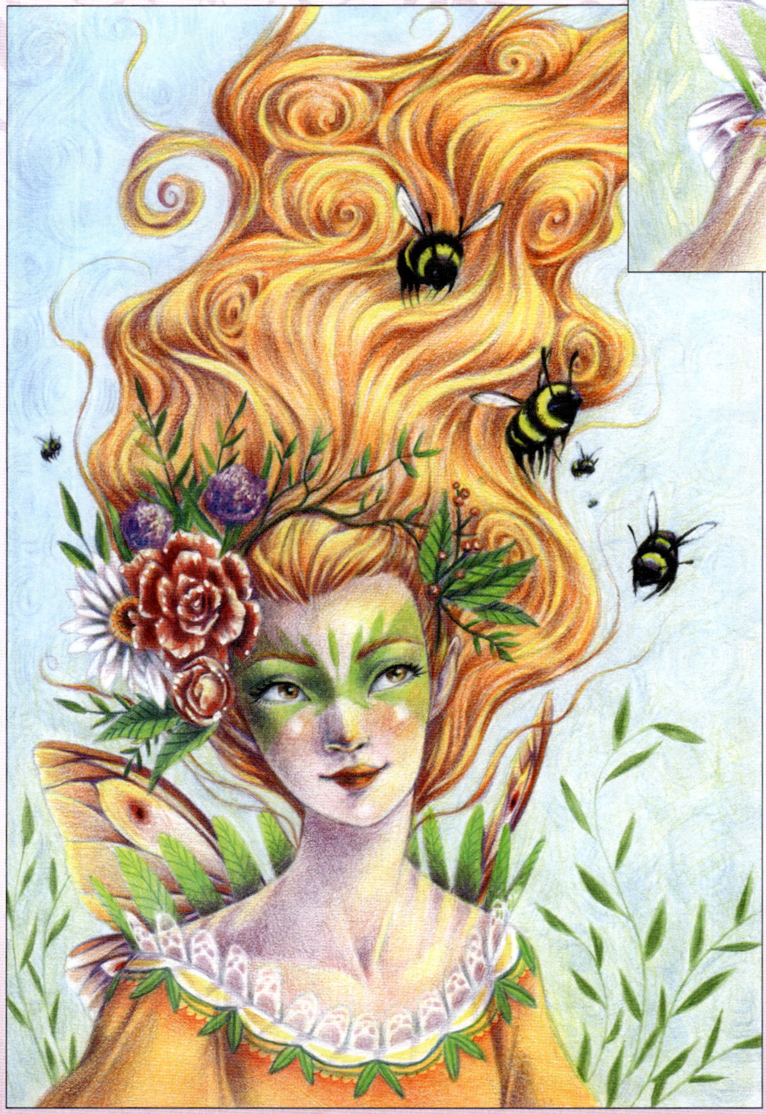

STEP 7 Use a kneaded eraser to lighten any areas by gently pressing down. Continue building up color and refining lines in the dress and leaf veins. Darken your shadows, and lay orange and lemon yellow into the clothes and wings. To brighten areas of highlight in the hair, add a layer of lemon yellow.

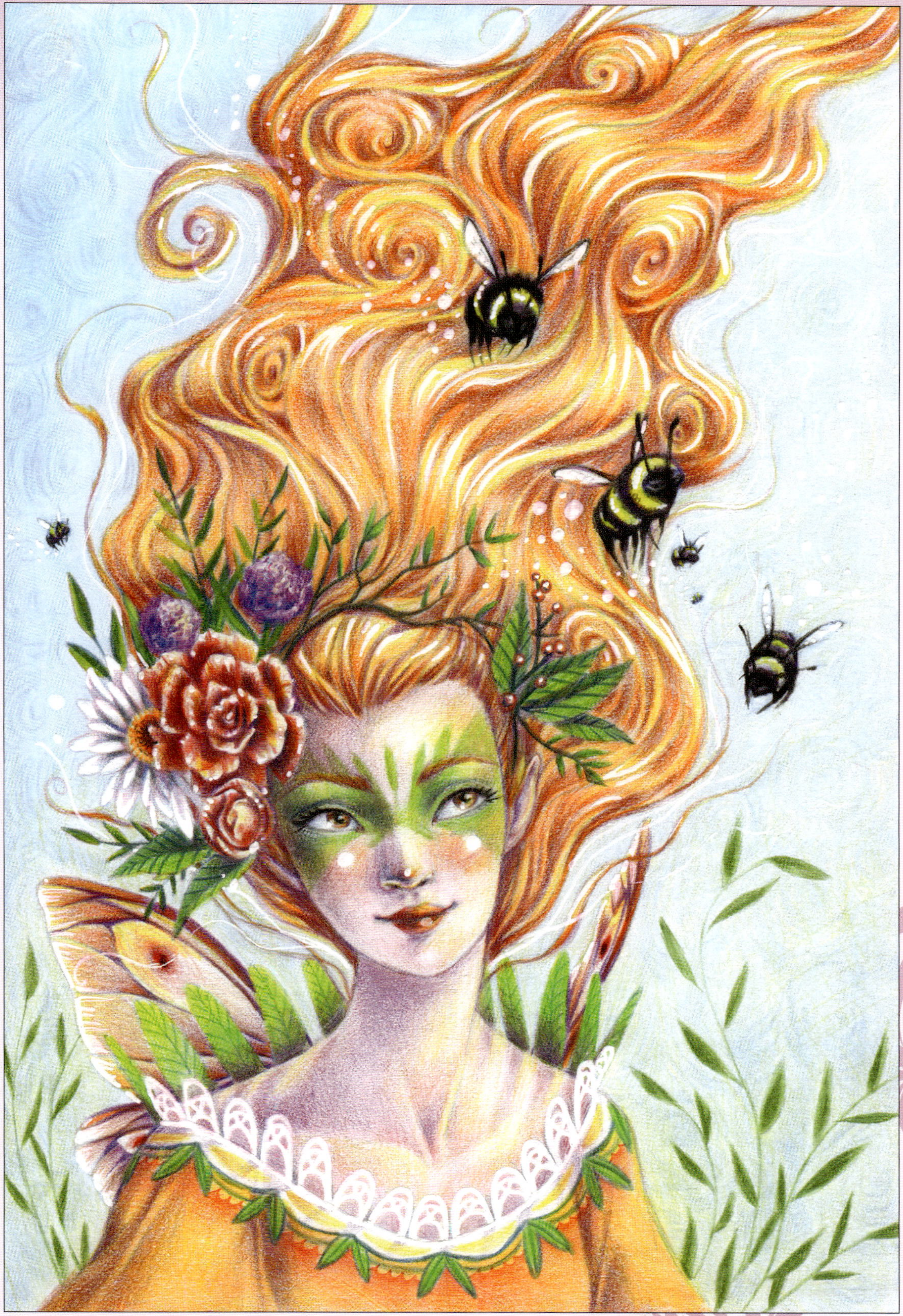

Step 8 Add finishing touches with a white gel pen, bringing out magical sparkles on the bumblebees, highlights on the nose and cheeks, and the lacy details of the dress. You can also use the white gel pen to intensify the shine of her hair.

Fairy Circle

with Sara Burrier

FOR THIS PROJECT, use a variety of application techniques to create a range of textures—from circular scribbling and feather-like strokes to smooth burnishes. You'll find that this eclectic look frees you of keeping every element consistent while still resulting in a cohesive work of art. In addition to the palette below, you'll also need a white gel pen to complete this project.

- 30% cool gray
- Black
- Canary yellow
- Chartreuse
- Dahlia purple
- Dark green
- Goldenrod
- Grass green
- Lemon yellow
- Light aqua
- Light peach
- Mulberry
- Olive green
- Orange
- Parma violet
- Peach
- Peacock blue
- Peacock green
- Poppy red
- Process red
- Sky blue
- Terra cotta
- Tuscan red
- Violet
- White

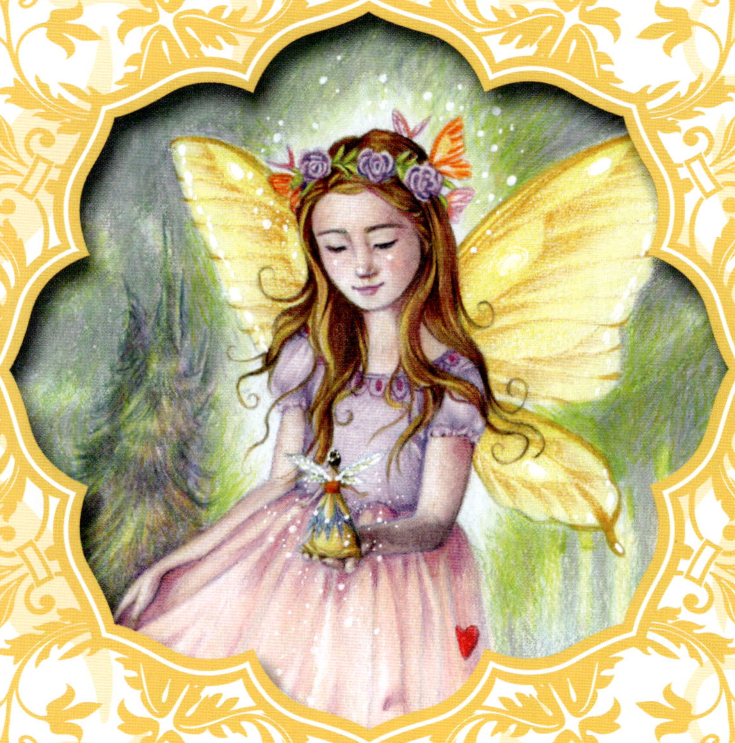

Sketch Sketch the scene with a peacock blue oil pencil. Lightly fill in some tree trunks, branches, and grass in the background, which will help them appear soft and distant. (To transfer the template for this project, see page 125.)

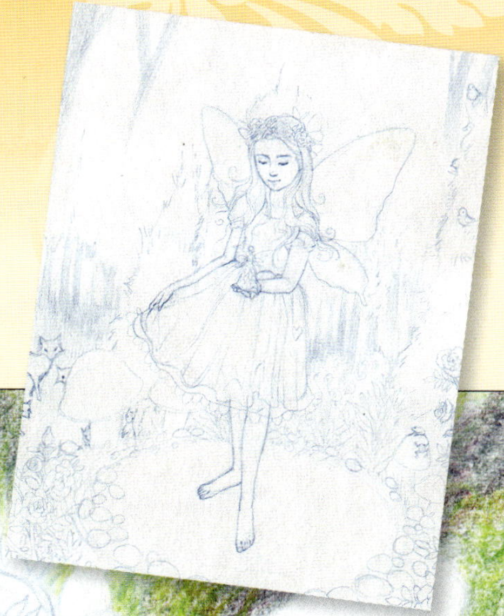

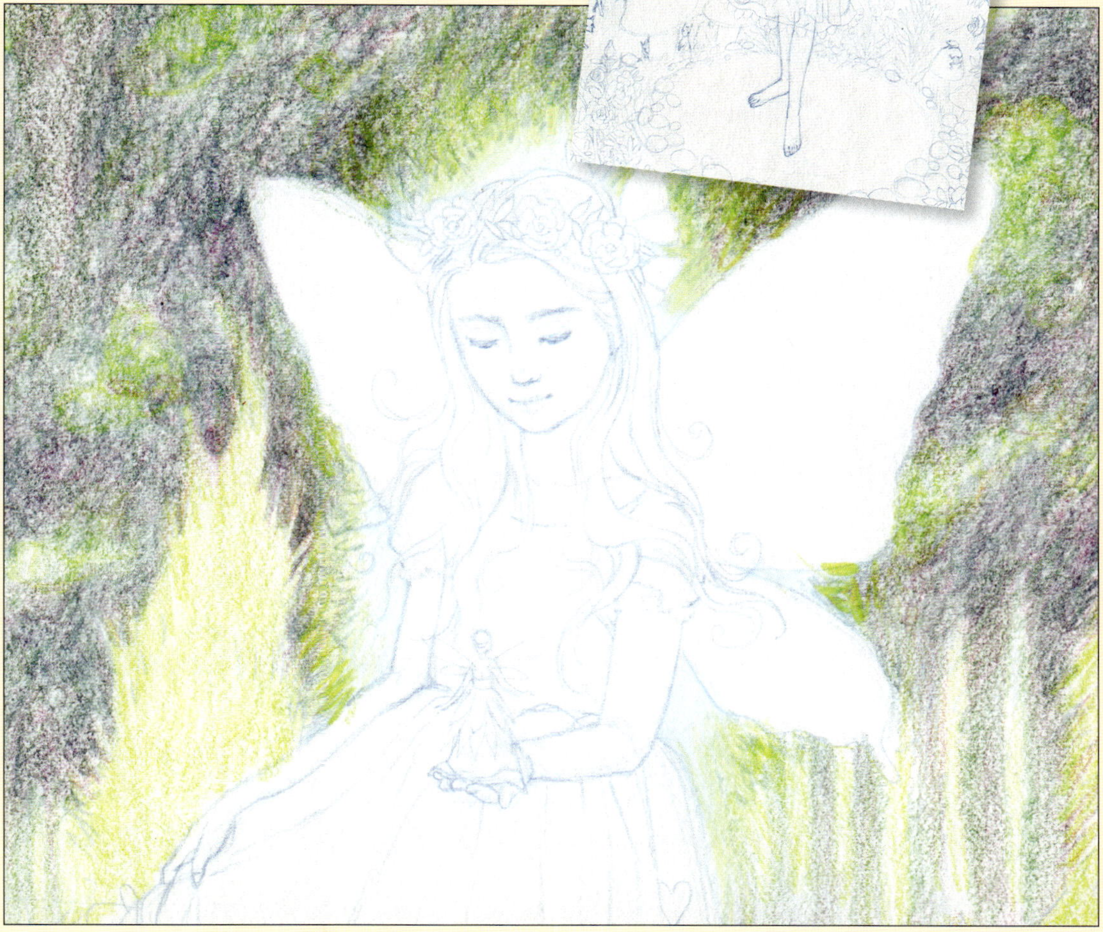

Step 1 Use scribbling strokes to apply grass green (oil) in the background, working from the top down to the tree trunks. With light to medium pressure, leave a few areas free of tone to represent light coming through. Using a vertical stroke technique, apply heavier pressure over the branches to separate them from the leaves. Fill in the areas of light with chartreuse, and add sky blue (oil) behind the fairy. Bring in mulberry and grass green for the darkest tree leaves.

Step 2 Burnish everything with white. Then add another light layer of grass green over the background leaves and a layer of mulberry over the tree branches. Finish off by burnishing everything with 30% cool gray. Using small fur-like strokes, fill in background grass and middle-ground trees with chartreuse.

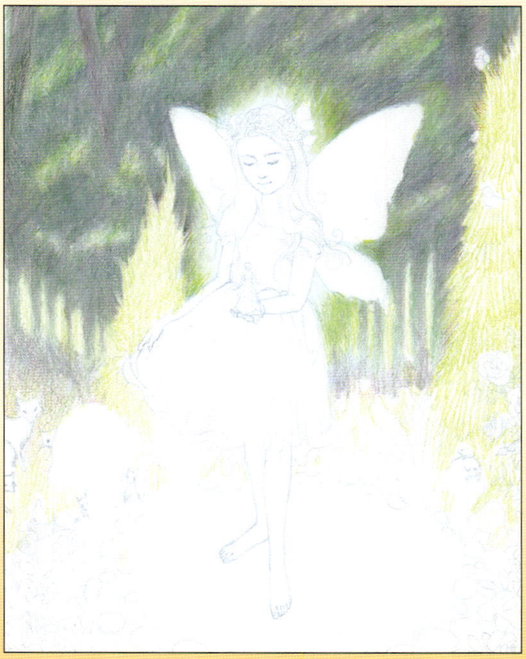

Tip

Use grass green throughout the piece to diminish any "halos" around the objects, such as the foxes and mushrooms.

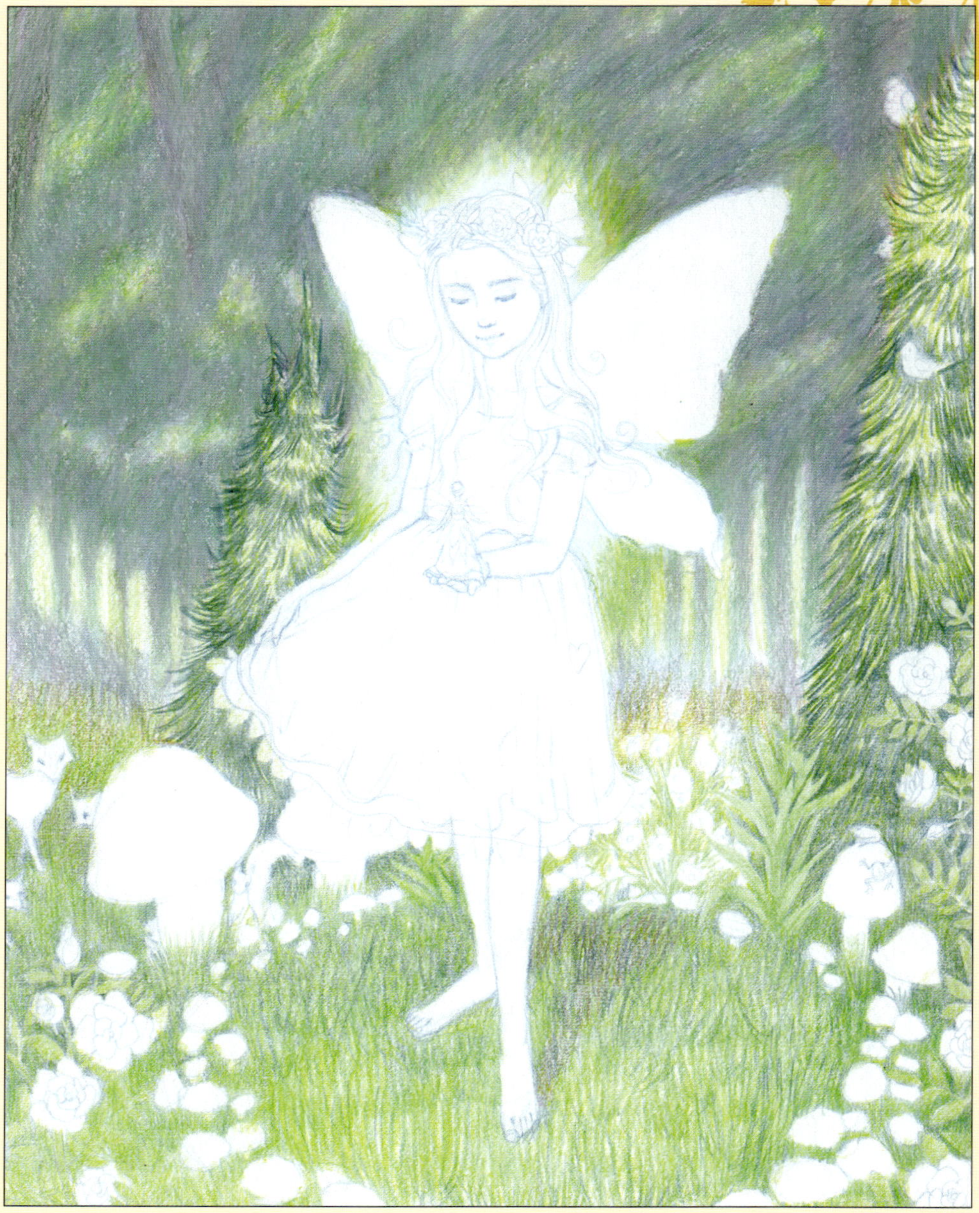

Step 3 Fill in the grass using chartreuse and small, vertical strokes, which allow for a consistent texture even in small areas. Create "pouches" of grass by adding grass green and olive green (oil). Keeping your strokes random will help the grass appear natural. Give the middle-ground trees depth using dark green (oil), and then create tall grasses and leaves with grass green and olive green.

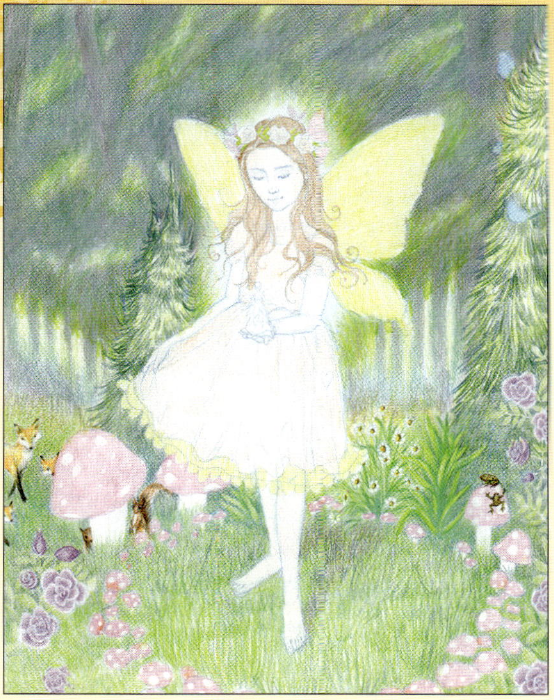

Step 4 To better determine how dark you should make the background, fill in as many white areas of your drawing as possible with oil pencils. Use process red for the mushrooms, and then dahlia purple (followed by burnishing with white) for the roses. For the daisies, use orange, grass green, lemon yellow, and peacock blue. Work in long strokes, filling in the dress and skin with light peach, the hair with terra cotta, and the wings and base of the skirt with canary yellow. To color the foxes, use short strokes of orange, lemon yellow, and black. For the squirrels and frogs, use orange, terra cotta, and black. Create the birds with peacock blue, followed by a burnish of white.

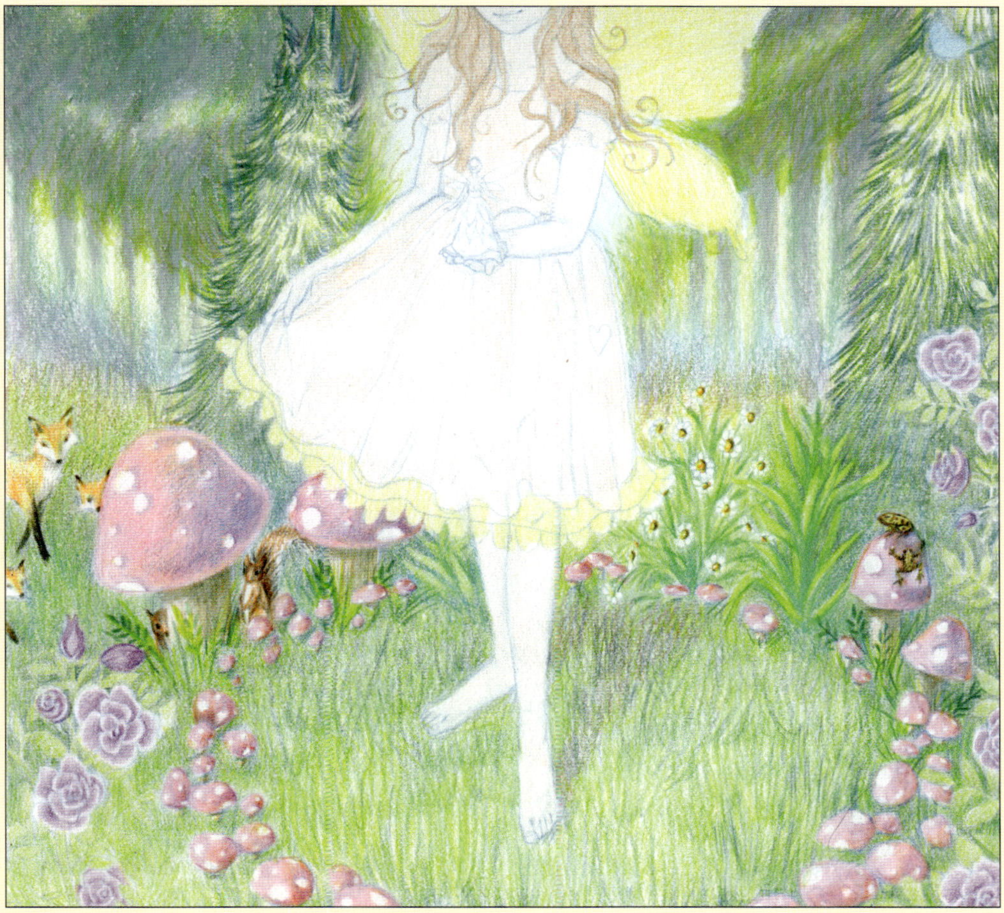

Step 5 Continue developing the scene with oil-based pencils. Using small, circular scribbles, build up the mushroom shadows with poppy red and dahlia purple, followed by a burnish of white. Use peacock blue to intensify the shadows of the large mushroom. Crosshatch more shadows using peach and peacock blue, and intensify the stems with light peach and terra cotta. Fill in the grass shadows with peacock blue and dahlia purple, adding sprigs of grass with peacock green and chartreuse to bring out the pink in the mushrooms.

Tip

Use fine sandpaper to fashion extra-sharp tips on your pencils. This will allow you to produce tiny, precise marks.

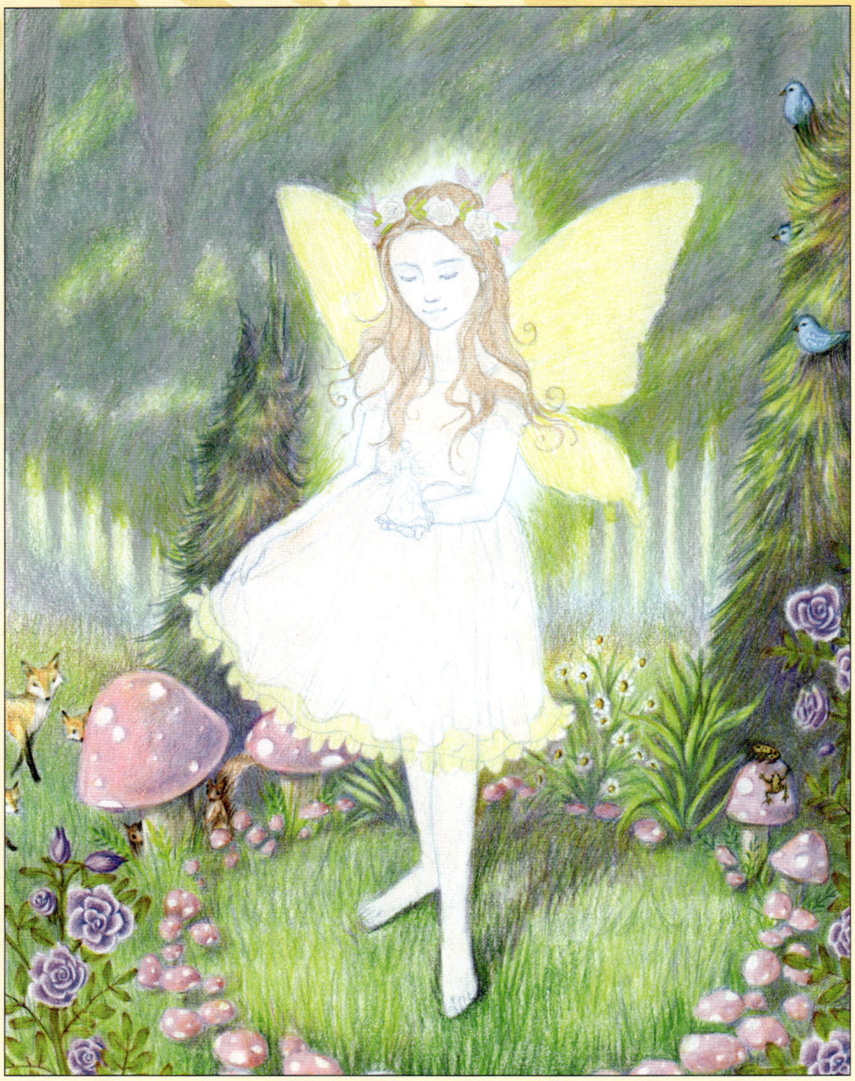

Step 6 Lightly outline the rose leaves and stems with Tuscan red. Using firm pressure, add olive green to all the leaves, followed by Tuscan red on the tips. Burnish each leaf with chartreuse. Build up the shadows in the roses with violet, working from the inside of the petals outward. Add a few heavy strokes of peacock blue in select spots to deepen the roses' shadows. Give the middle-ground trees some heavier shadow with violet, fading the bottoms into the grass with short strokes. Burnish the trees with a colorless blender. Finish the birds using peacock blue for the darkest areas, stippling light aqua (wax) for the wings, and adding black to the eyes and cast shadows.

Step 7 Now build up the skin. Use a light layer of terra cotta in the shadows; then lightly add peach over most of the skin, working around the brightest highlights. Next, use process red for the fleshy areas, such as the wrist, knees, nose, and cheeks; burnish with white. Deepen the shadows with Tuscan red, and burnish with light peach (wax). Use terra cotta for hair shadows, burnish it with lemon yellow, and then apply Tuscan red and a bit of black for the darkest areas. With the skin and hair finished, apply peach and mulberry to the skirt. Burnish with white, and return with dahlia purple and violet to intensify the shadows. Use soft pressure and keep your strokes close together for a blended look.

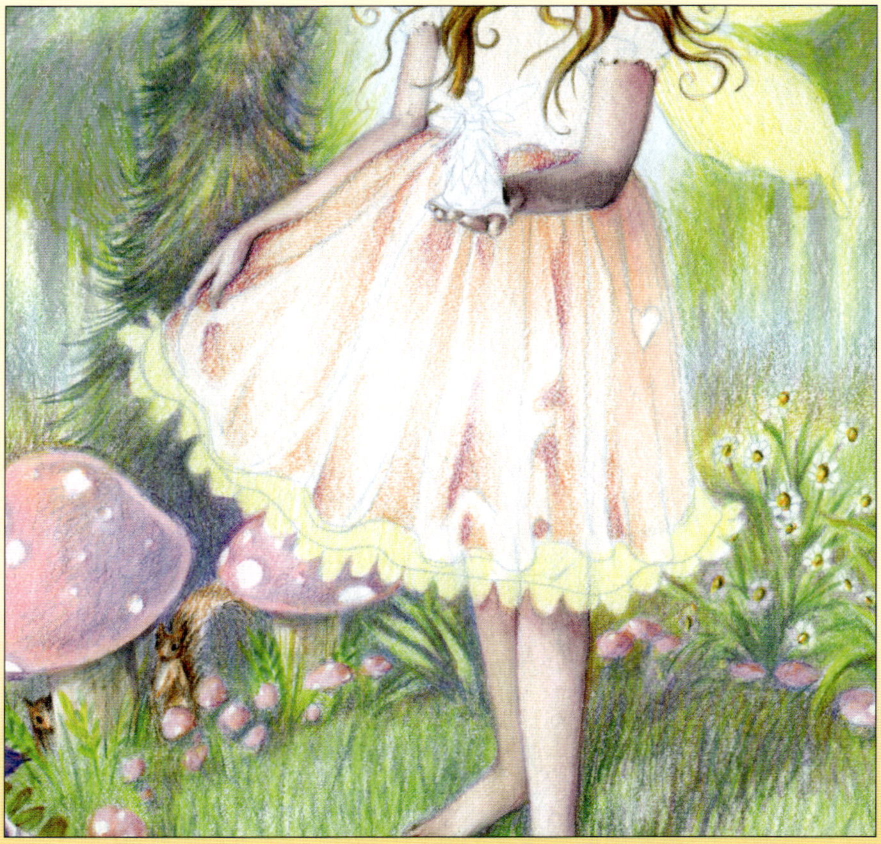

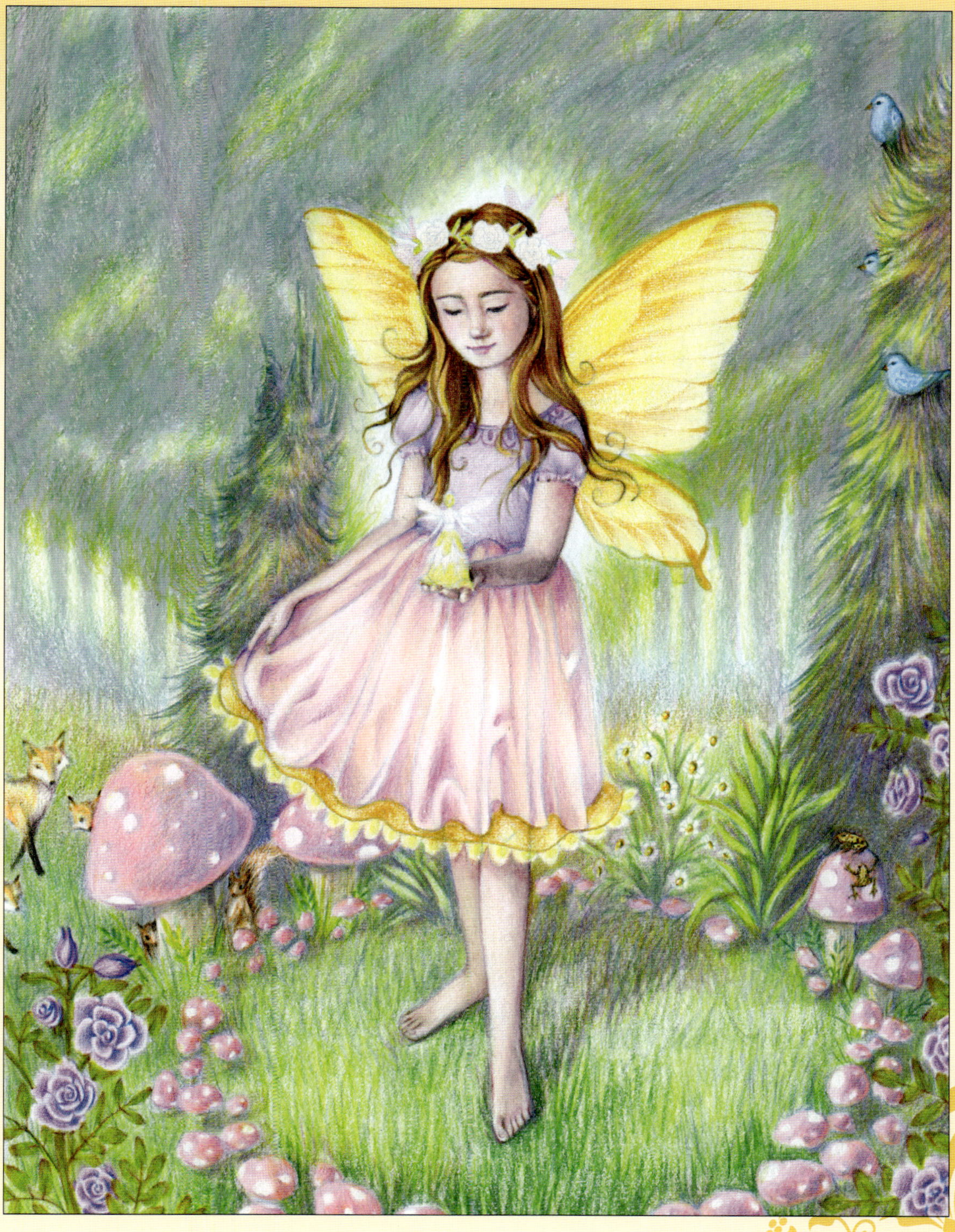

Step 8 Fill in the top half of the dress with parma violet (oil), using dahlia purple for the darks and burnishing with white. Then use peacock blue to add light shadows. Add another layer of purple; then switch to goldenrod and add shadows to the skirt, working from the base and blending outward to a lighter pressure. To finish the skirt's scalloped edge, use lemon yellow. Use goldenrod on the wings, applying heavy pressure on the upper edges. Working from the inside outward, apply feathered, hair-like strokes. Then work in lemon yellow from the top down, lessening your pressure as you move toward the tips. Burnish the outer edges with white.

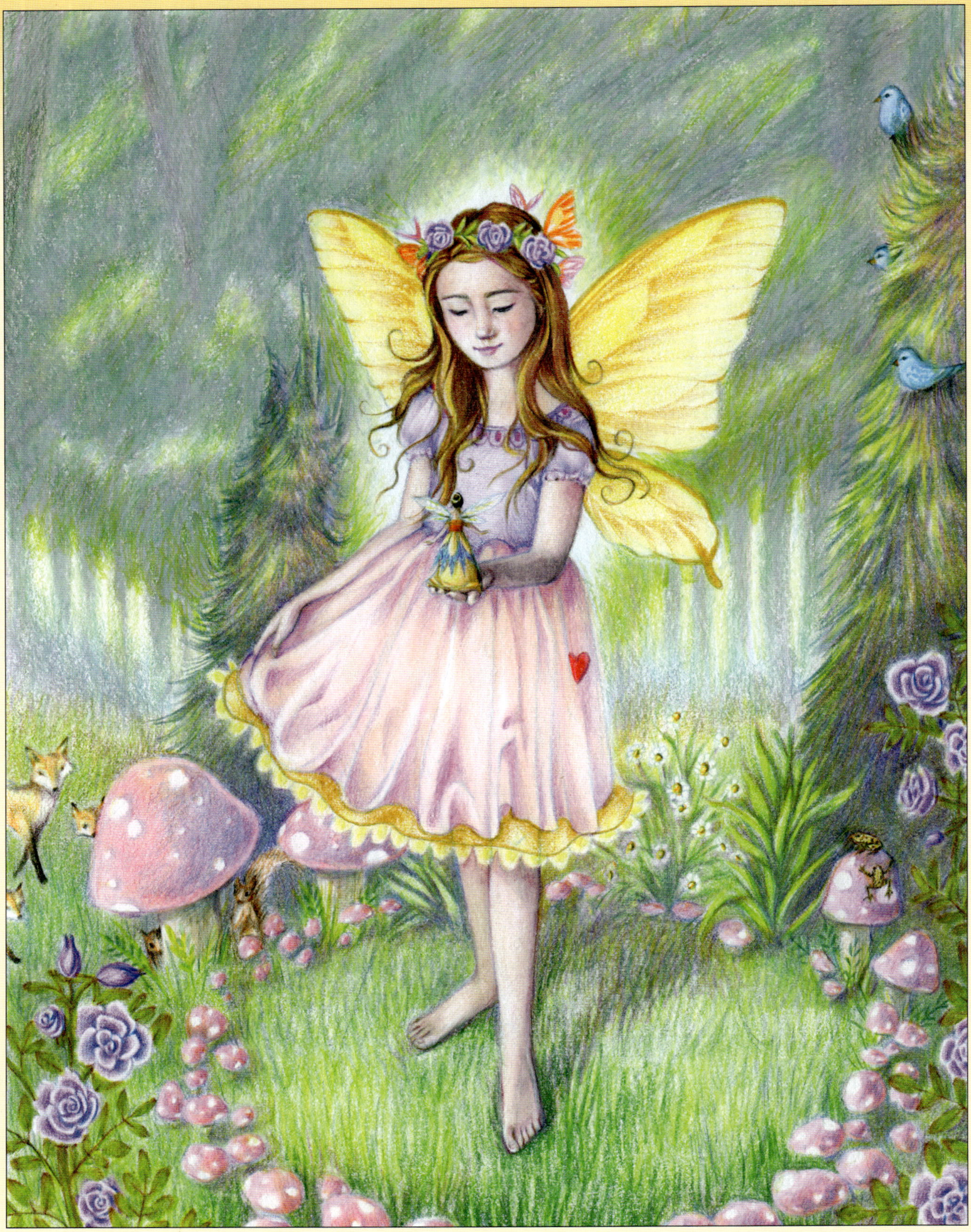

Step 9 Fill in the heart on the large fairy's skirt with process red. Now develop the small, handheld fairy. Apply lemon yellow to the skirt and light aqua to its blue leaf design. Detail it with violet. Apply orange for her top and light aqua for the wings, detailing them with peacock blue. Use terra cotta for shadows and black for the hair. Fill in her skin with terra cotta, burnishing with light peach. Now finish the large fairy's flower crown by developing the foreground roses as you did in previous steps. Use olive green for the leaves, followed by orange, lemon yellow, and process red for the butterflies. Build up shadows with dahlia purple and violet throughout, especially in the grasses and trees.

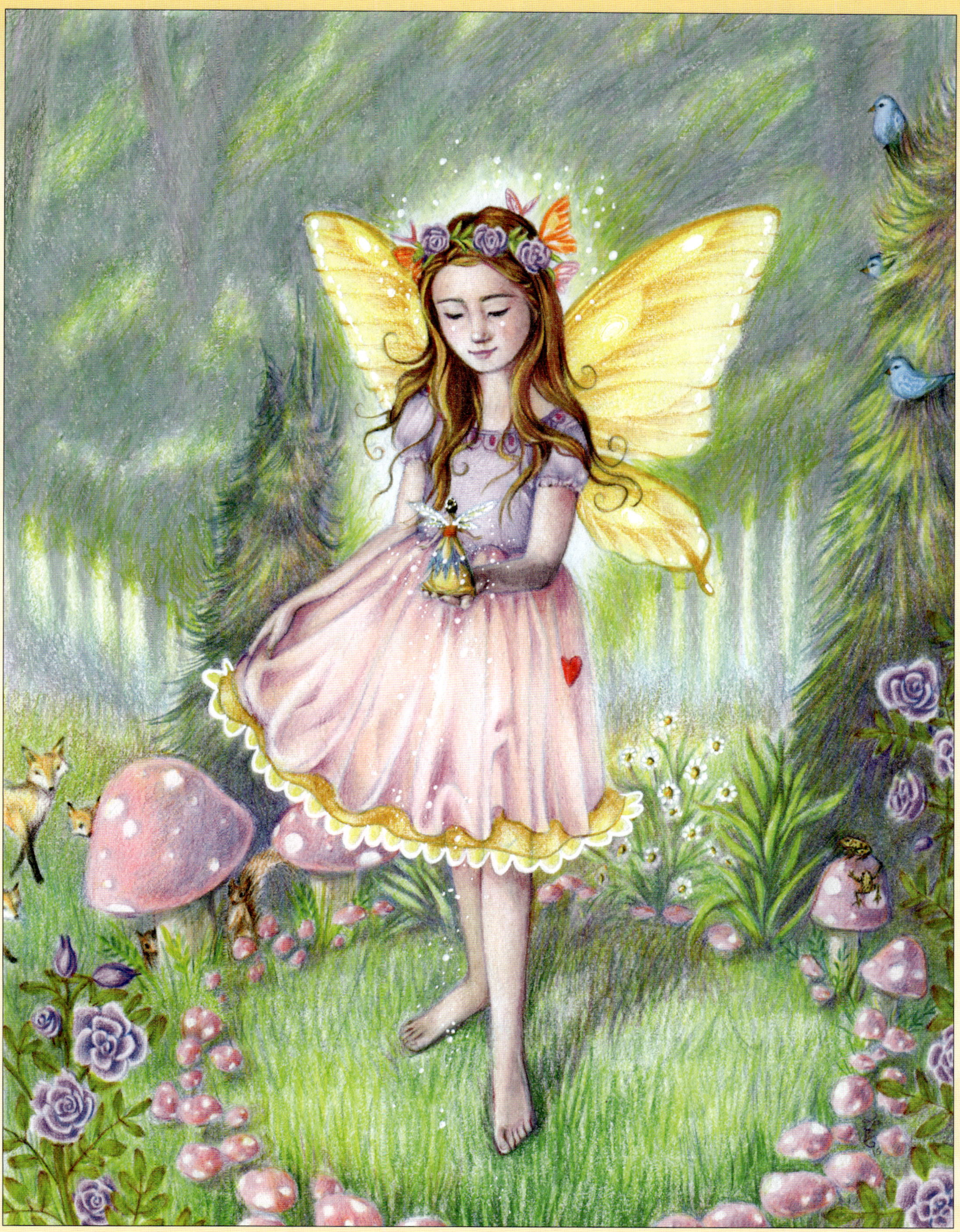

Step 10 To finish, use a white gel pen to add sparkles of fairy dust on the large fairy's face, within her "halo," and around the small fairy.

Poppy Fairy

with Sara Burrier

WHEN DRAWING FAIRIES AND OTHER WORLDS OF THE IMAGINATION, you won't want to copy a reference exactly. In this project, I use a reference for the basic positions of the face, hands, and shoulders; the rest is open to changing form as the drawing develops. When working from the imagination, remember to keep your light source consistent throughout so you can build realistic highlights and shadows.

30% cool gray	Black	Crimson red	Deco pink	Grass green	Lemon yellow	Light aqua	Olive green	Orange	Peach
Peacock blue	Peacock green	Poppy red	Process red	Sky blue	Terra cotta	Tuscan red	Ultramarine	Violet	White

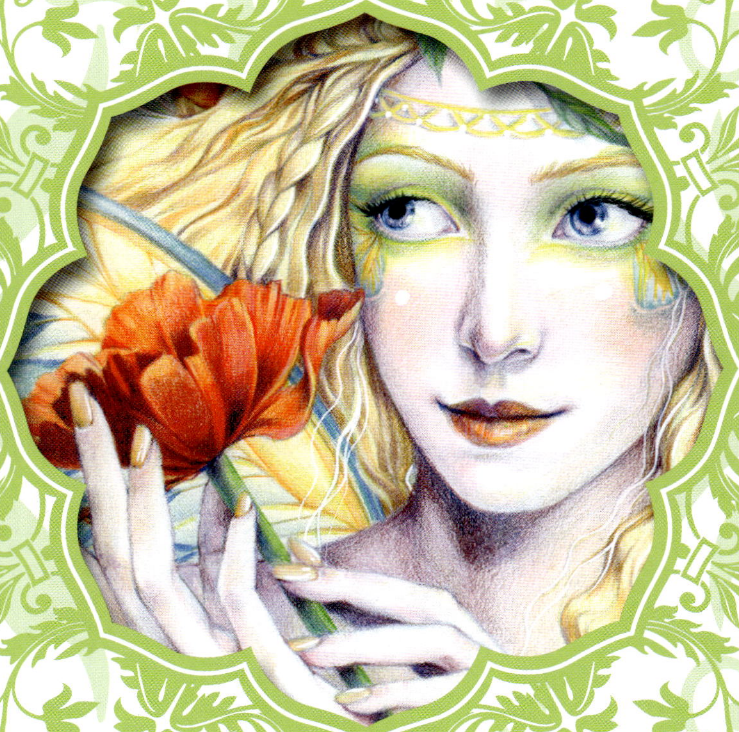

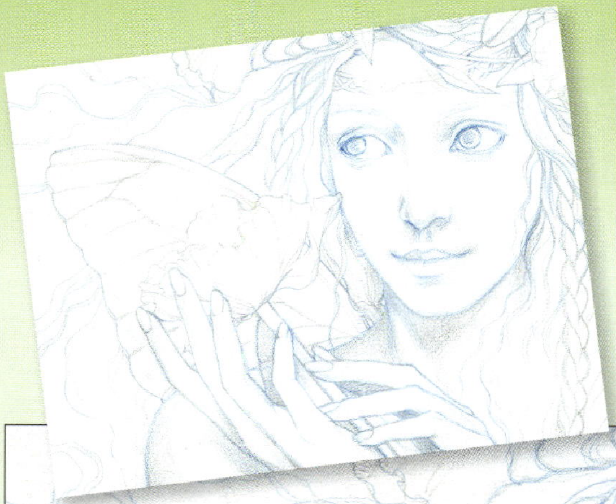

Sketch Start by lightly sketching most outlines in peacock blue (oil). For the lines that need to disappear into the final piece, such as the poppies, headband, and inside of the wing, use a 30% cool gray pencil. (For the remainder of the project, use oil pencils and burnish with a white wax pencil.)

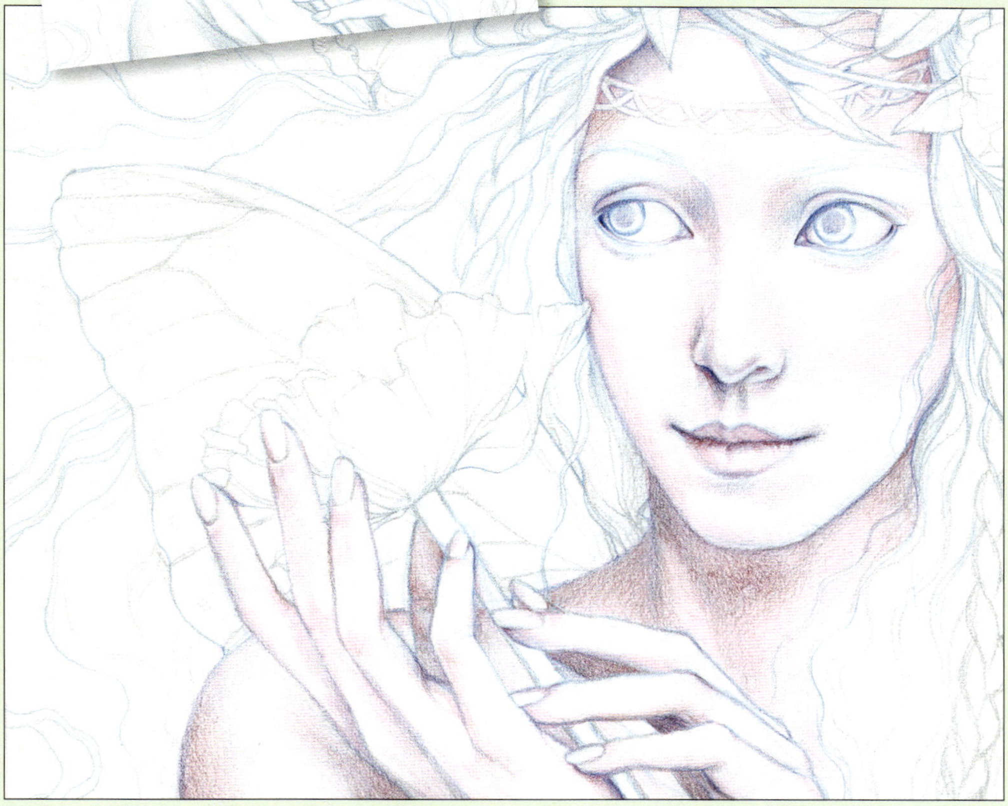

Step 1 The blues of the underdrawing will allow for some soft purples as you apply the pinks of the skin. With light pressure, hatch Tuscan red into the darkest parts of the face, shoulders, and hands. The Tuscan red over the gray will create a muted purple. Next, use process red to hatch the flesh tones, lightly hatching toward the Tuscan red. Allow the creamy color of the paper to come through for highlights.

Step 2 Build up your skin tones using deco pink, process red, and Tuscan red, intensifying the shadows with ultramarine (such as within the nostrils). Layer process red more intensely on the tip of the nose, cheeks, neck, and knuckles.

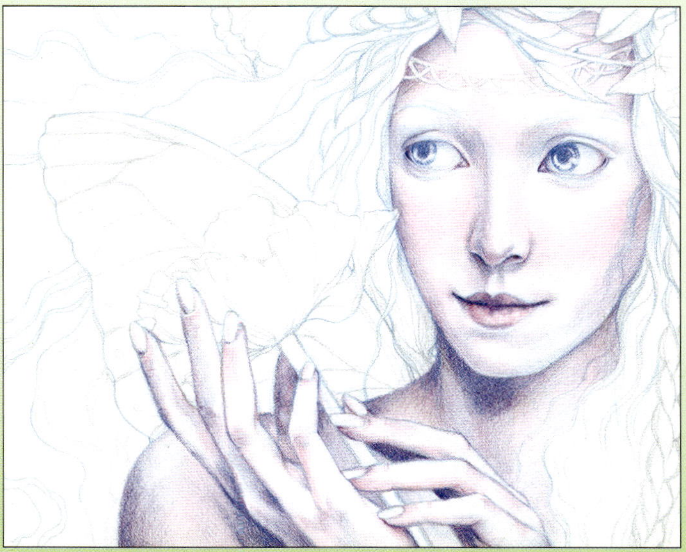

Tip:

Use cool gray to crosshatch areas where the deepest shadows will go. This engages you in the drawing at an early stage by allowing you to see more form.

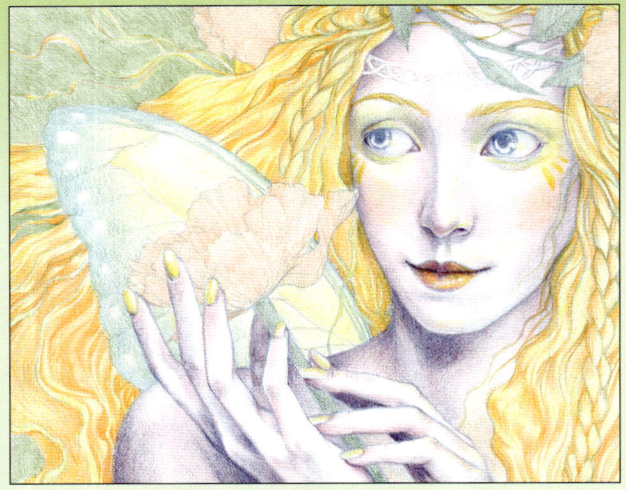

Step 3 Use lemon yellow to fill in the hair, lessening the pressure as you finish each broad stroke. Follow the direction of the hair's wave, letting your imagination flow within the sketch. The light source comes from the right; keep this in mind as you add orange shadows in the hair with medium pressure. Bring lemon yellow to the outer eyes and over the nails. Apply a light layer of olive green over the background using diagonal strokes, and bring this color into the eyelids and under the eyes. Fill in the poppies with poppy red, stroking in the direction of the petals. Color the crown of leaves with peacock green. Using medium pressure, crosshatch lemon yellow inside the wing and switch to aqua near the edges. Use poppy red and lemon yellow for the lips, and bring out the eyebrows with orange.

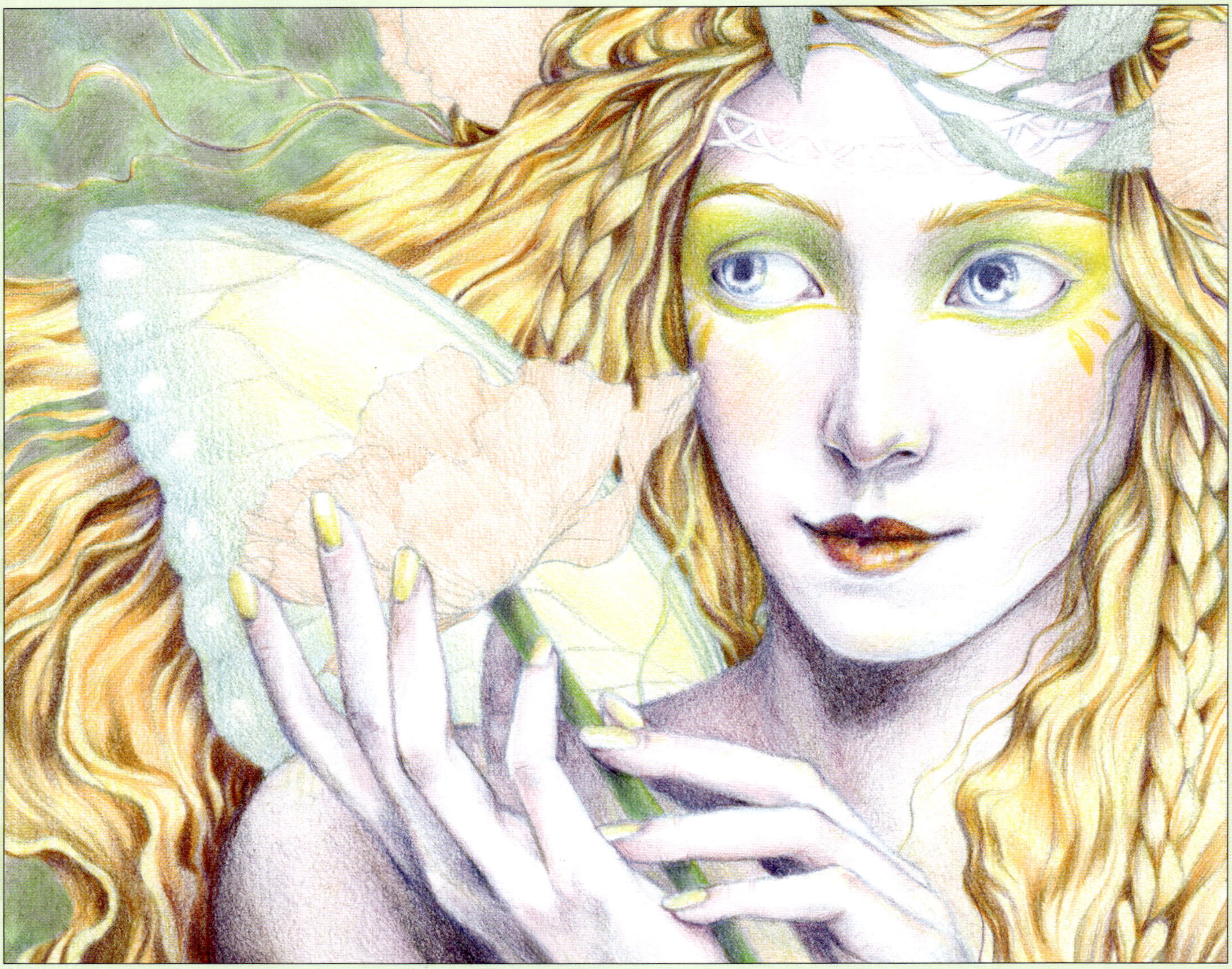

Step 4 Moving in the same direction as the olive green, enhance the darks of the background with violet and ultramarine. Burnish with white to blur and fade out the details. With light pressure, work in the opposite direction of your previous strokes and intensify the background with grass green. Bring violet into the foreground by adding it to the deepest shadows of the hair. To finish, give it volume by adding terra cotta over the violet and to the base of each wave. Intensify the color of her eyes with lemon yellow, grass green, and olive green. Add grass green above the ends of the eyebrows. Next, develop the poppy stem with ultramarine shadows and lemon yellow highlights. Burnish with white, and then coat the stem with grass green.

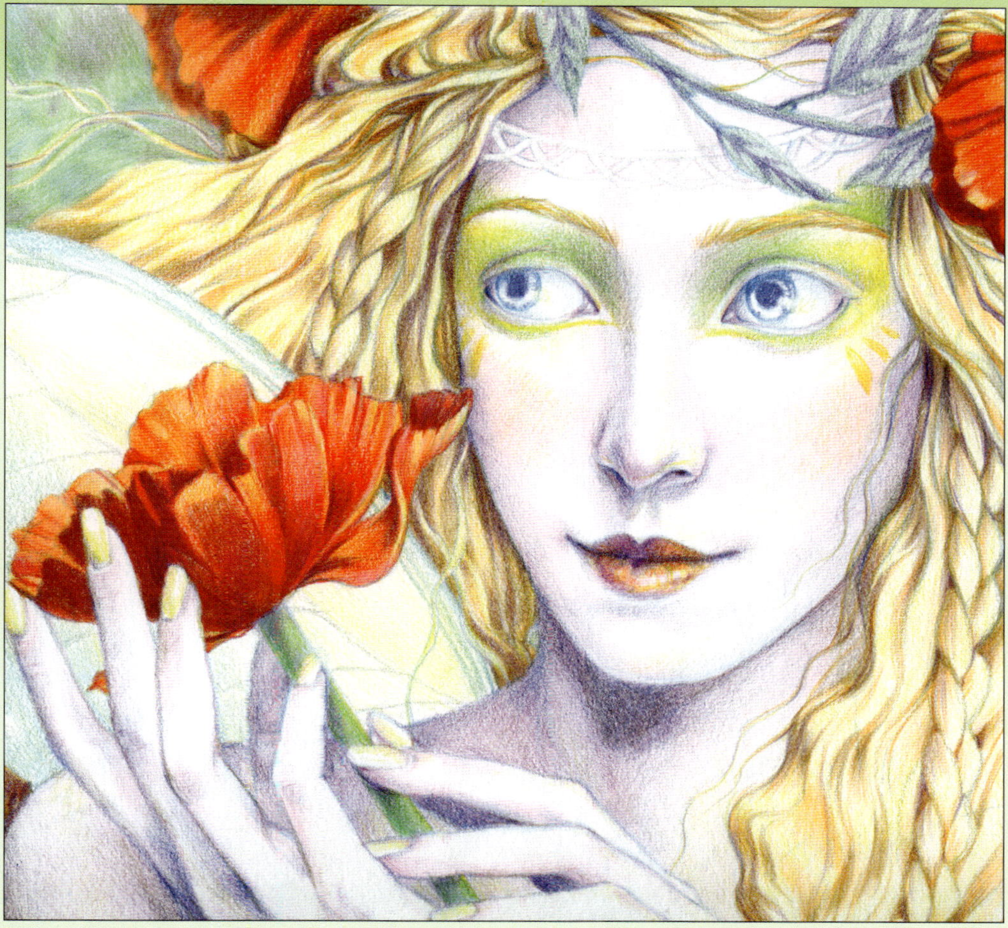

Step 5 Add a layer of poppy red over the poppies, using heavy pressure over the areas of shadow and leaving the lightest areas free of tone. Use lemon yellow and firm pressure over the highlights, fading softly into the richer red. Apply crimson over the deepest shadows, followed by violet in the darkest areas. Use white to burnish the tips and petals in the light. Where needed, redefine your edges with crimson. To blend and push back the upper left poppy, burnish the entire flower with white.

Tip:

Before this step, it's a good idea to observe a general reference of a poppy to understand the forms of its petals.

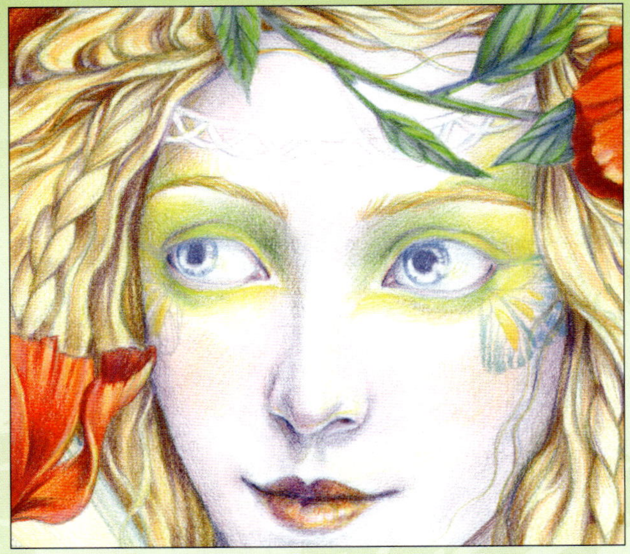

Detail Add "eye wings" to give more character to your fairy. Draw them using 30% cool gray, and add veins using orange. Add light aqua to the tips, burnishing with white. Fill in the gaps and veins with lemon yellow. For the eyes, use process red and pink over the tear duct and skin, adding violet for the shadows within the whites of the eyes. To color the irises, start with process red around the pupil and fade outward; then add sky blue and ultramarine over the iris. Fill in the pupils with ultramarine and a layer of black. Using checkmark-like strokes, draw the lashes with black. Bring out the cheeks with some poppy red.

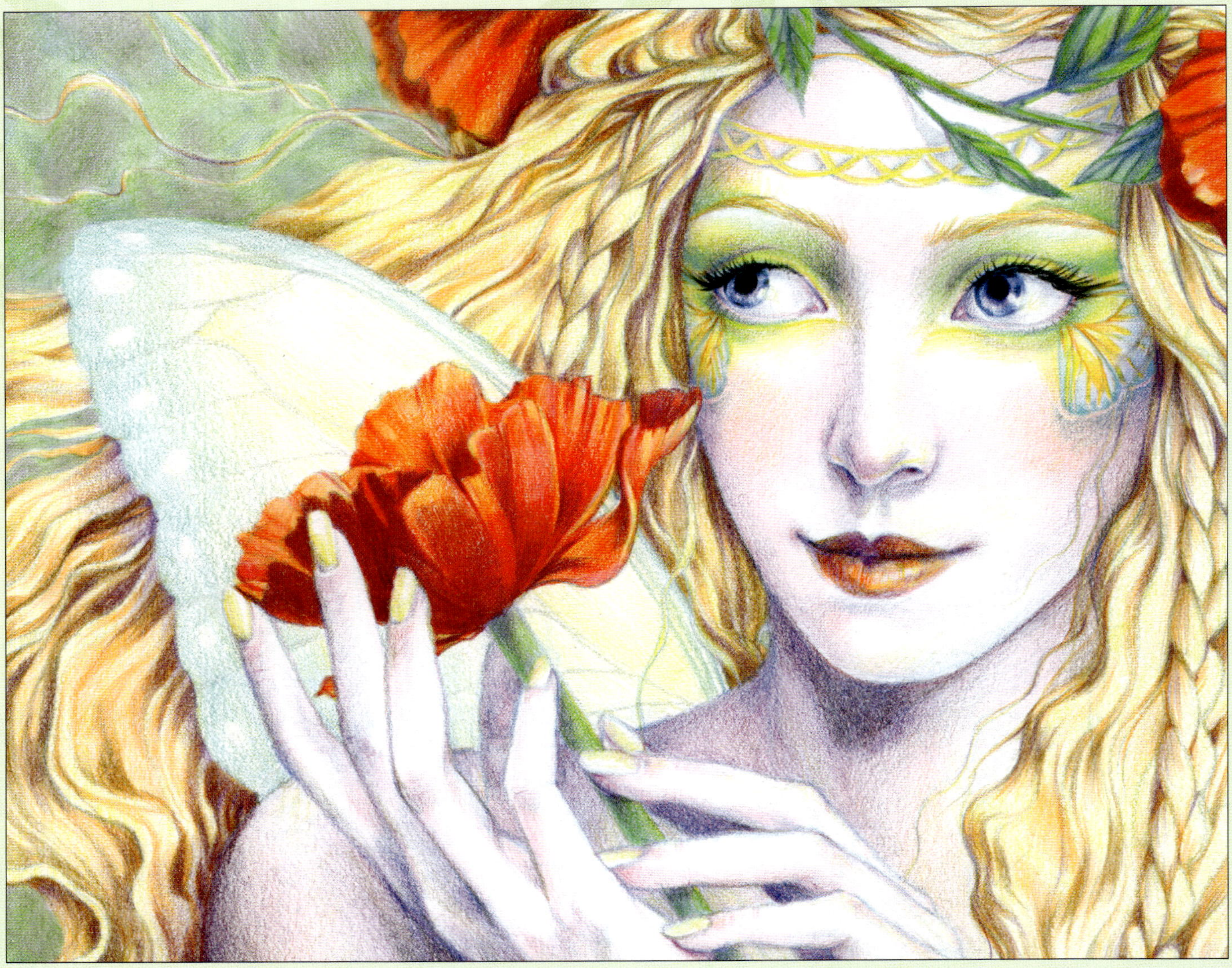

Step 6 Finish the crown of leaves using the same colors as the poppy's stem; use ultramarine for the shadows, lemon yellow for the highlights, and white to burnish. Then go over each leaf with grass green. Add a touch of aqua in the veins for more roundness and dimension. To develop the headband, begin with a layer of lemon yellow, followed by peach for the shadows. Lightly apply peacock blue on the skin along the headband, giving it lift and dimension.

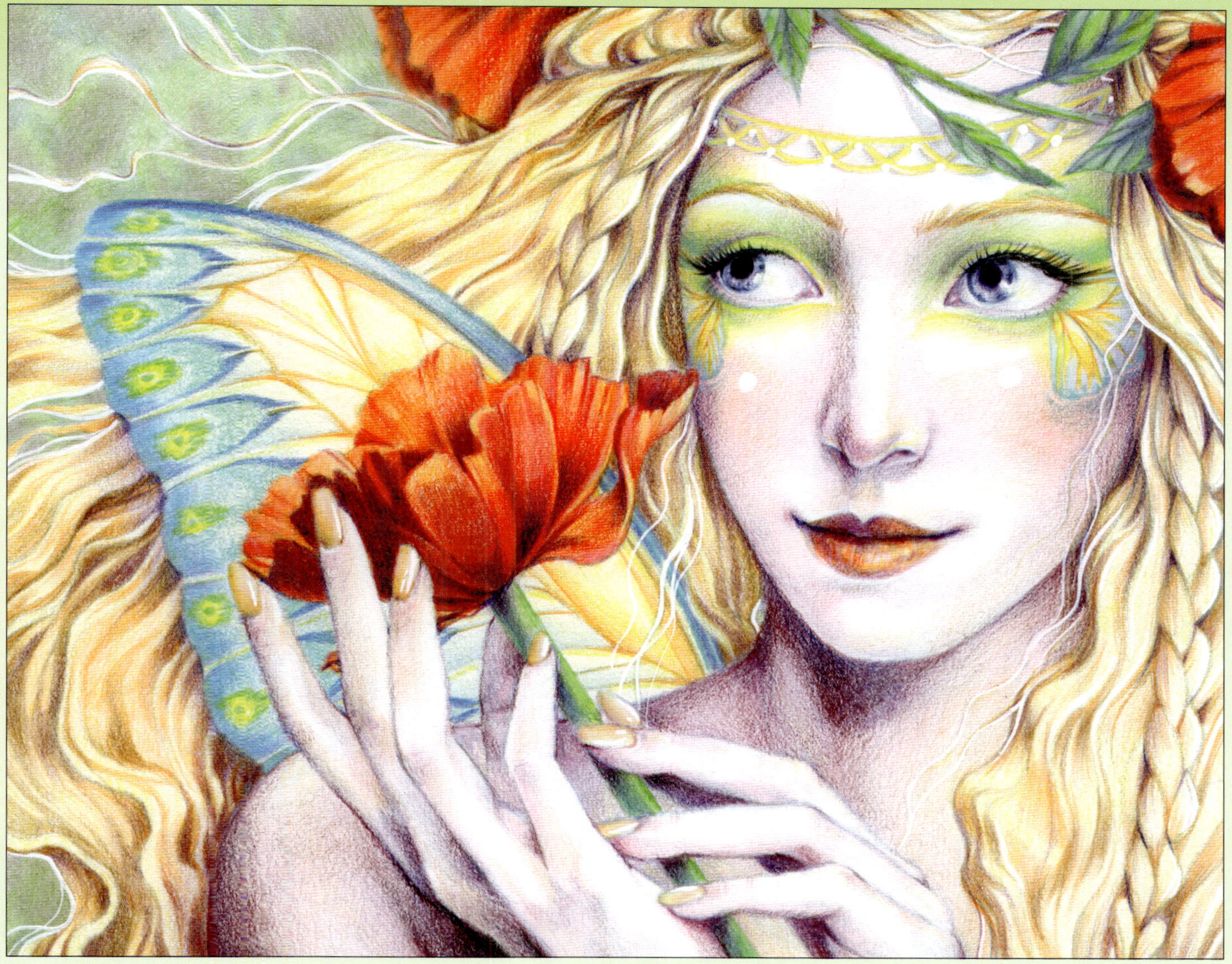

STEP 7 Use firm pressure to build up the outer edges of the wings with light aqua, lightening as you move toward the center. Next add sky blue and burnish the edges up to the white dots and along the bottom of each section to suggest some shadow. Use ultramarine and firm pressure to add the darkest blue details. Fill in the dots with lemon yellow, and use orange to shadow the inside of the wing and outline the veins. To finish, build up the shadows throughout using Tuscan red and black, and use a white gel pen to add any final decorative details.

Butterfly Fairy

with Sara Burrier

USING A TONED (OR COLORED) DRAWING SURFACE pushes you out of the comfort zone of white paper. It is a great way to fill the background at an early stage, and it helps you understand the process of working from dark to light. Contrast and light bring the image to life almost instantly as the fairy emerges out of the darkness.

Apple green · Black · Blackberry · Blue violet · Chartreuse · Emerald · Lavender · Lemon yellow · Light aqua · Light peach · Magenta · Mulberry

Orange · Peach · Peacock green · Pink · Poppy red · Spanish orange · True blue · True green · Tuscan red · Violet · White

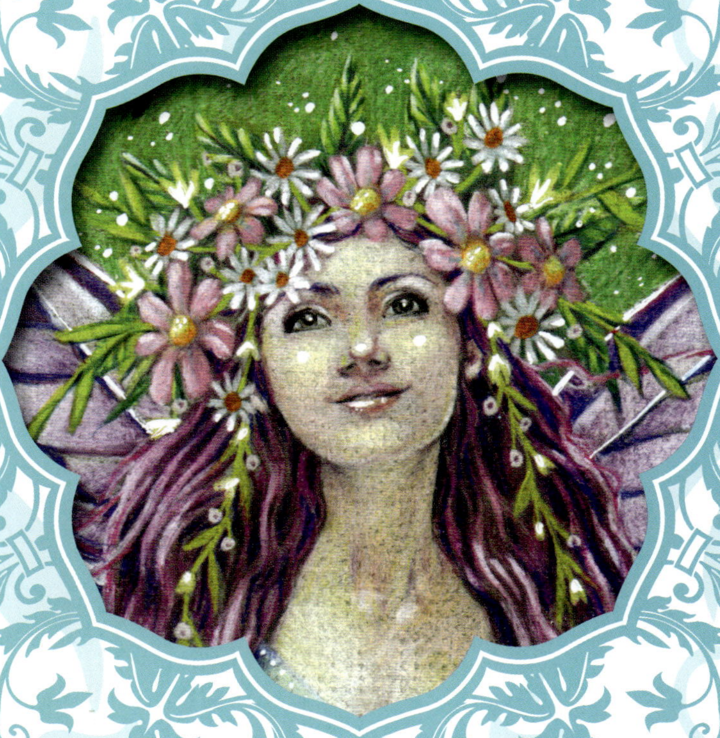

SKETCH Using a white oil pencil, sketch your subject matter on textured green mat board. You can base your drawing on a reference, but change out some features to make the fairy unique. Keep your lines soft and general. Don't let the white lines get in your way; keep in mind that they will fade later in the process. (To transfer the template for this project, see page 126.)

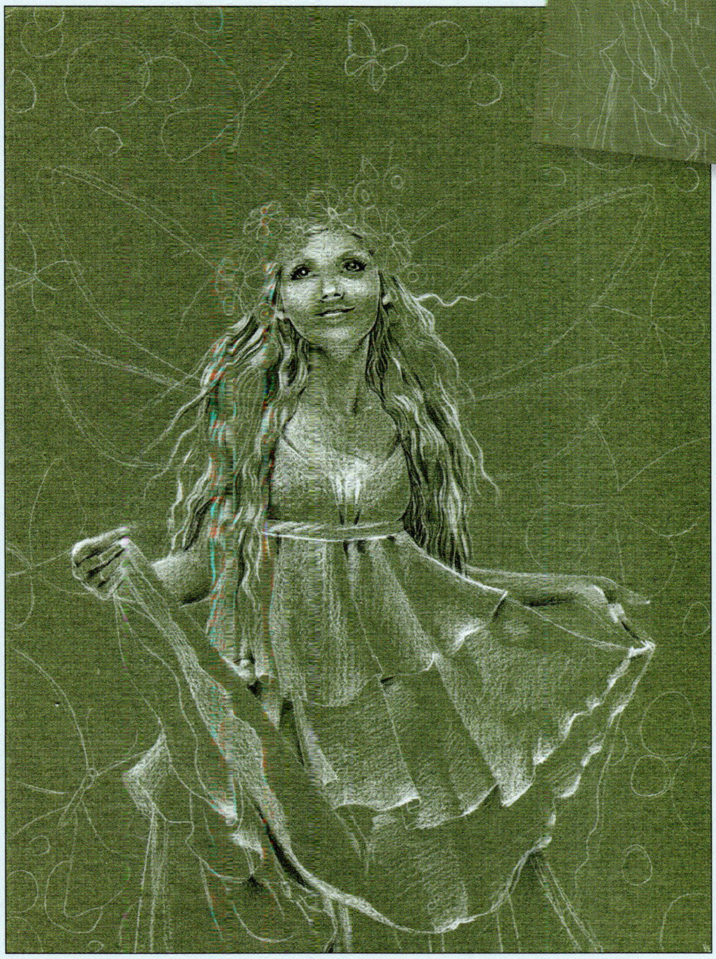

STEP 1 Now build the highlights and map out the darks. Following the light source, add highlights using medium to heavy pressure for the brightest areas, followed by softer pressure for areas that fade into the midtones of the colored paper. Add black for the darkest shadows, taking care not to leave outlines, which can flatten the image. Instead, blend the black lines into the paper with light to medium pressure.

STEP 2 With a very sharp peach pencil (oil), cover the skin using light pressure. Switch to a peach wax pencil and use medium pressure for the highlights, followed by white and lemon yellow. Burnish with light peach for a solid, silky surface. Lay in the shadows with poppy red and use chartreuse under the chin for reflective light. Use blackberry to darken the darkest shadows and use white for highlights. Keep your strokes short and small so they blend easily.

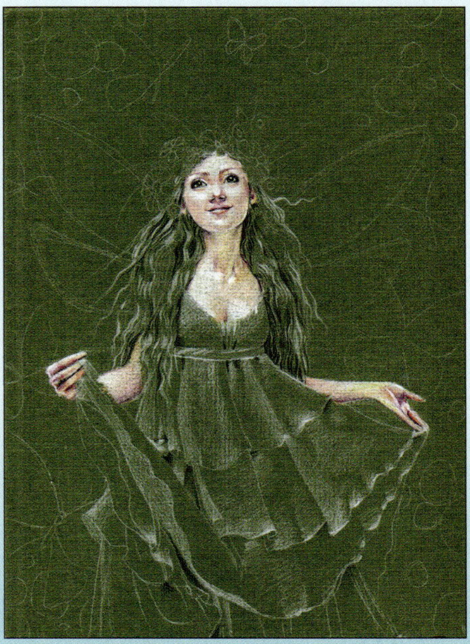

Tip

KEEP IN MIND THAT YOUR DRAWING WILL NOT LOOK REALISTIC IN THE FIRST FEW STEPS. TRY TO DEVELOP THE SUBJECT'S FACE FIRST SO THAT YOU HAVE SOMETHING RECOGNIZABLE TO RETURN TO.

Tip

To fill in the spots that get "missed" because of the surface's texture, stroke in the direction of surface grain. Always keep your pencil tips very sharp.

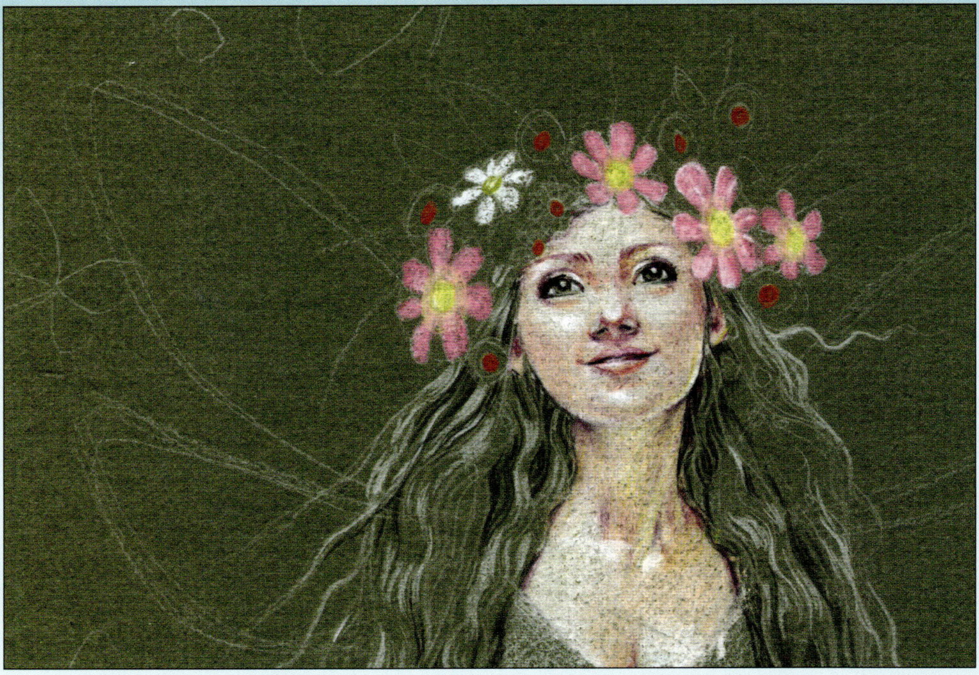

Step 3 Map out the centers of the flowers with lemon yellow and orange oil pencils. In the largest flowers, apply white (oil) and pink. Add blackberry in the shadows for dimension and finish with lemon yellow in the center. Build up the daisies using white (oil) and light peach, with lemon in the centers. Bring in light aqua for the petals in shadow. Working around the flowers, draw the large leaves using true green and light pressure. Use chartreuse to connect all the flowers with a vine, adding volume with sprigs of leaves. Add leaf veins with emerald, highlights with lemon yellow, and shadows with blackberry.

Step 4 Stroke over the darkest parts of the hair with blackberry, followed by the entire hair with mulberry. Redefine some shadows using a sharp blue violet pencil. To brighten the highlights, use pink with medium pressure followed by white to make it "pop." Then apply darker midtones with blackberry using medium to light pressure, blending the lines together.

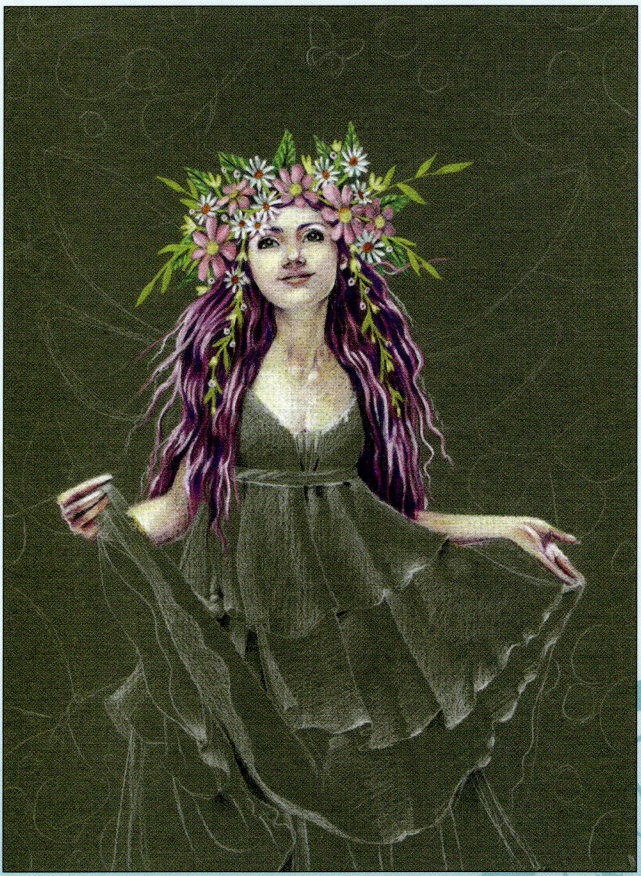

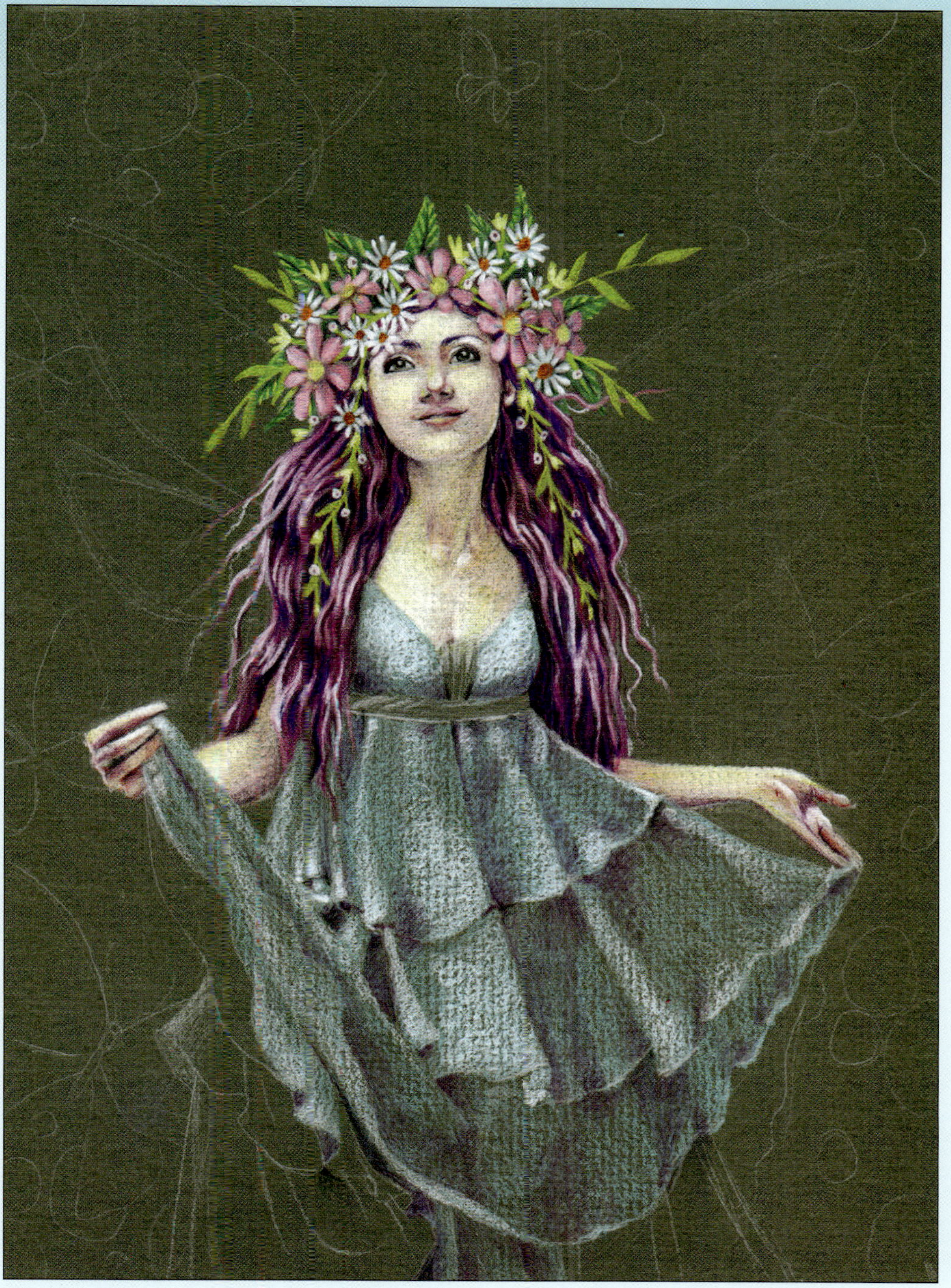

STEP 5 Begin filling in the dress using light aqua and light pressure. Color the sections one at a time, keeping the folds visually manageable as you work. Add blackberry in the shadows using small, soft, circles. In areas of highlight, add white using small, soft circles. In the brightest areas, add light aqua using medium pressure. Add true green to the bottom of the skirt to suggest back lighting.

Tip

LET THE FLOWERS OF THE CROWN SHOW YOU WHERE TO PUSH THE BRIGHTS. ADD LEMON AND WHITE TO BRIGHTEN THE SKIN, USING HEAVY PRESSURE ON YOUR LAST LAYER.

Step 6 Burnish the dress with white using medium to heavy pressure, lightening the pressure as you move into the shadows. Avoid placing any white over blackberry and allow the paper's color to keep the darks dark. Burnish the shadows with light aqua and lightly crosshatch blue violet in the deepest shadows. Fill in the belt with true green, using blue violet for shadows and white for highlights.

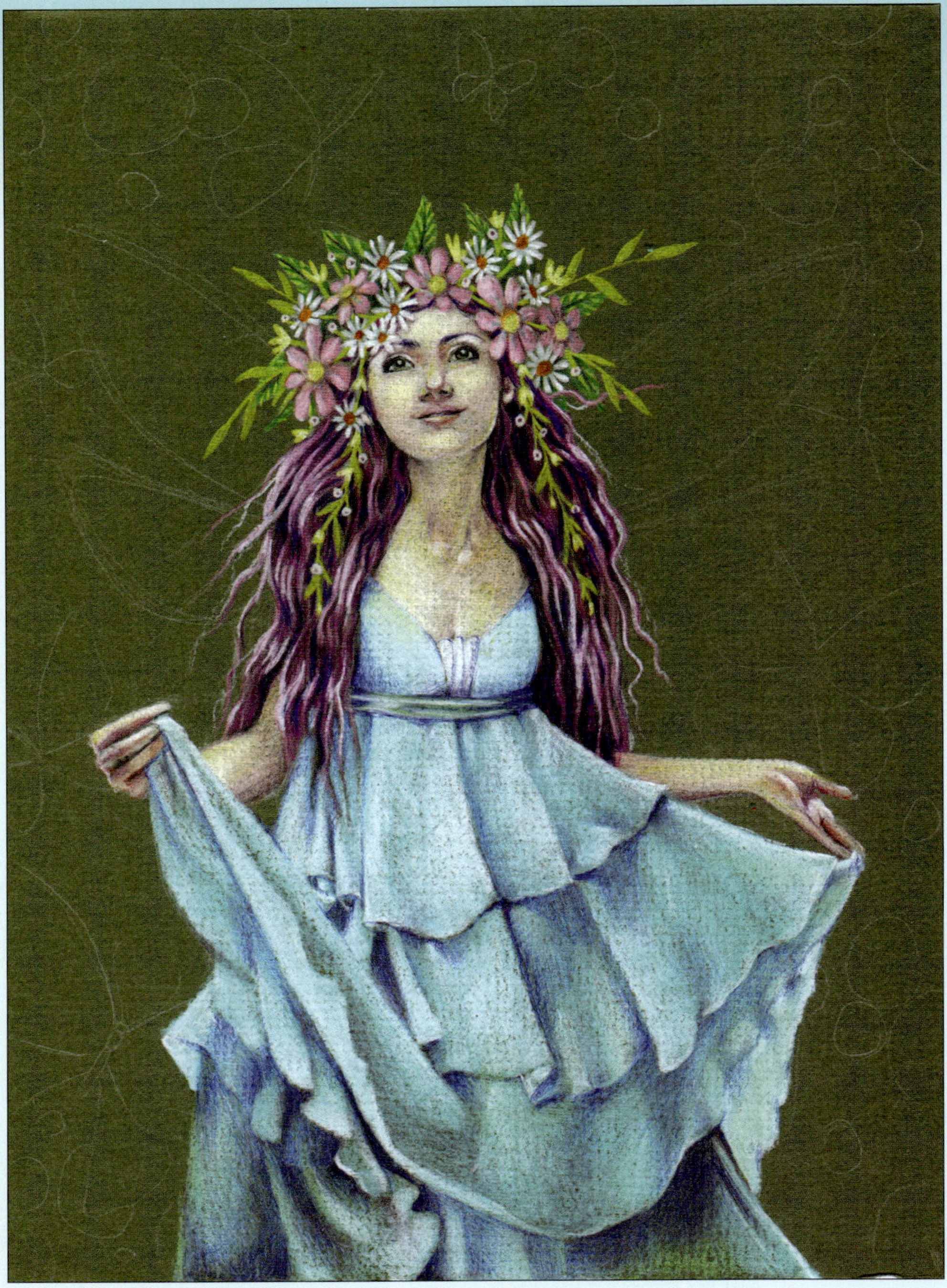

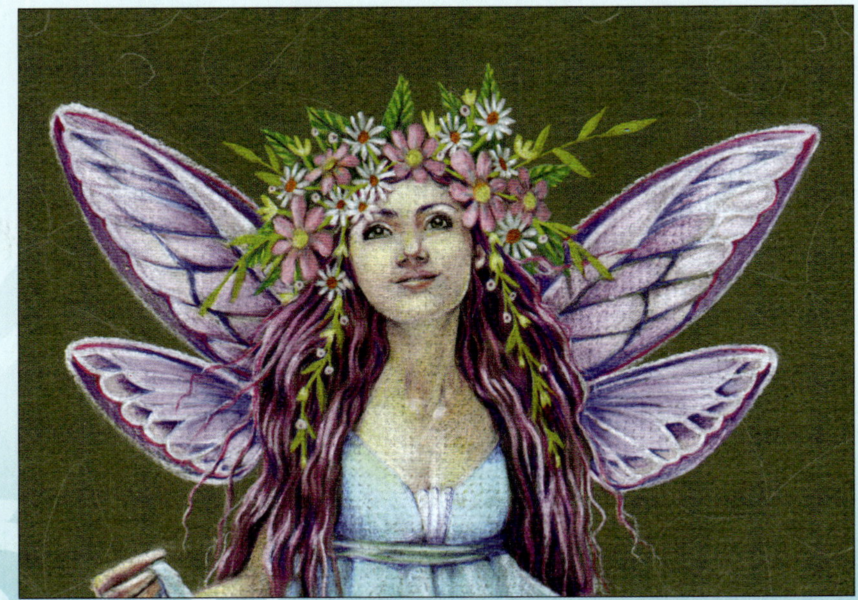

Step 7 After observing a few references of wings, place the images out of sight and use peach (oil) to sketch the fairy's wings from your imagination. Use violet (oil) and light pressure to fill in the top set of wings and then burnish with wax white. Add peach to the tips and outline the inner sections with blue violet. In the bottom set of wings, add peach to the tips instead of white. Begin with hard pressure and fade out the color. Return with violet as an accent and then fill in the outline using white. Add some magenta detail along the scalloped edges to bring it all together. Finish by burnishing the sections with white.

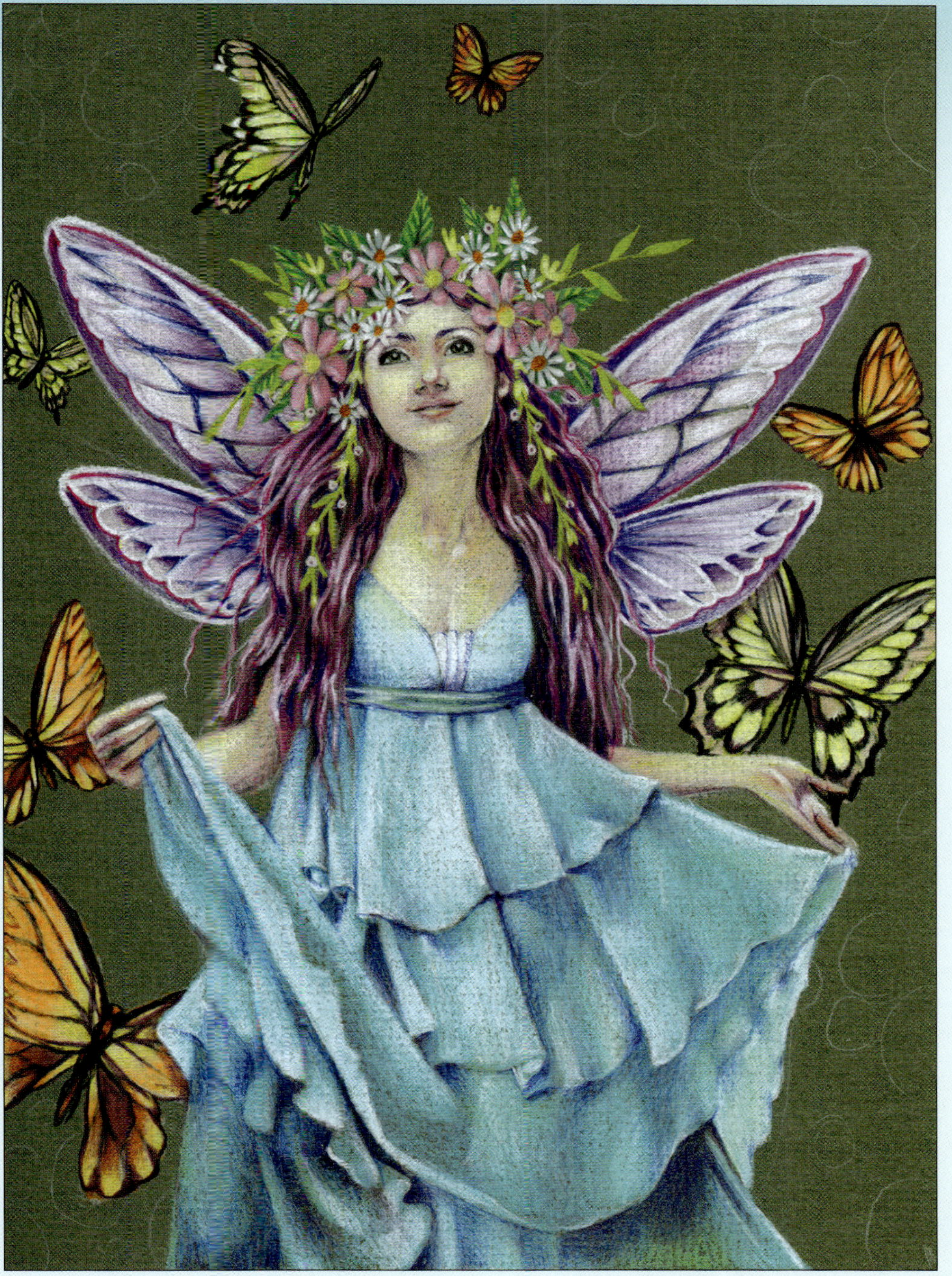

Step 8 Choose a few butterfly references and work loosely from them. Begin by adding white (oil) to all the butterfly shapes first, which will keep your colors bright. Then follow up with orange or yellow, stroking horizontally with medium pressure. Cross these strokes vertically with a wax white pencil to create a smooth surface. Outline wing veins using black (oil). In the yellow butterflies, add peach to the tips and inner sections. Place lemon yellow (oil) around the peach and brighten with white. Outline and fill in the details with black. In the orange butterflies, use lemon yellow on the insides and tips, orange (oil) within the sections, and white to burnish. Touch up the darks in the yellow butterflies with blackberry and in the orange butterflies with black.

Step 9 Use lavender to fill in the background flowers. Add white (oil) behind the fairy's head with light pressure; over this apply a light layer of apple green. Fade out this color into the dark green of the surface.

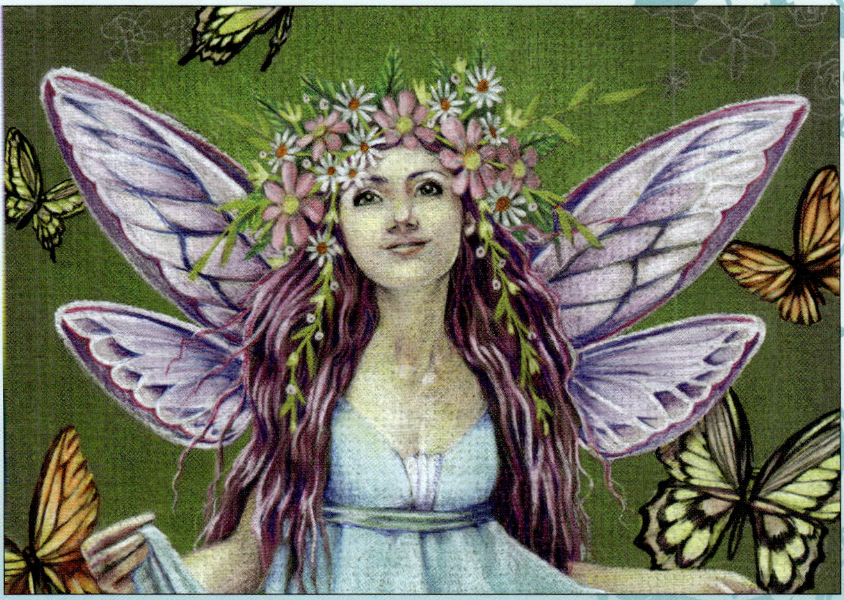

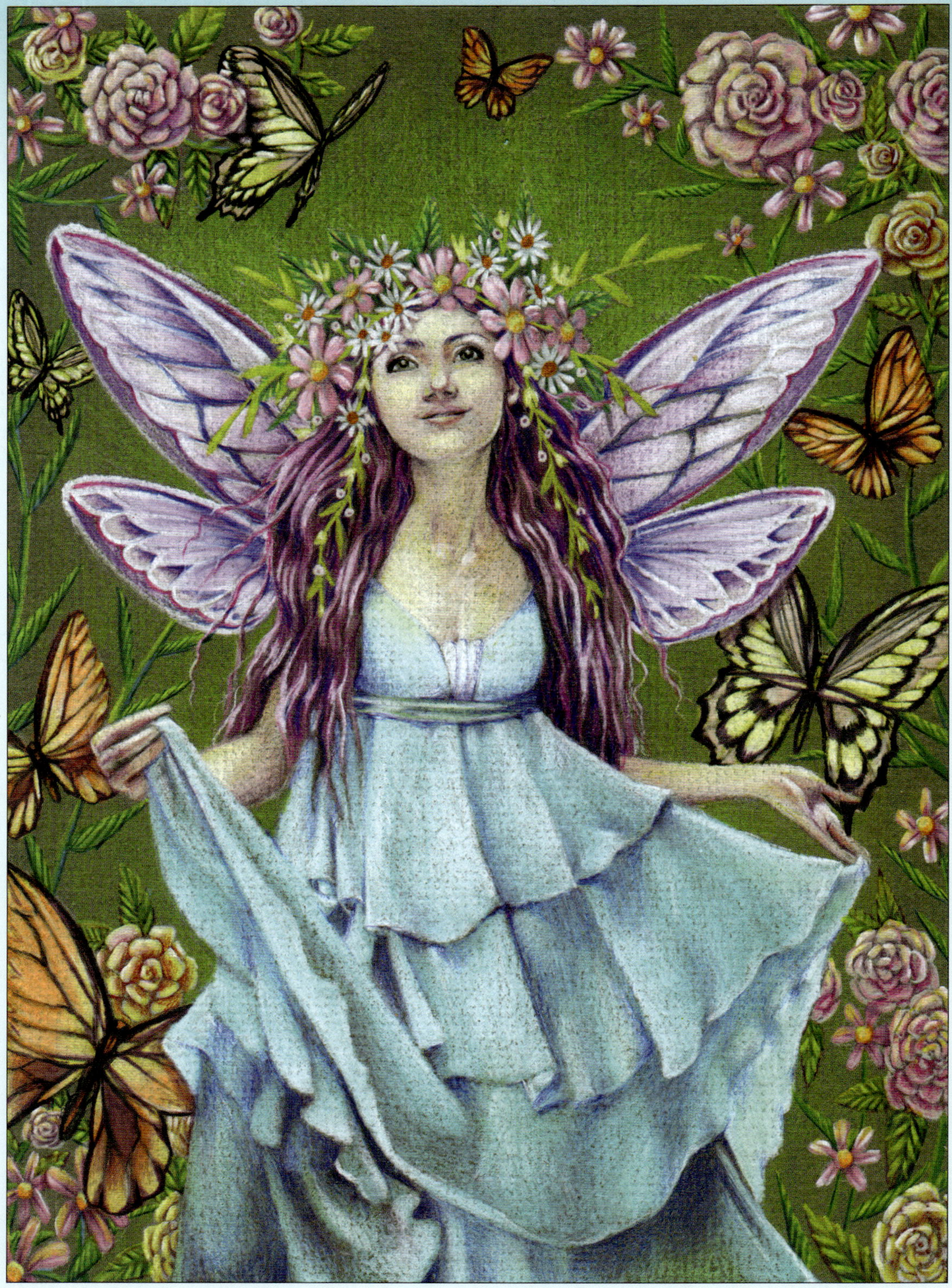

Step 10 Add white (oil) to the tip of each petal with heavy pressure, lightening as you move toward the inside. For the roses, fill in each petal with peach, again working from heavy to light pressure. For the daisies, apply pink with medium pressure. Fill in the centers using lemon yellow and orange. Returning to pink, accent the tips of the roses with heavy pressure and lay in shadows using blackberry, working from heavy (near the centers) to light (near the petal tips). Burnish highlights with lemon yellow and white. For the yellow roses, use lemon yellow in place of peach and Tuscan red in place of blackberry. Add magenta to boost shadows in all the flowers.

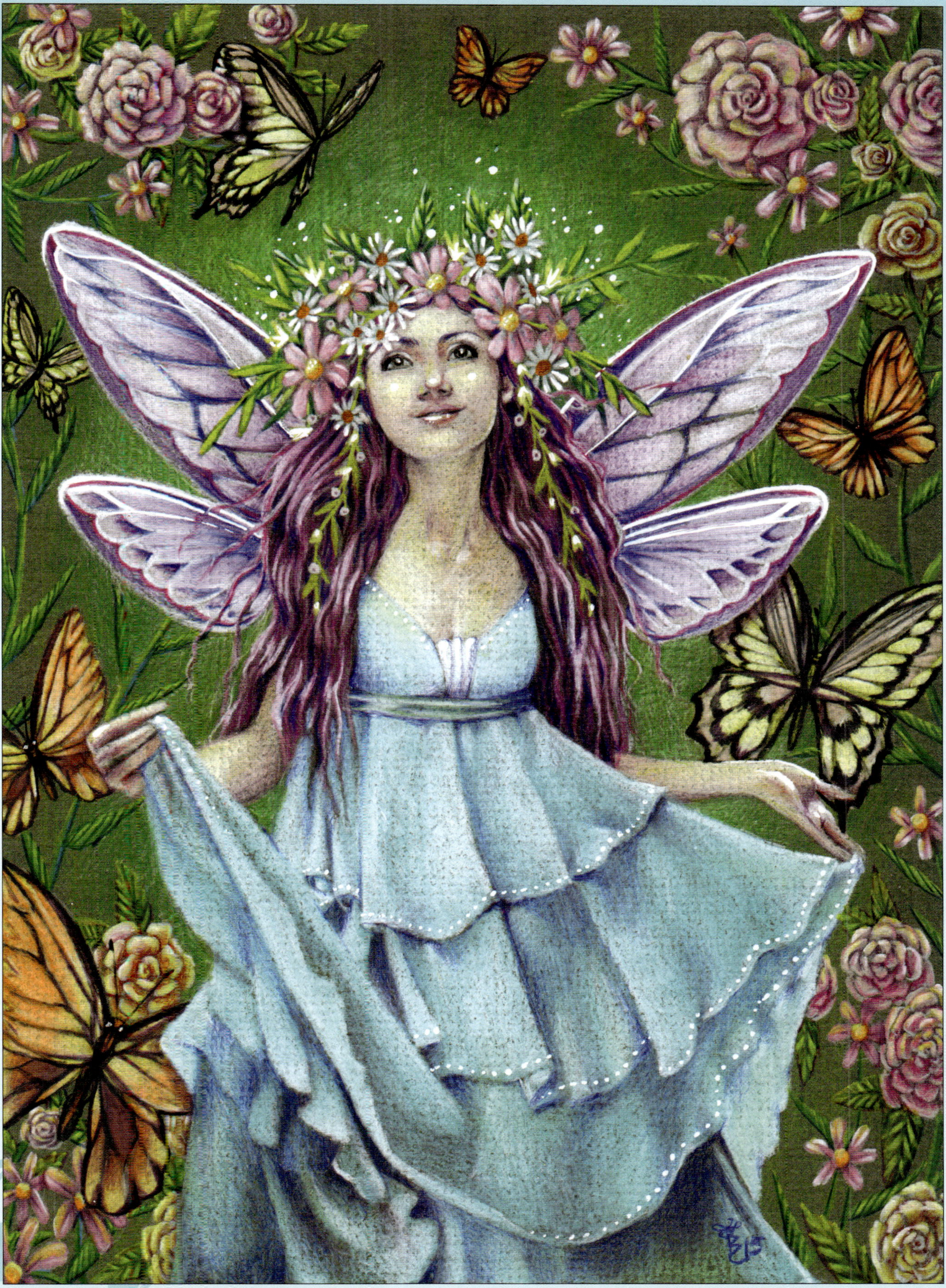

Step 11 Draw the leaves from your imagination with apple green, using light to medium pressure. Apply Spanish orange to show where the light is coming from, and draw the veins using chartreuse. For the skinny daisy leaves, use apple green with chartreuse for highlights and peacock green for veins. Finish all the leaves by working blackberry and true blue into the darkest shadows.

Cherry Blossom Fairy

with Lindsay Archer

IN THIS PROJECT, LEARN HOW TO USE A RANGE OF GRAYS to build soft, muted tones. By receding into the background, these neutral tones create a dynamic image by making the reds and yellows of the leaflike wings appear to "pop" from the scene. In addition to the pencils below, you'll need a colorless blender to complete this project.

10% French gray	50% cool gray	70% French gray	90% French gray	Beige	Beige sienna	Black grape	Blush pink	Bronze	Burnt ochre	Clay rose	Celadon green	Eggshell
Ginger root	Grayed lavender	Light cerulean blue	Light umber	Moss green	Peach beige	Pink rose	Rosy beige	Sandbar brown	Sky blue light	Sunburst yellow	Tuscan red	White

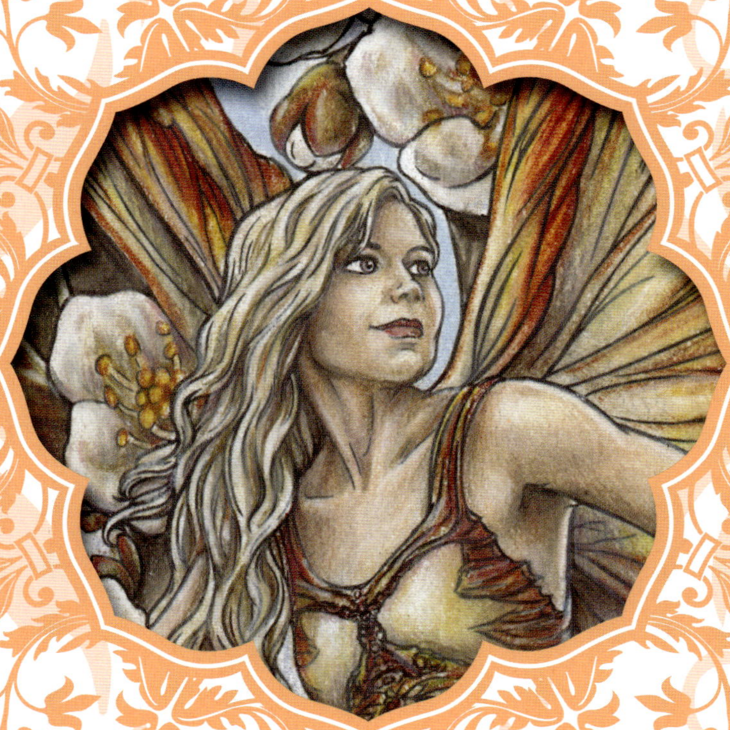

SKETCH Begin by creating a line drawing of the scene. You can do this simply using a pencil; however, I prefer to plan and create my drawings digitally using Adobe® Photoshop®. This allows me to print out my drawing on Bristol board—and if anything goes wrong during the course of the drawing, I can easily print it again and start over.

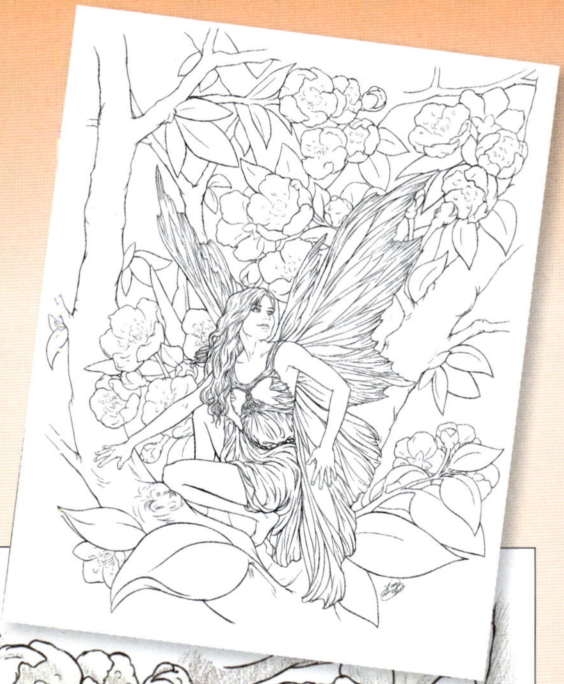

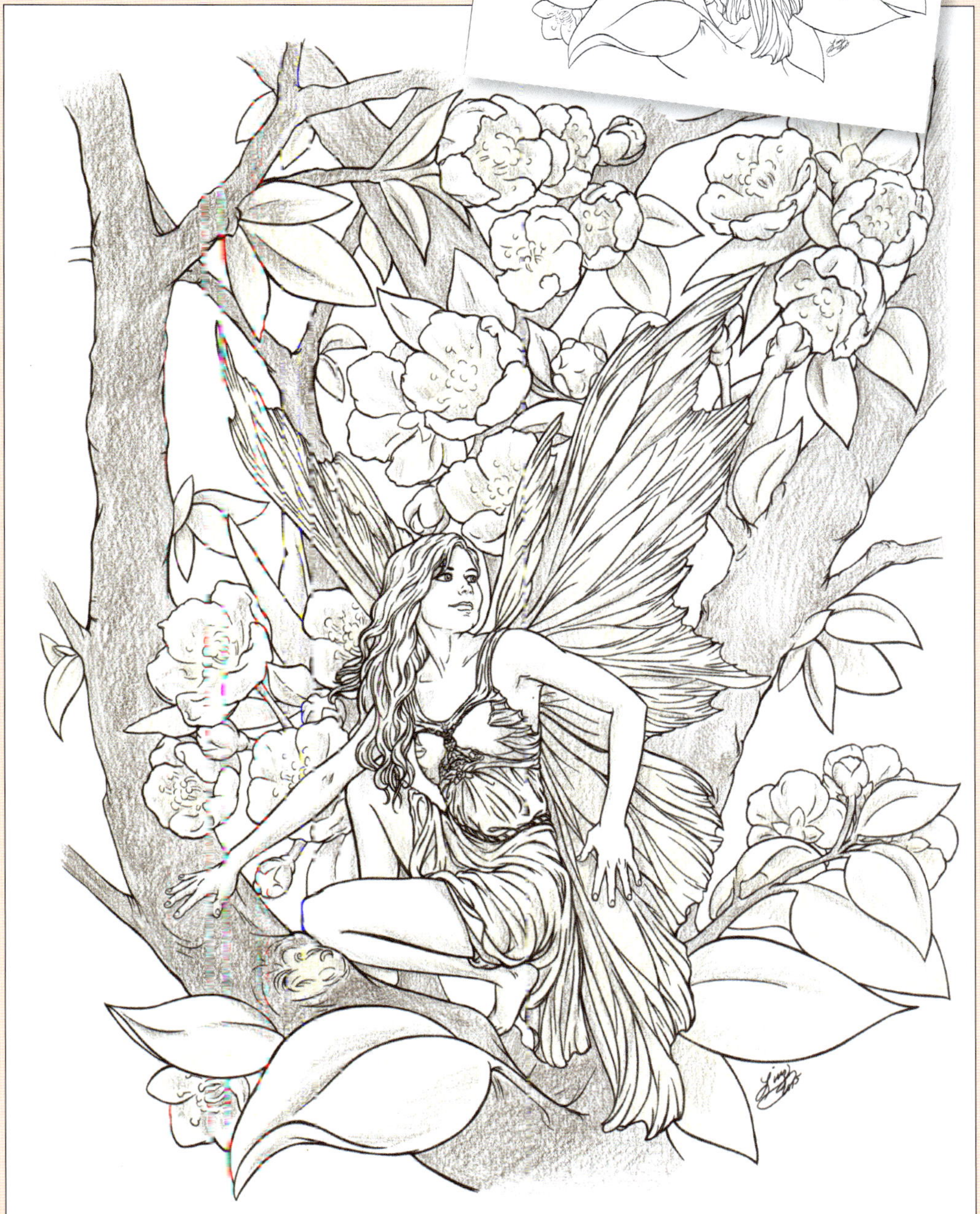

STEP 1 Using light to medium pressure, fill in the tree bark using 70% French gray. This provides a simple, neutral base over which you can layer colors later. Then use the gray to fill in shadows throughout the piece. Layer in the base color of the wings and leaves using eggshell, and then use this color to shade the body and interior of the blossoms.

Tip

AS YOU USE A COLOR, IT'S A GOOD IDEA TO WORK IT INTO THE REST OF THE SCENE WHERE POSSIBLE. CARRYING COLORS THROUGHOUT A WORK, INSTEAD OF LIMITING THEM TO SINGLE OBJECTS, CREATES VISUAL UNITY.

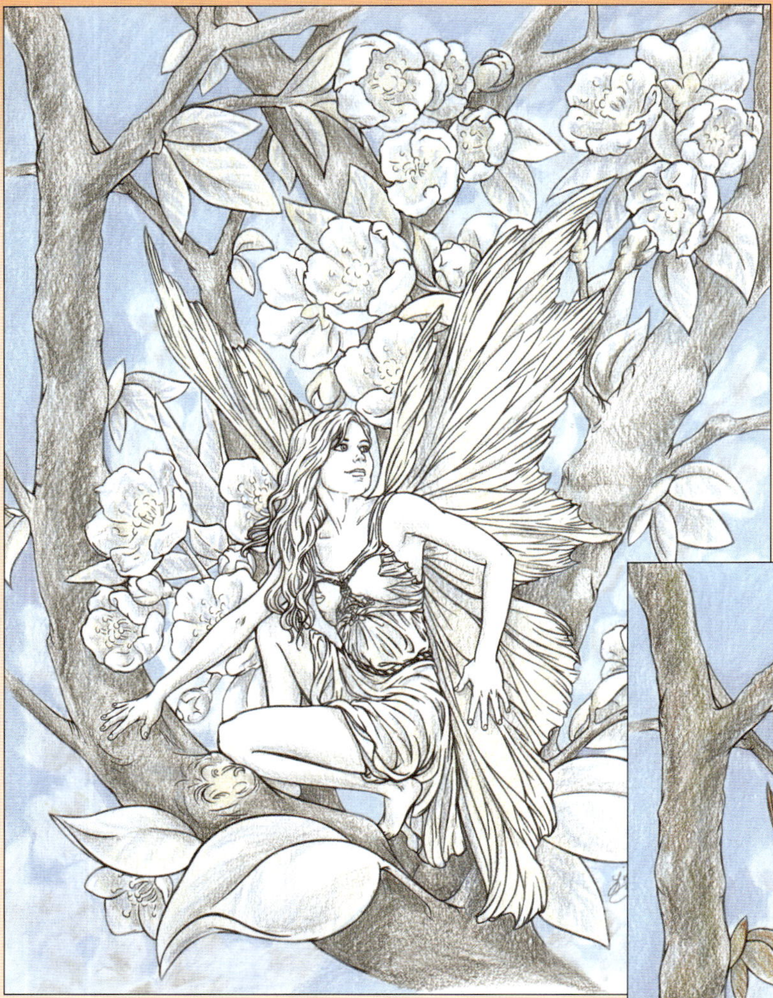

Step 2 Lightly fill in the background using light cerulean blue and sky blue light. To hint at the blossoms in the background, cover these shapes with firm strokes of white. For areas of pure sky, use firm strokes of sky blue light. Returning to the background blossoms, lightly apply 10% French gray to create the sense of soft focus. Then carry the light blues throughout the rest of the piece, adding them to shadows for depth. Bring in more 70% French gray to shade the tree branches.

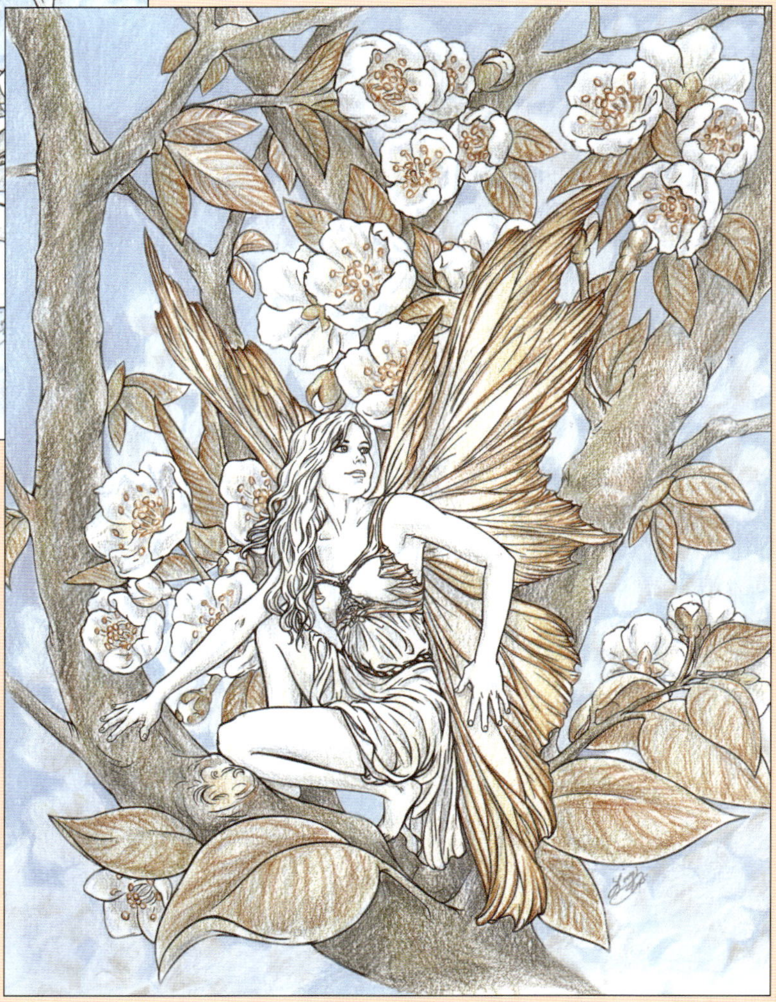

Step 3 At this point, lightly cover the bark and leaves with bronze. Switch to burnt ochre to color the stamens of the blossoms and to highlight the veins in the leaves. Then use it to accent the wings of the fairy, following the outlines and pulling the color from the edges inward. Taper and lighten your pressure as you stroke. Now layer the wings with eggshell, applying a gradient by pressing firmly around the edges and lightening as you move toward the fairy's back.

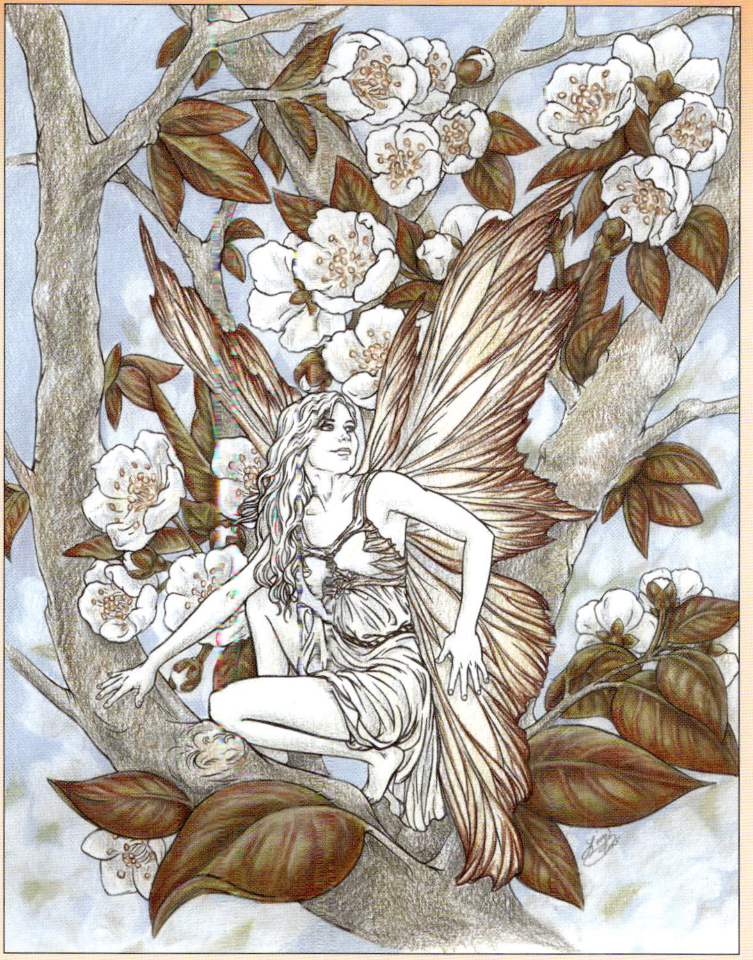

Step 4 Finish the leaves and buds by covering them with moss green, followed by a colorless blender. Then use Tuscan red to accent the edges of the leaves and fairy wings. Note that the young cherry blossom leaves contain more red than green at this stage of life. Next use eggshell and firm strokes to lighten the ridges of the leaves. Further develop the form of each leaf by shading with 70% and 90% French gray, finishing with white highlights.

Tip

As you develop the trunk and branches, stroke along the forms and ridges to suggest the bark's irregular surface.

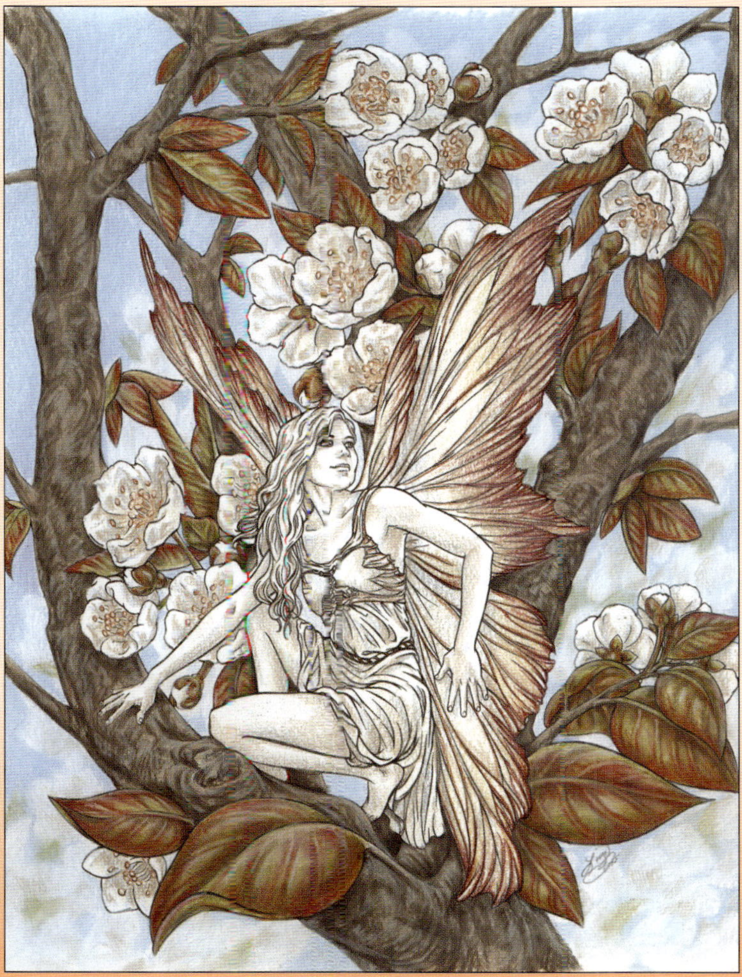

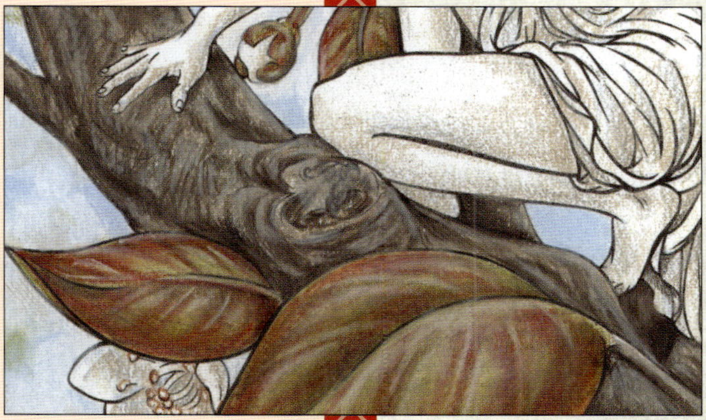

Step 5 Using ginger root, cover the bark with firm strokes and accent both the blossoms and fairy. Add depth to the bark by shading with 70% and 90% French gray. Use 10% French gray to add highlights to the bark.

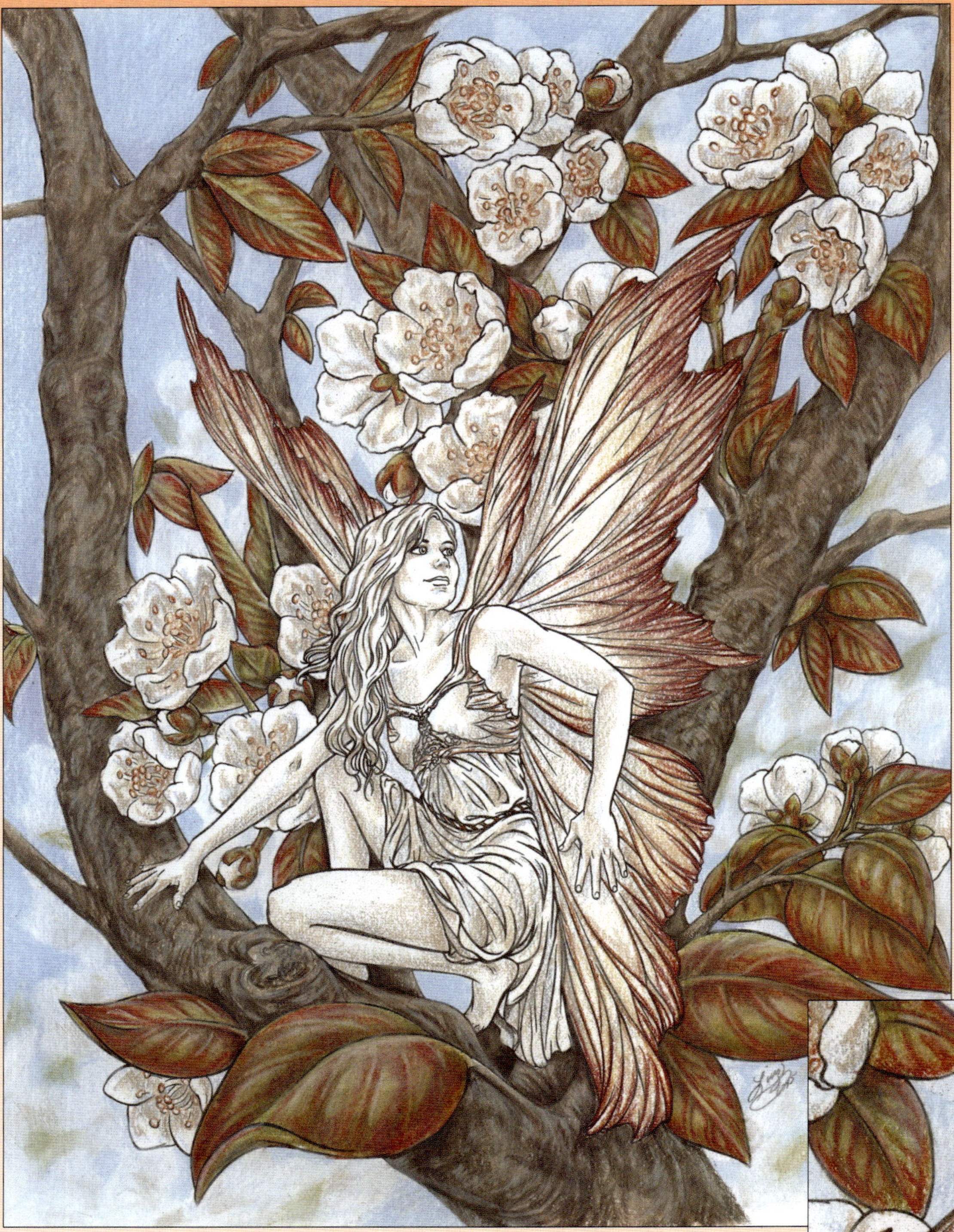

STEP 6 Use sunburst yellow to accent the stamens and fairy wings. Now use a colorless blender over the blossoms, wings, and dress. Detail the blossoms using light umber and 50% cool gray. For the fairy's base skin tone, use peach beige and beige, also using these colors to accent throughout the work.

TIP Colorless blenders help you smooth the strokes without altering the brightness of your colors. Here you can achieve a soft gradation of red to orange to yellow.

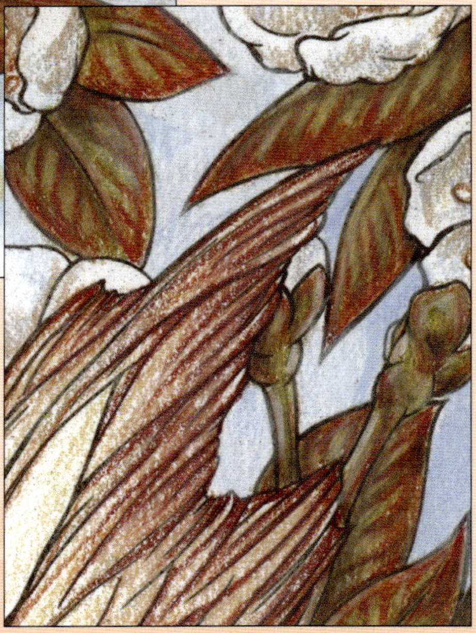

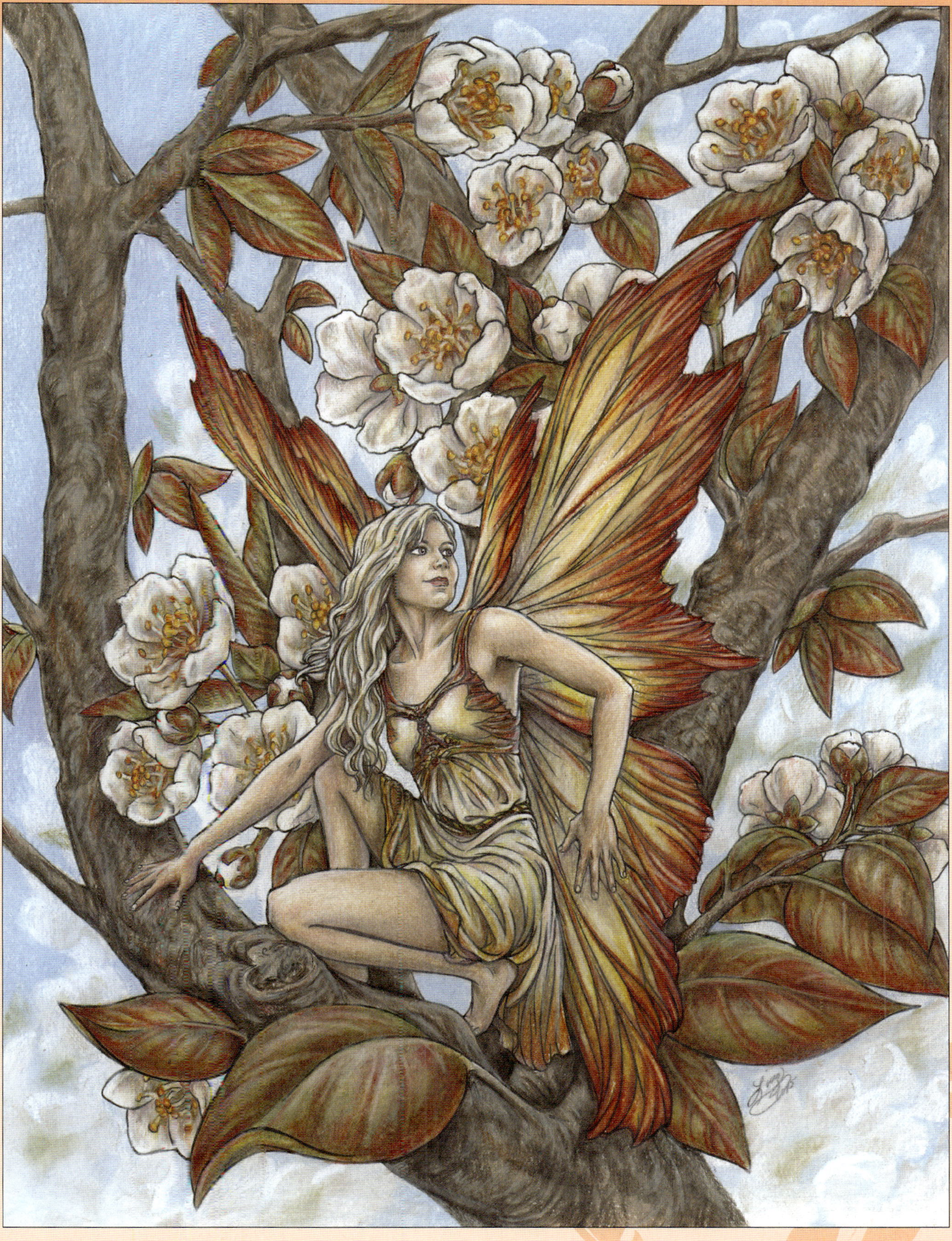

Step 7 For the final stage, use a blender on the fairy's skin to smooth the strokes. Then use several different pinks to build the skin tone—from muted pinks like beige sienna, clay rose, and rosy beige to bright hues like pink rose and blush pink. Then work over the entire drawing with purples to complement and balance the yellow in the scene. Use grayed lavender in the skin shadows and blossoms, and apply black grape to the leaves. To bring out highlights, use white and firm pressure or a colorless blender. For shadows, use various percentages of French gray and sandbar. Tone down the reds of the leaves using celadon green. To recover any final highlights, use an electric eraser.

Runestone Fairy

with Lindsay Archer

THIS NORTHERN EUROPEAN-INSPIRED SCENE features a runestone (or rock carving) set in an aged forest. Muted tones and overgrown moss contribute to the overall ancient feel.

- 10% cool gray
- 20% cool gray
- 20% warm gray
- 70% cool gray
- 70% French gray
- 70% warm gray
- 90% cool gray
- Black
- Black grape
- Deco peach
- Eggshell
- Goldenrod
- Grayed lavender
- Indigo blue
- Jade green
- Kelly green
- Kelp green
- Light peach
- Light umber
- Nectar
- Parma violet
- Peach beige
- Putty beige
- Rosy beige
- Sage green
- Seashell pink
- Sienna brown
- Slate gray
- White

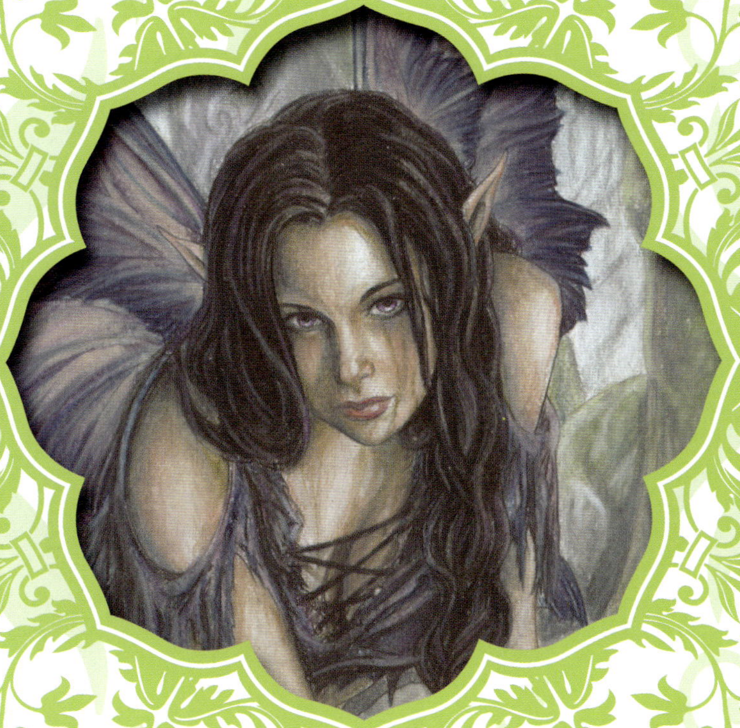

Sketch Begin by creating a line drawing of the scene. (To transfer the template for this project, see page 127.)

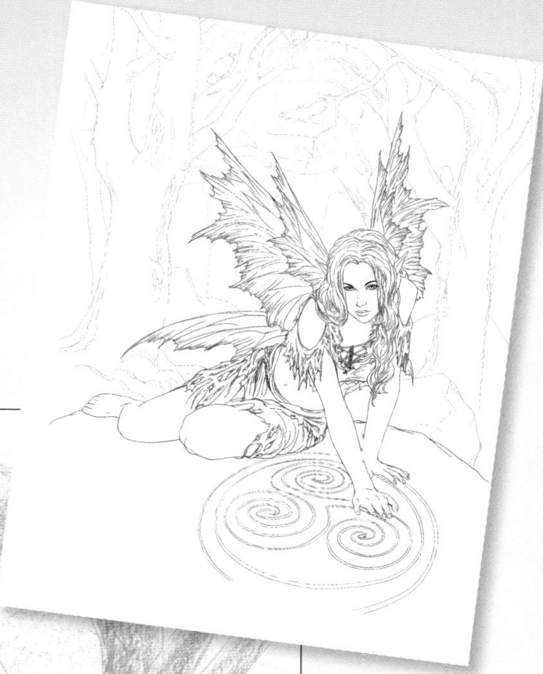

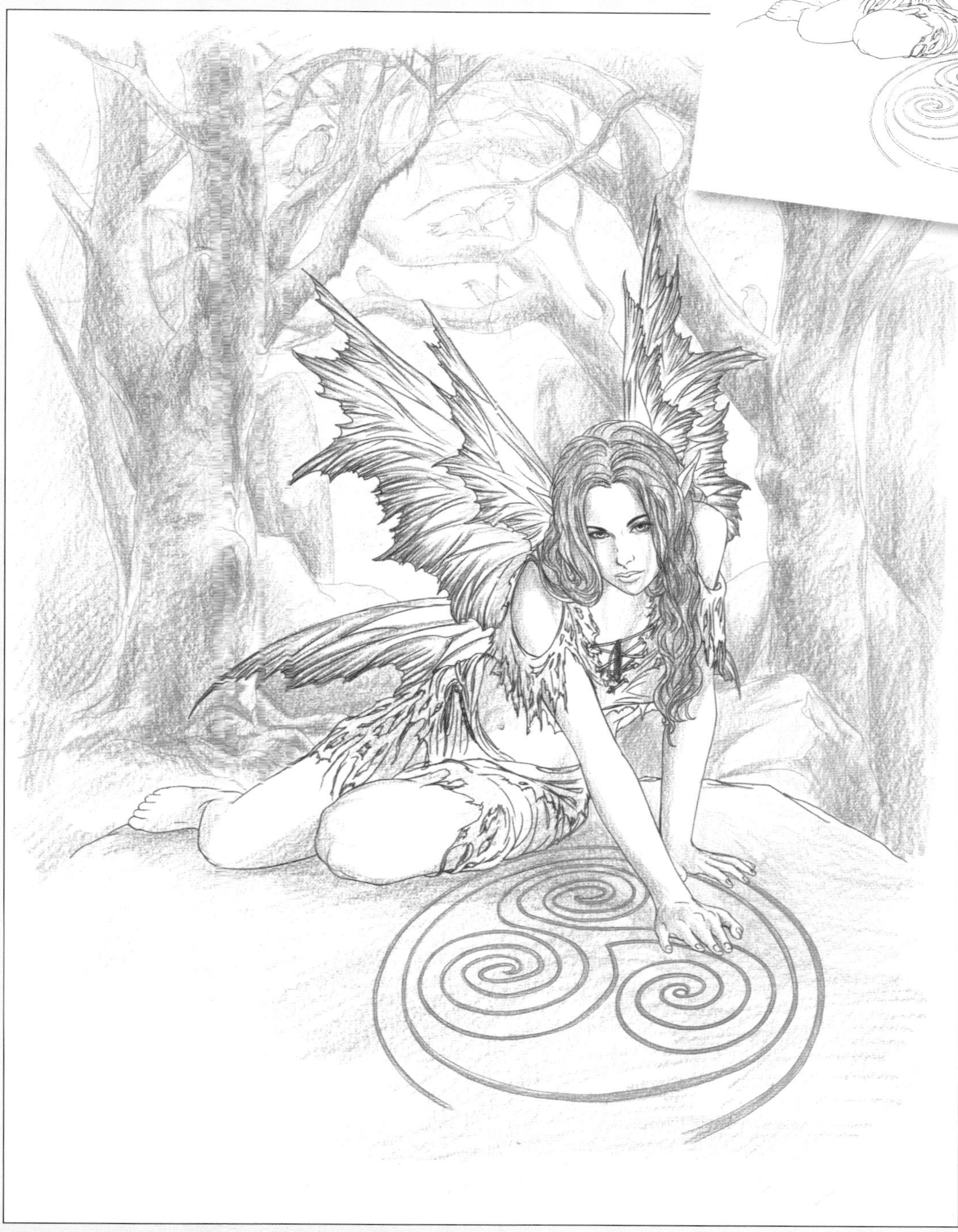

Step 1 Begin by applying a light basecoat of 20% warm gray over the background, along with sage green over the edges of the branches. To make the forest atmospheric and old, like the Black Forest, cover the trees and rocks in moss and ferns. Using kelp green and kelly green, fill in the center of each branch with a dark green. Then shade them with 20% cool gray, followed by indigo blue in the darker shadows. For the shadows on the flesh of the fairy, use 70% French gray.

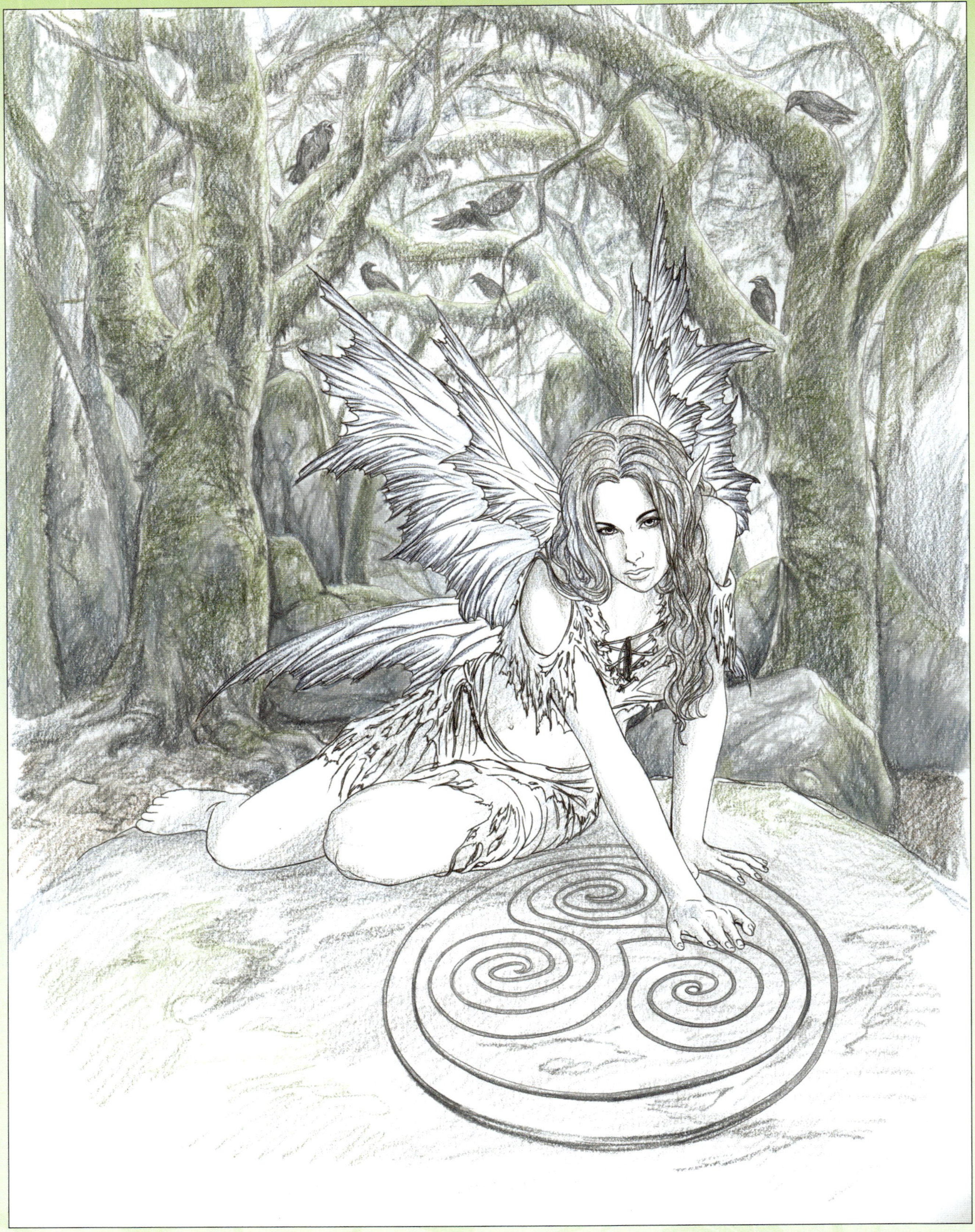

Step 2 To build the green moss and ferns in the background, use jade green and kelp green to bring out the color. Using 70% cool gray, shade the bottoms of the branches, pulling down strokes for hanging moss. For the tree ravens, use 70% cool gray, as black would overpower the foreground. Now use sienna brown for the ground leaves and indigo blue for the shadows throughout. To add depth and a misty feel, layer light gray over the background, alternating between 10% and 20% cool gray.

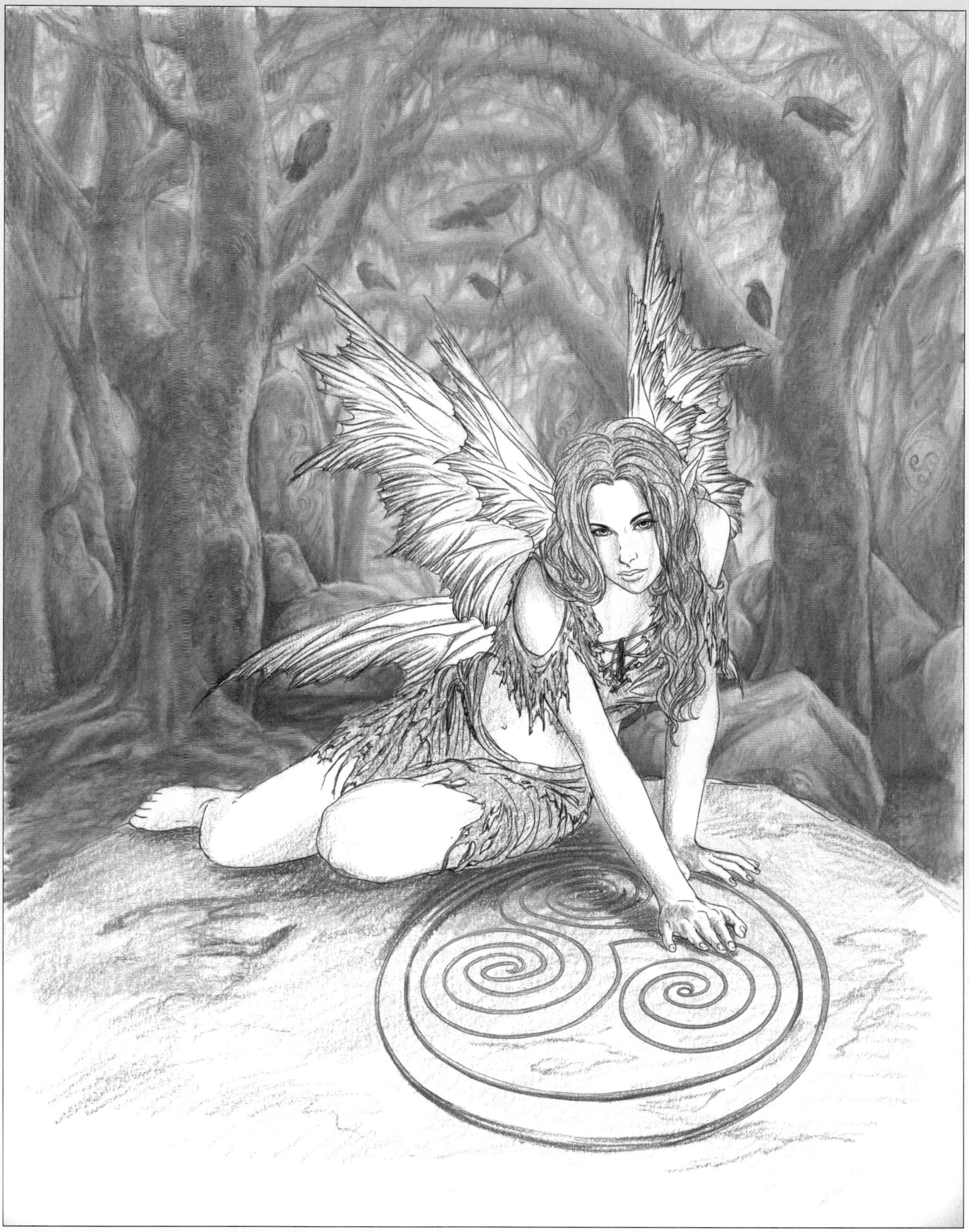

Step 3 Now reuse all the colors from the previous step to blend your colors, adding slate gray for shading and parma violet for some color in the shadows. Continue using 10% and 20% cool gray over any branches that stand out and take away from the misty atmosphere. Then use 70% cool gray to add details, and use firm strokes of white to bring out highlights.

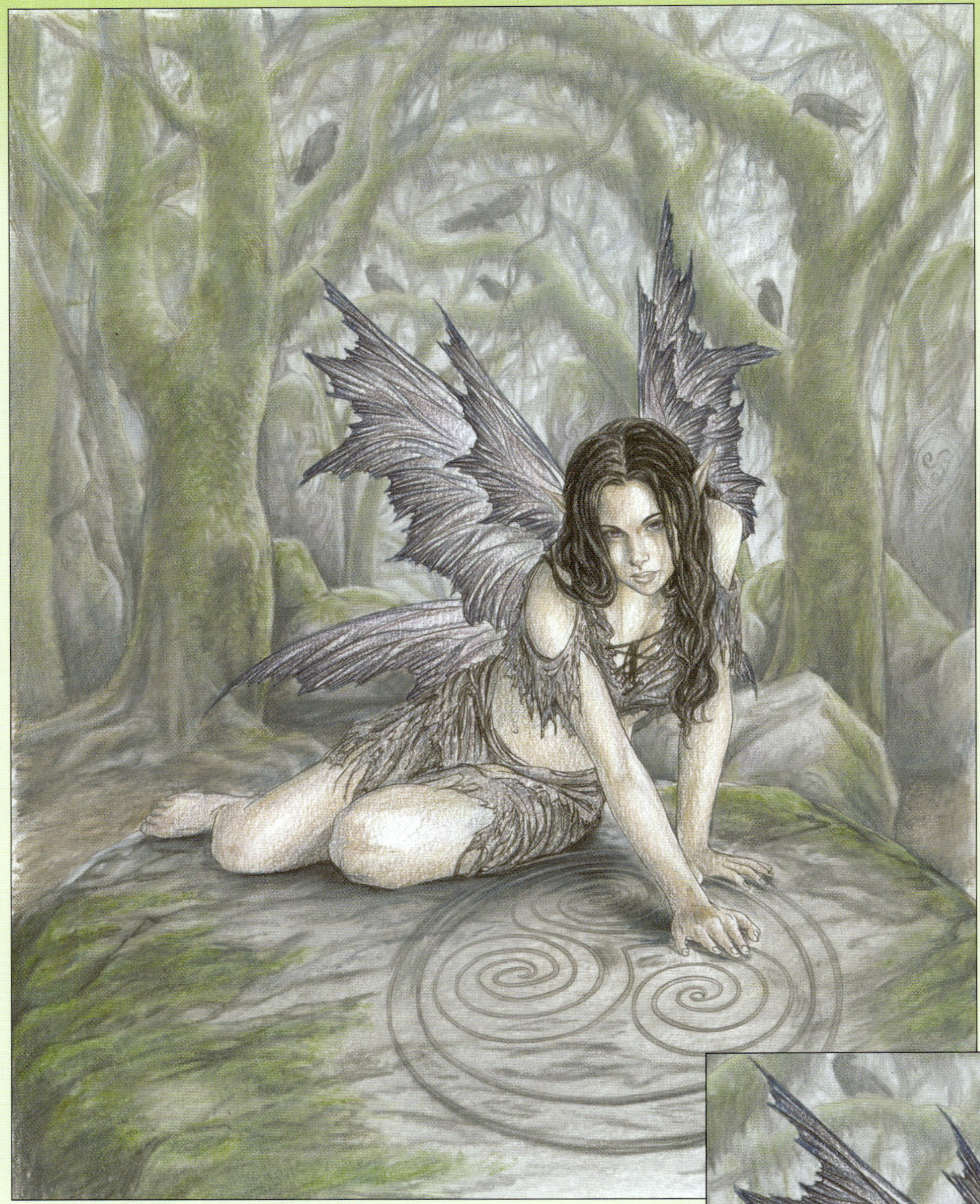

Step 4 Cover the foreground stone with 10% cool gray, switching to Kelly green and kelp green for the moss. Use black to develop the rock shadows and the fairy's hair. Within the hair shadows, mix in indigo blue; for the hair in light, add black grape. Now develop the wings (see "Detail" below). For the fairy's body, fill in the shadows with a mixture of indigo blue, light umber, and rosy beige. Use light peach and eggshell for the lightest areas, along with goldenrod for the warmer shadows.

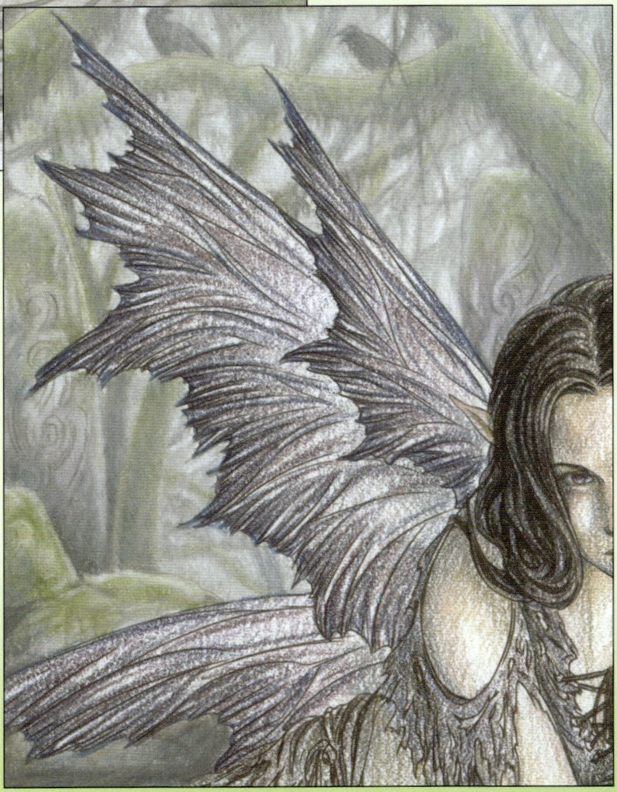

Detail To begin the wings, lay down a light layer of putty beige and then trace the outer edges with indigo blue. Use black grape to add strokes moving from the edges inward. For the center of the wings, apply parma violet. To add a shadow separating the wings from the body, use slate gray.

STEP 5 Use a colorless blender to smooth out your strokes. Then bring texture and highlights to the wings using peach beige and rosy beige. With black grape and parma violet, add color to the wings and then shade with slate gray. Use these colors to develop her clothing, along with 70% and 90% cool gray for the shadows. Blend the hair using parma violet for the shadows and peach beige with white for the lightest areas. For the skin, first blend the colors and then add deco peach, nectar, and seashell pink over the lit areas, followed by 70% warm gray and 70% cool gray in the shadows. Use grayed lavender for lighter, softer shadows. To finish the runestone carving, use white to highlight any edges that catch the light.

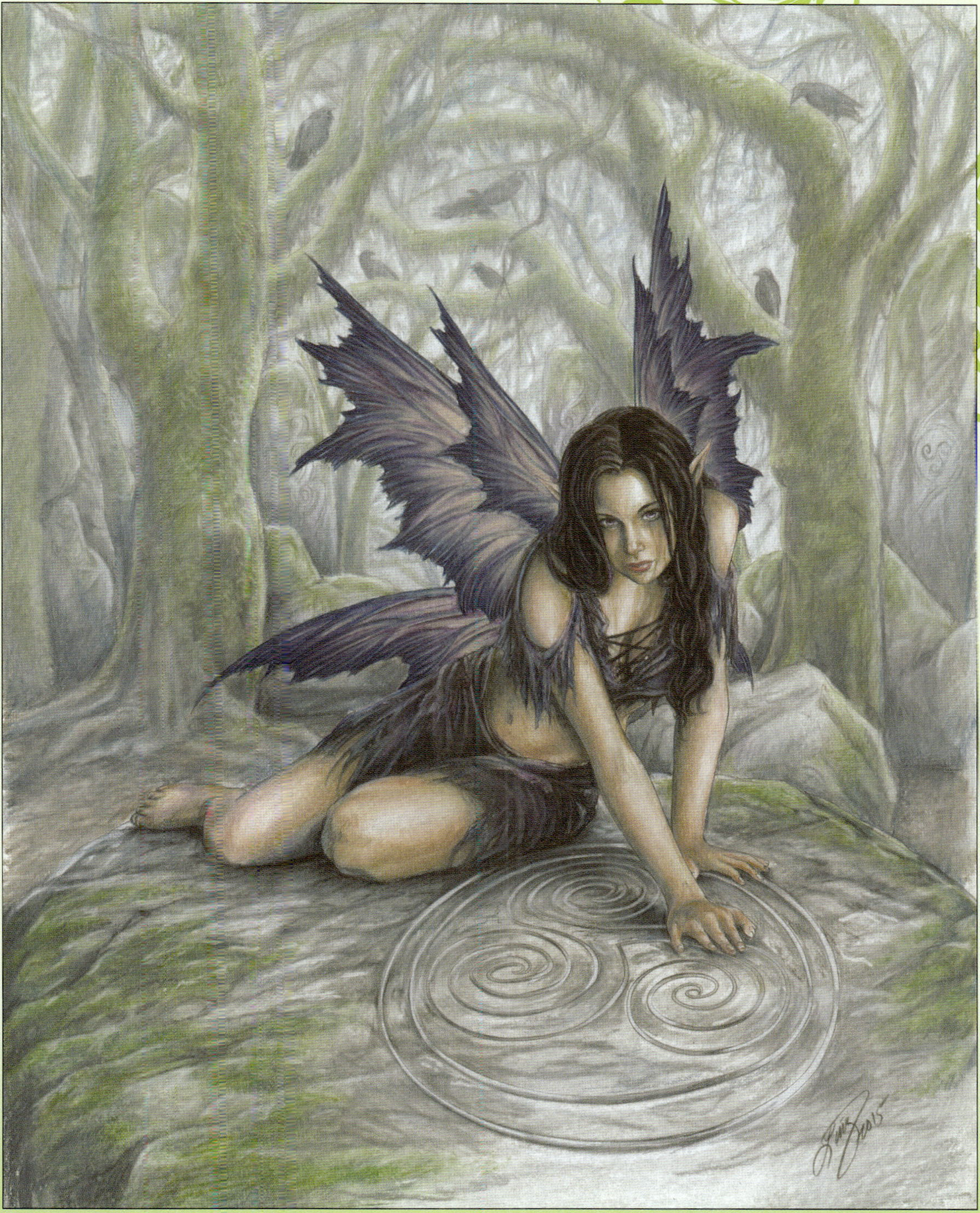

Forest Guardian

with Lindsay Archer

IT'S A GOOD IDEA TO OCCASIONALLY RETHINK THE BORDERS OF YOUR ARTWORK; you are not limited to the edges of your paper! In this project, plan your drawing to include a lovely leaf frame that ties into the greens of the scene, complementing the reds of the fairy's dress.

- 20% cool gray
- 20% warm gray
- 50% cool gray
- 70% French gray
- 90% cool gray
- Beige sienna
- Black
- Black raspberry
- Bright green
- Bronze
- Celadon green
- Chestnut
- Cloud blue
- Deco yellow
- Eggshell
- Ginger root
- Grayed lavender
- Gray-green light
- Indigo blue
- Kelly green
- Light umber
- Limepeel
- Moss green
- Pale sage
- Pink rose
- Poppy red
- Prussian green
- Rosy beige
- Sage green
- Seashell pink
- Slate gray
- Spring green
- Terra cotta
- White

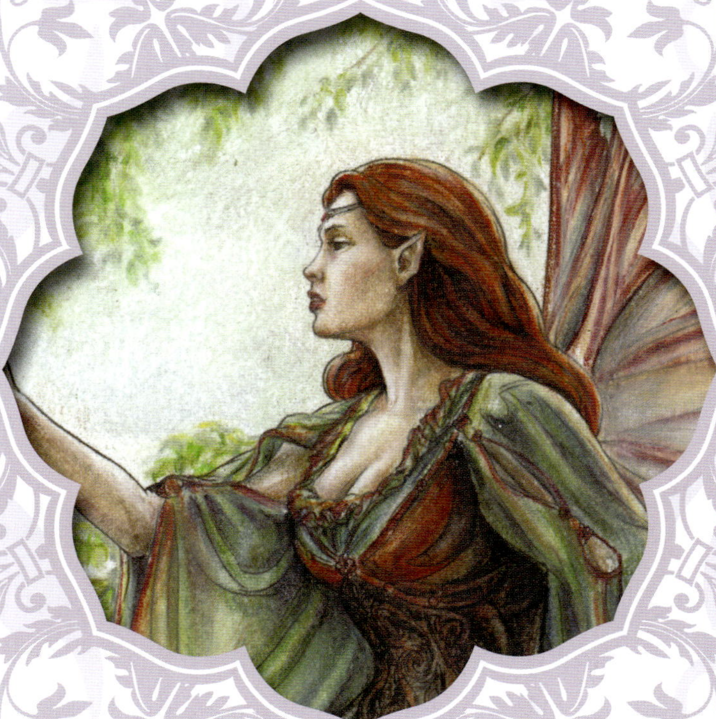

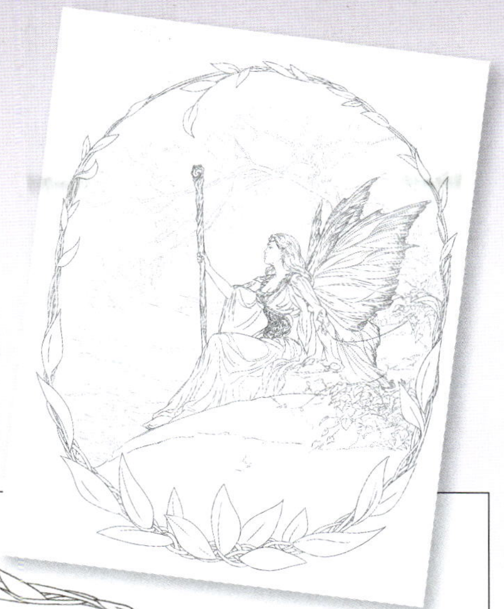

Sketch Begin by creating a line drawing of the scene.

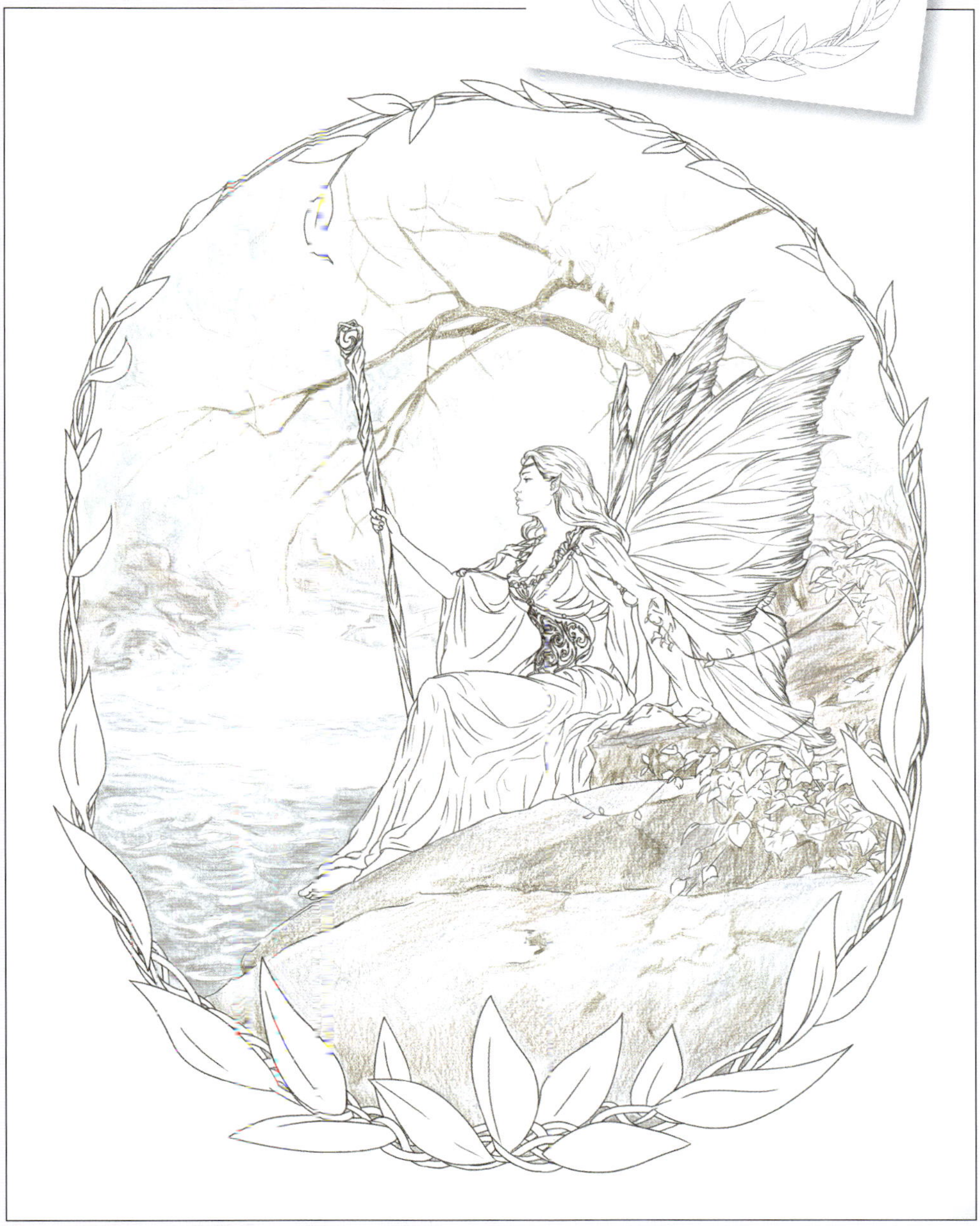

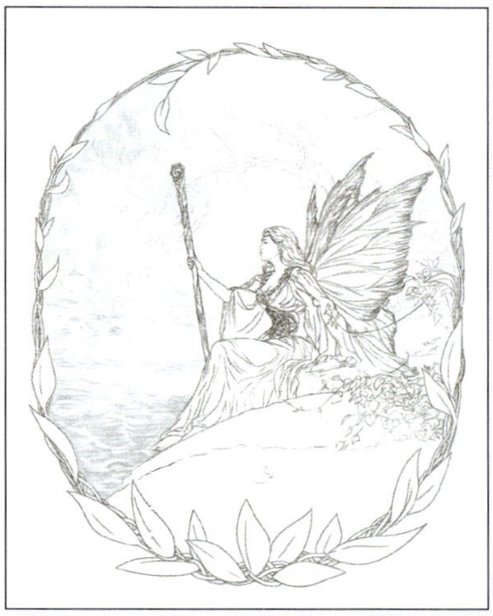

Step 1 The moisture in the air makes the background colors faint, so begin with a light base layer of gray-green light within the trees. Then shift to a light layer of cloud blue near the water and above the cloud line, blending over the gray-green light to create a gradation. For the water at the bottom, apply 20% cool gray, working around white highlights or removing them with an electric eraser. Use heavier pressure to bring out water ripples. Continue using 20% cool gray to give depth to the tree line and foliage, hinting at tree trunks. This background gray will help your truest colors "pop" in the foreground.

Step 2 Apply beige sienna and 20% warm gray to the rocks, increasing pressure to create the cracks. In the water nearest to the figure, work 20% cool gray into the water. Use this same pencil to add depth to the rocks, and then complete the majority of your shading with sandbar brown. Use this color as the base layer for the tree trunk and branches. Then use cloud blue to rework the background with another layer.

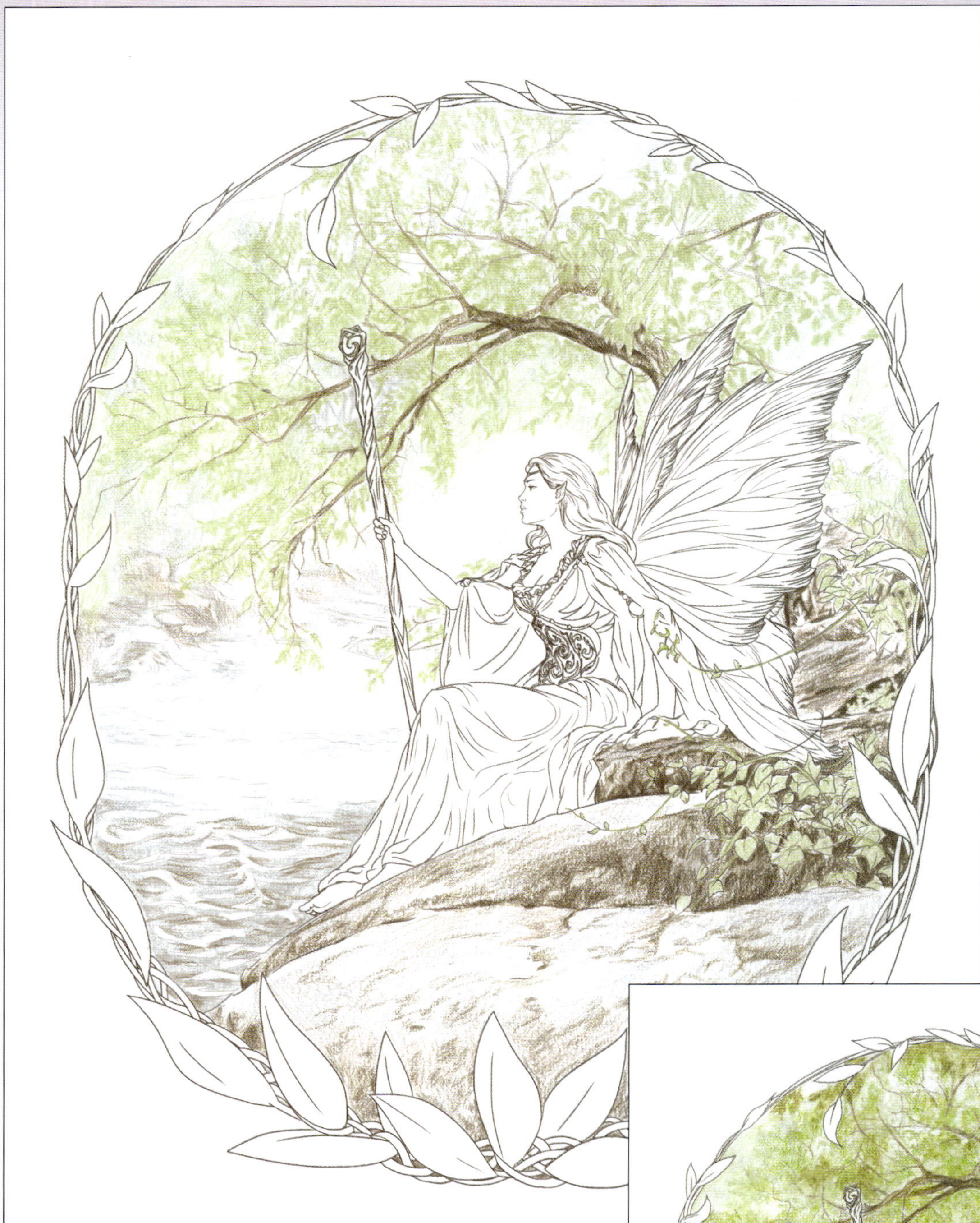

Step 3 Darken the background using a light coat of pale sage. Use this same color to draw the first layer of leaves, using short strokes and firm pressure to form the leaves. Fill in some of the branches with 70% French gray and shade the tree, rocks, and water.

Step 4 Now tackle the foliage. Apply spring green and deco yellow over the sage green and just outside of it. For midtones, use limepeel and moss green. As you continue to develop the leaves, shade more with 70% French gray where needed. Next, use ginger root and seashell pink to give the rocks some color. Now that the background colors are in place, use a colorless blender to smooth out the strokes.

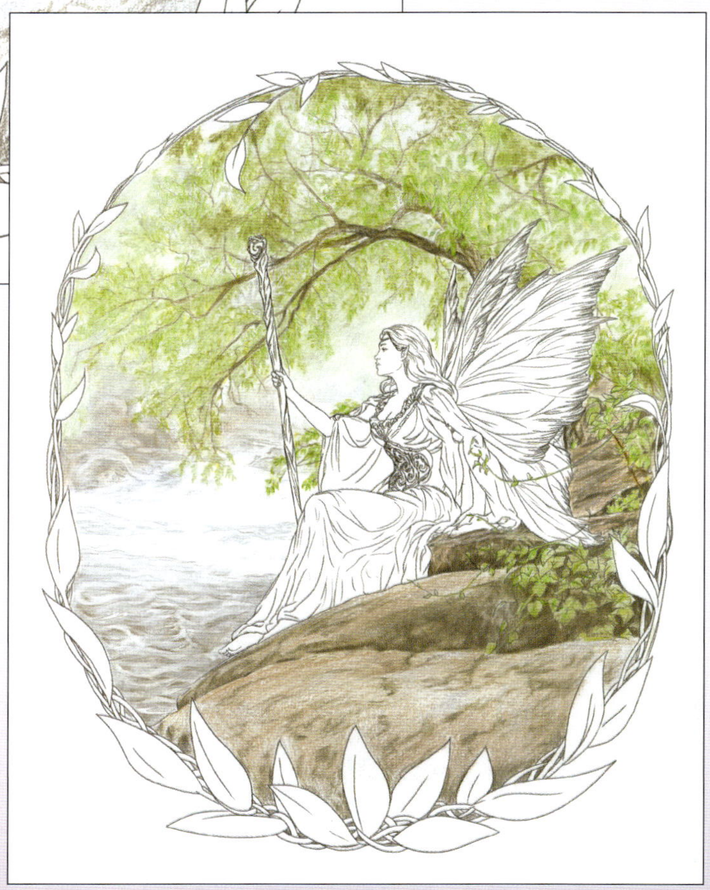

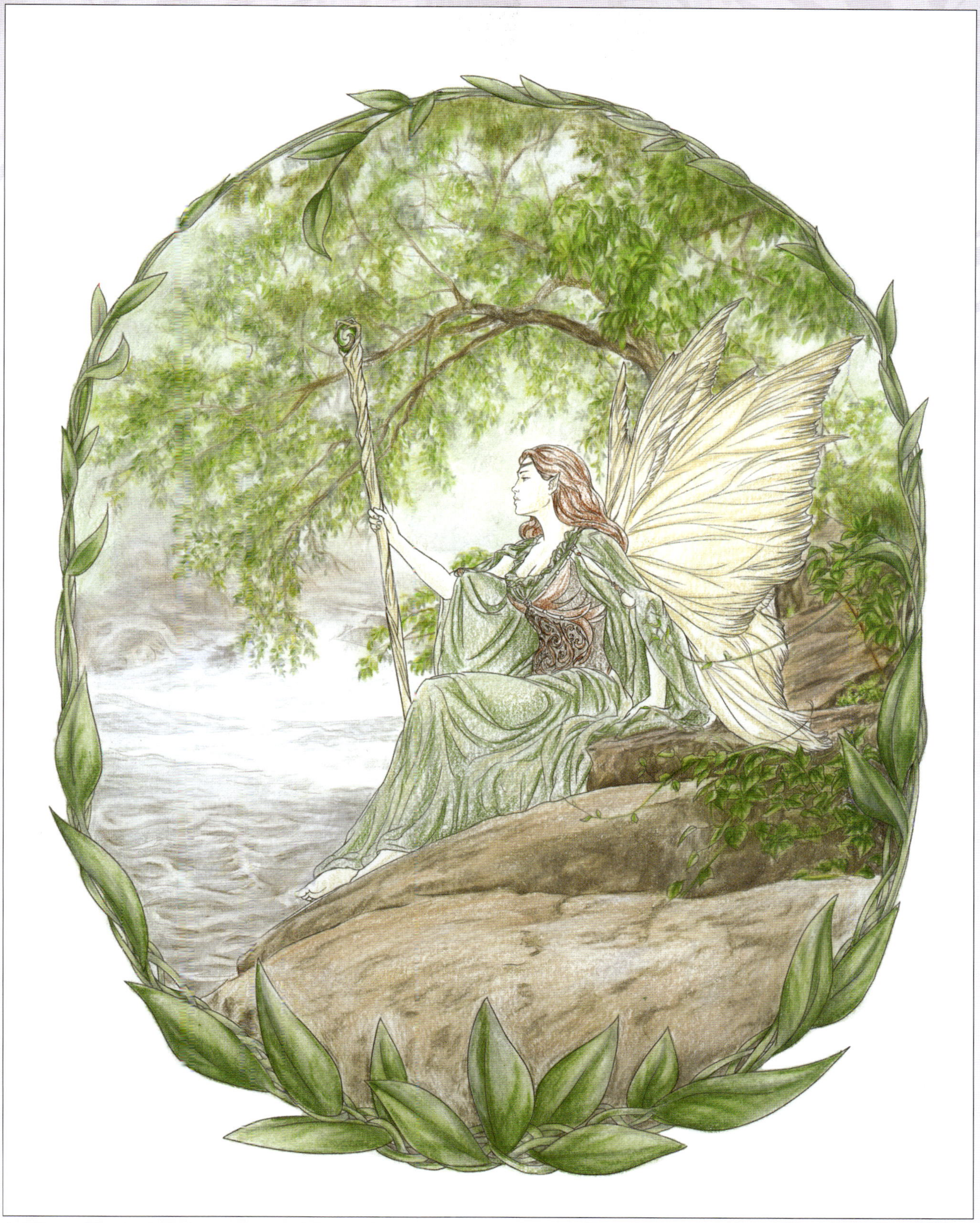

Step 5 Develop the foliage with short strokes of celadon green, working it into the foreground leaves. Bring in sage green for the lighter tones, and blend the colors with a colorless blender. Shade the foliage with Kelly green and Prussian green. Next, move on to the figure (see "Detail" on page 106).

Detail Use eggshell for flesh shadows and to fill in the wings, using dark strokes near the edges and light strokes near the center. Use terra cotta for the hair and bodice, shading with 70% French gray. Revisit the greens for the dress, using celadon as a base color, lightening with eggshell, and darkening with Kelly green. If necessary, use an electric eraser to lighten areas that have already been blended.

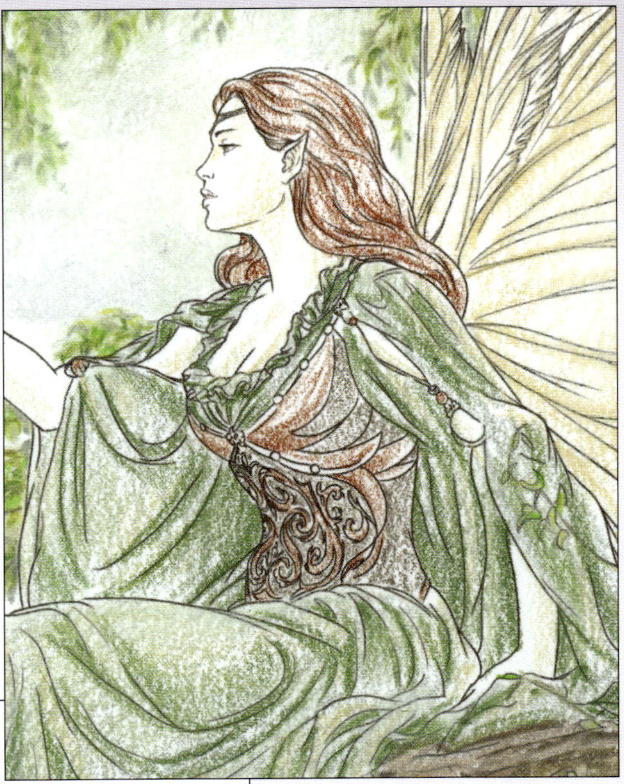

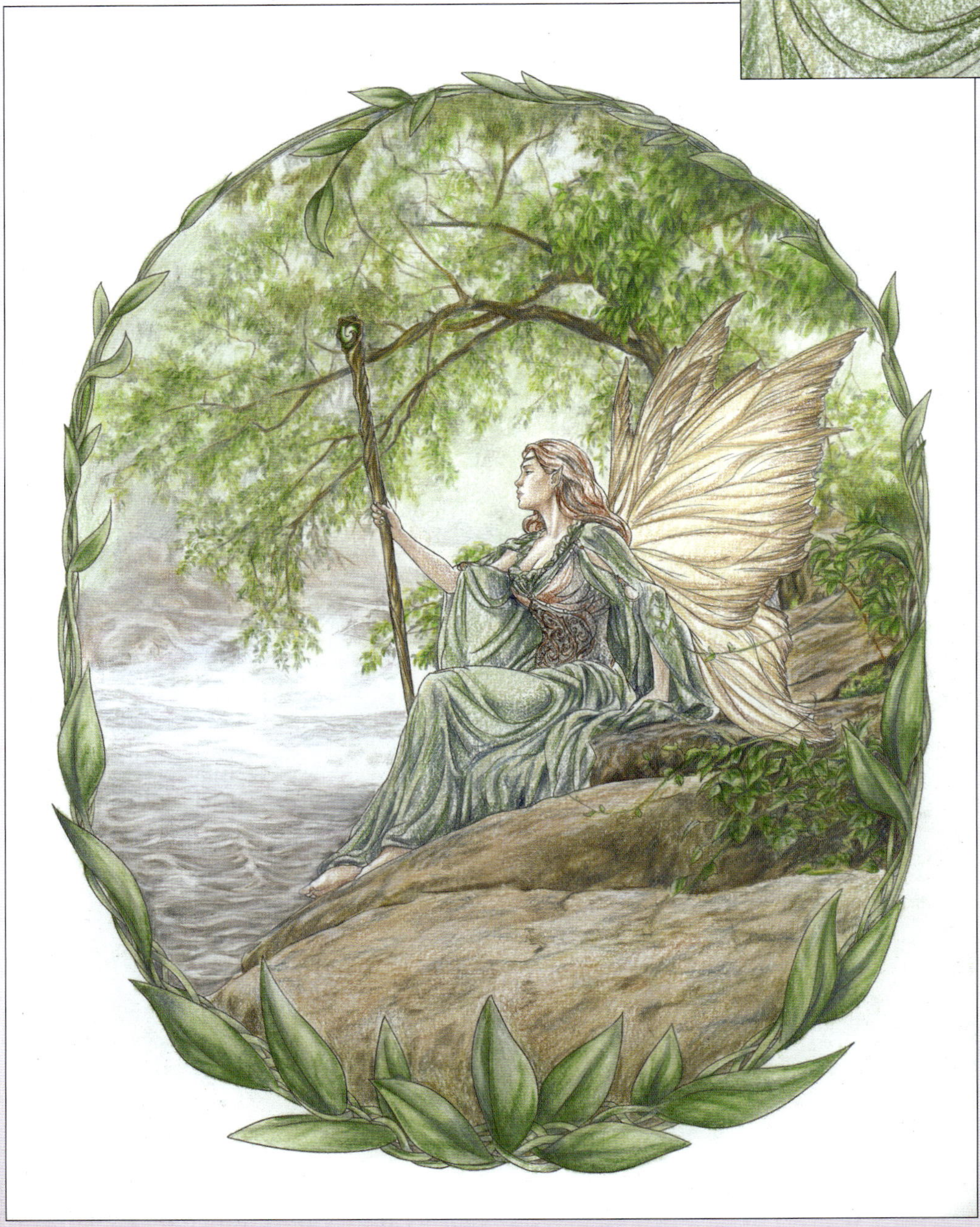

Step 6 Develop the staff using bronze and 70% French gray, finishing with a bright green for the stone. Then work the entire piece by shading with slate gray and indigo blue, focusing on the dress and leaves. Enhance the figure's shadows using grayed lavender and seashell pink. Apply the grayed lavender to the water and the seashell pink to the rocks. Using 50% cool gray and white, add highlights and shadows to the water and blend. For flesh shadows and dark accents on the wings, use beige sienna. Use a little pink rose and rosy beige to bring color into the fairy's face.

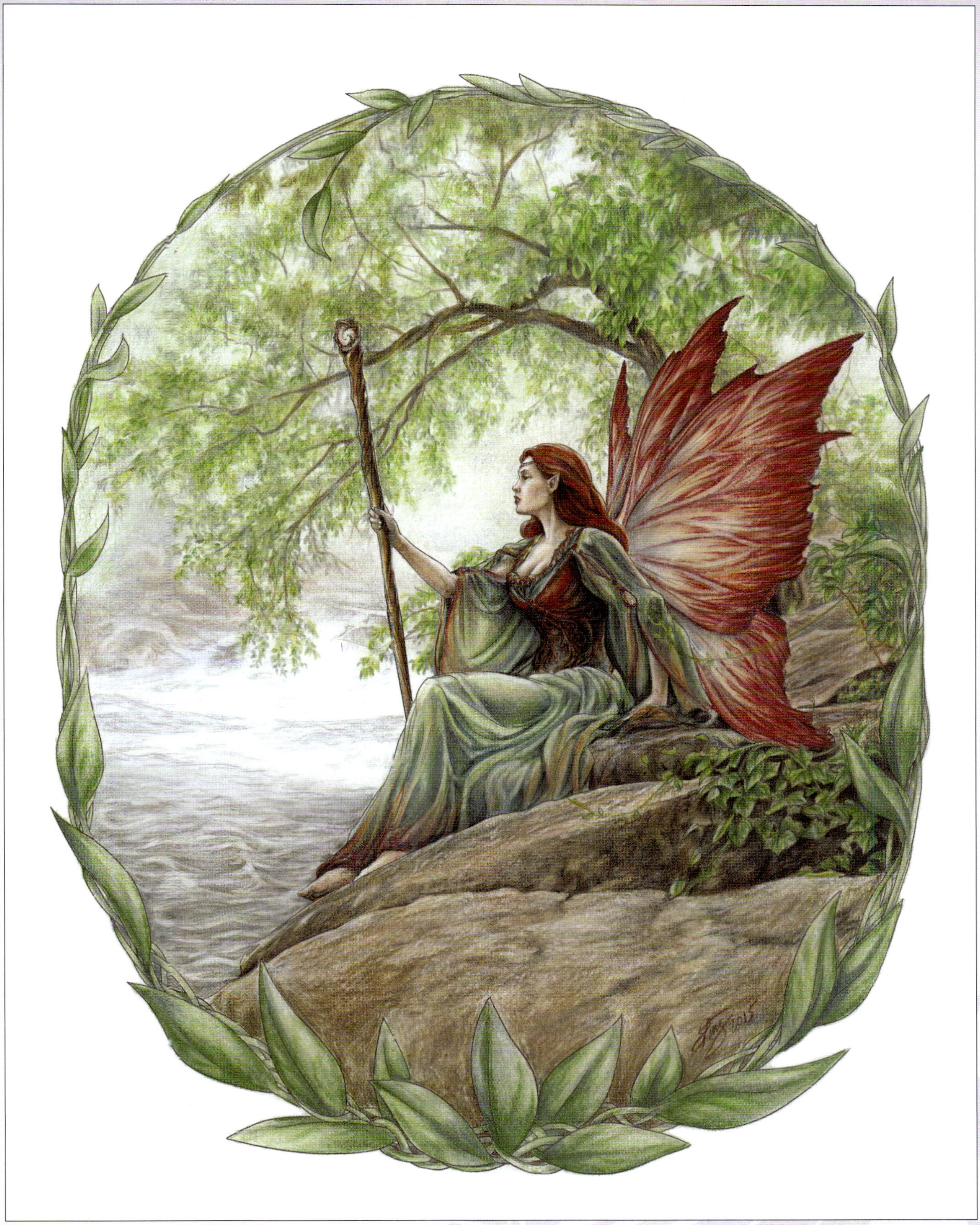

Step 7 Blend the colors of the figure and tighten up the details of the clothing. Add a light gradation of black raspberry on the fabric's edges, moving inward with poppy red and eggshell. Use the same colors used for the hair on the bodice, adding bronze and chestnut. For the face, add rosy beige and shade with dark and light umber. To develop the wings, use slate gray to add a shadow near the body. Then use black raspberry along the edges, moving inward with pink rose and nectar for a light center. Add accents with poppy red. Blend the wings and highlight some of the veins with white. To finish, add any final shadows with slate gray, 90% cool gray, and black.

Come Away

with Lindsay Archer

IN THIS PROJECT, I create a dreamy feel with a vague, out-of-focus background, leaving the sharpest details for the fairy and girl. I also embellish the edges with vines and allow the fairy's wing to penetrate the golden border for a sense of depth.

10% warm gray	30% warm gray	50% cool gray	50% warm gray	70% cool gray	90% cool gray	Apple green	Artichoke	Beige sienna	Black	Bronze
Chestnut	Cloud blue	Dark green	French gray	Ginger root	Goldenrod	Grayed lavender	Indigo blue	Jade green	Jasmine	Light umber
Limepeel	Nectar	Olive green	Peach beige	Sable	Sand	Sandbar brown	Sap green light	Sepia	Spring green	White

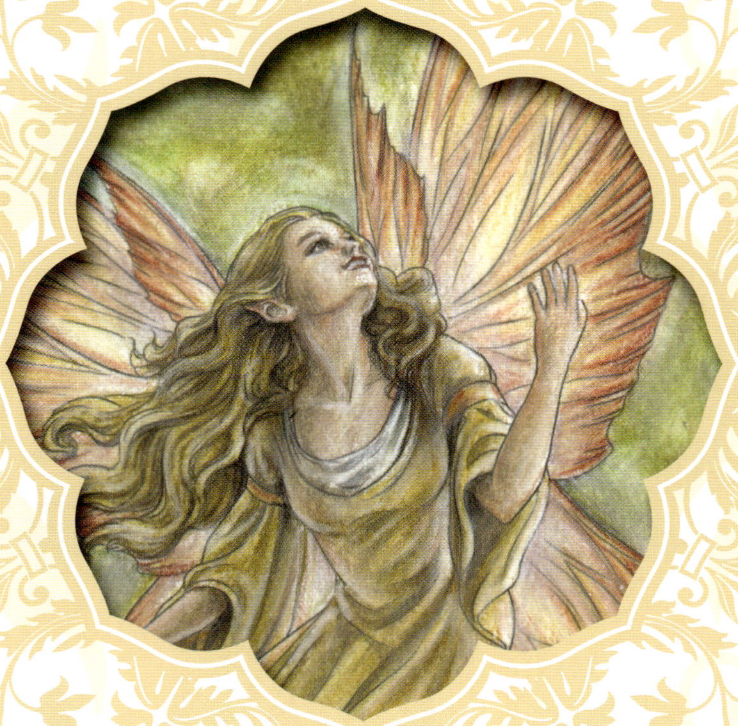

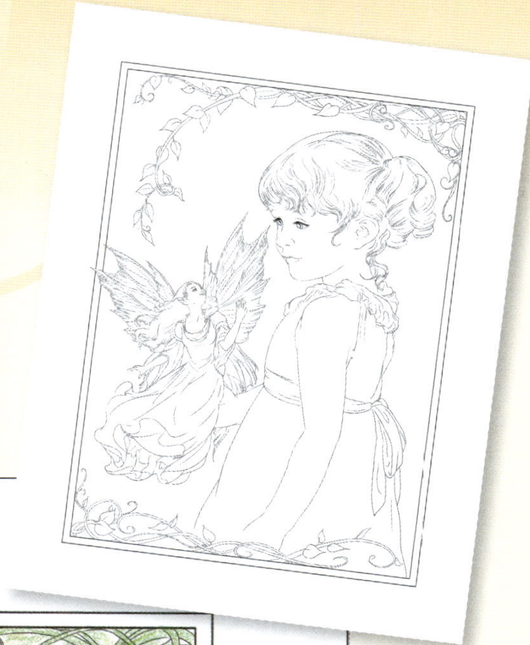

SKETCH Begin by creating a line drawing of the scene.

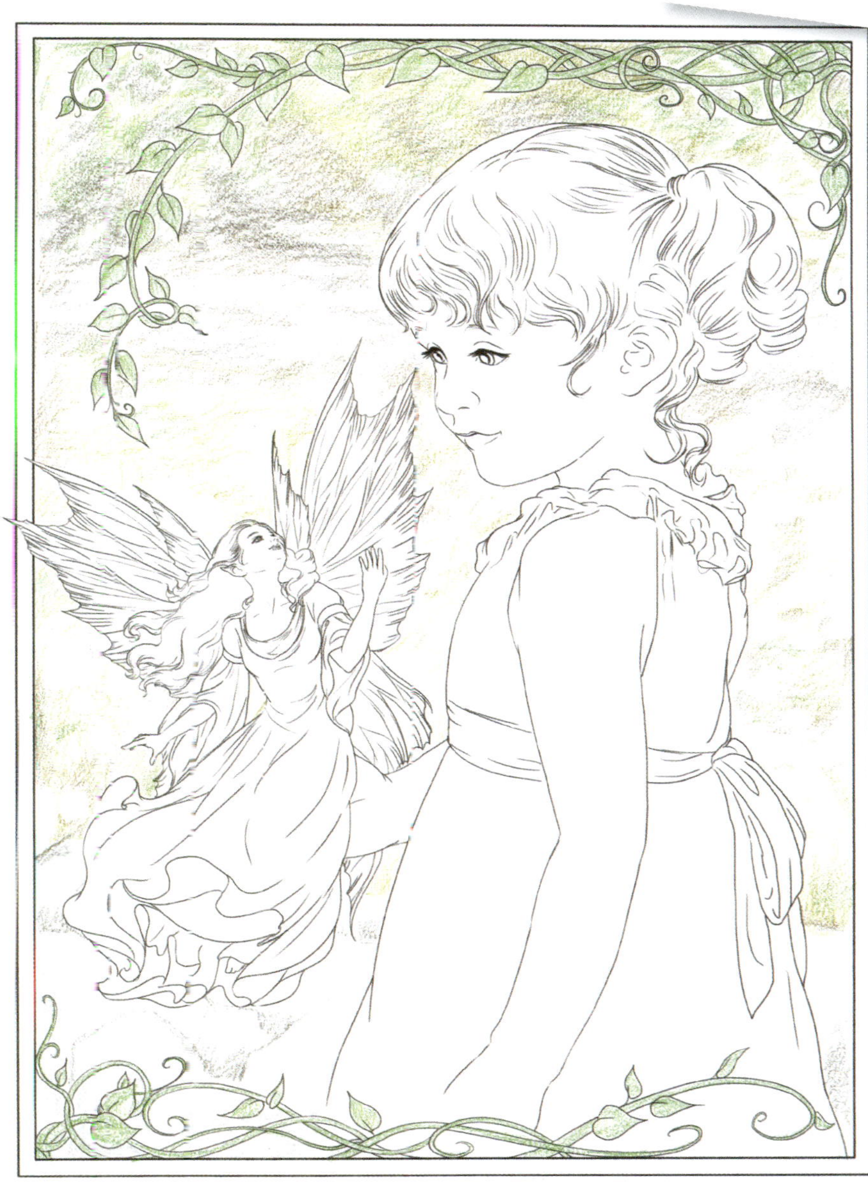

STEP 1 To begin the background, use limepeel to lightly fill in the greens of the water and woods. Then use sepia to begin filling in the darker base colors. Using artichoke, layer over some of the limepeel and sepia, working it into the water. Leave sketchy circles to suggest light reflecting off the water. With light umber and sandbar brown, work the water and background to darken the edges of the water. Use apple green and spring green to apply a layer to the knotwork leaves.

Step 2 Reapply many of the same colors to tighten up the image, darkening and mixing them for just the right effect. Also use ginger root, bronze, and jasmine on the background. With 50% cool gray, work the shadows in the water and add midtones to the rocks. Then use 70% and 90% cool gray for the dark shadows at the top and bottom, blending to bring out the colors. Next, to tame some of the colors, apply sap green light and jade green.

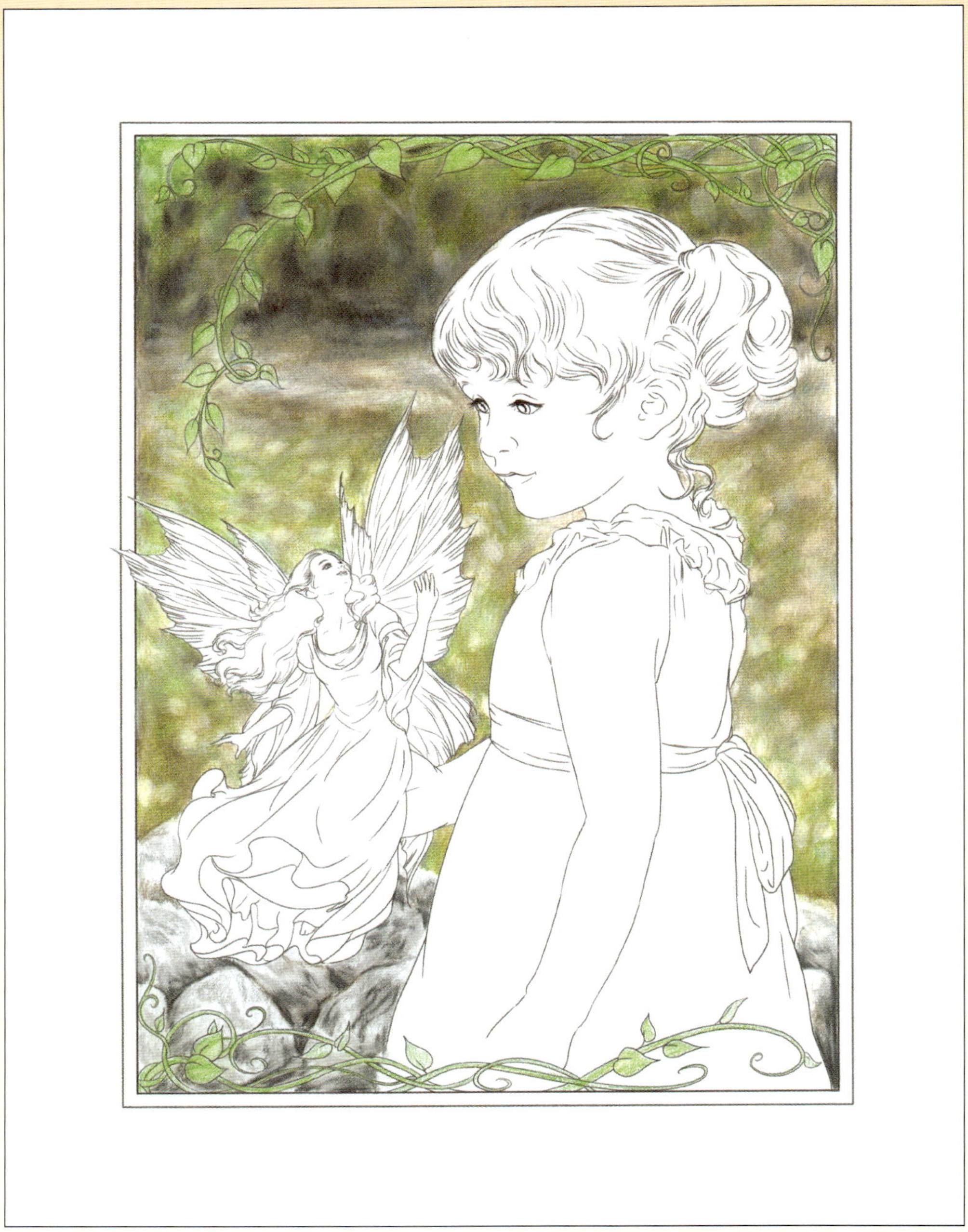

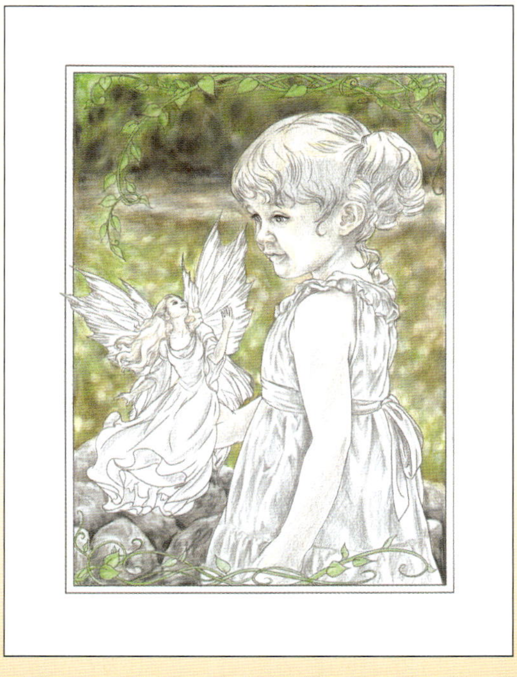

Step 3 Switching your focus to the figures, use 10% warm gray for an initial layer of light shading. Move to 30% warm gray for some of the darker areas and 50% warm gray for even darker areas, creating a gradient. For the flesh, use beige sienna for dark tones and peach beige for midtones. Use sand to create the warm reflection of light on the child's face.

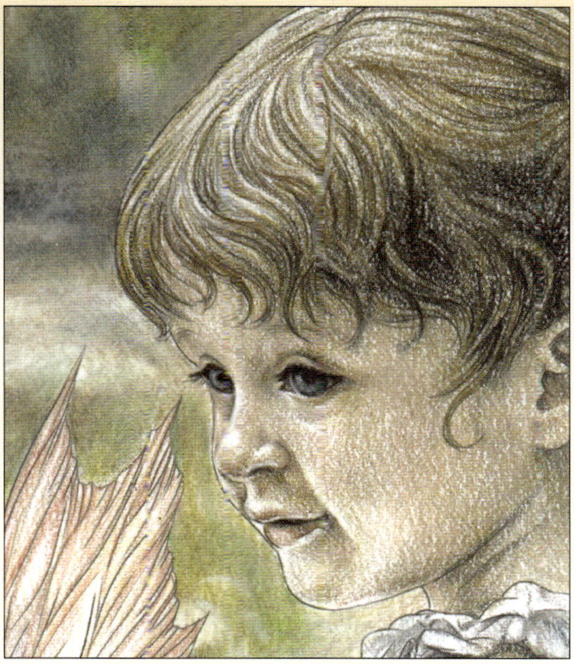

DETAIL At this point in my drawing, I decide that I'm unhappy with the girl's eyes, so I change the iris and pupil so that she is looking more forward, as though the fairy is luring her to fairyland. I use white to diminish some of the lines. To develop her eyes, use black for the pupils and around the iris, followed by indigo blue. Return to the iris with jade green in short, hard strokes over the indigo blue, working from the outside of the iris toward the pupil. Then use white to lighten the irises around the pupil.

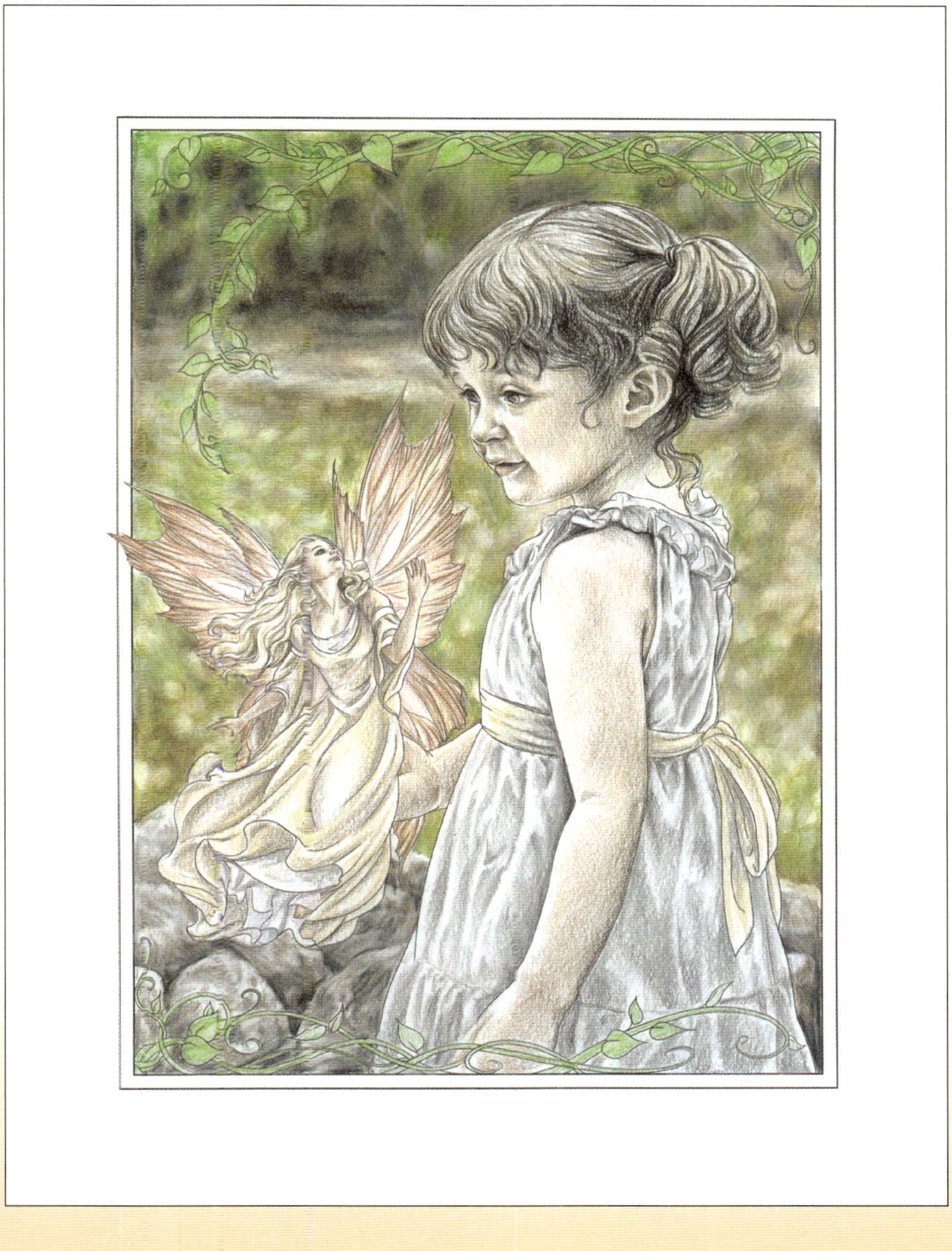

STEP 4 Continue working on the skin tones with peach beige, and then work this color into the fairy's wings and dress. For the darker areas and the wing tips and veins, use beige sienna. With nectar, which is a more vibrant pink, bring life into the flesh tones. Now establish the darker tones with 90% cool gray and sepia in the dress, rocks, fairy, and the girl's hair curls. This helps bring the foreground to life, separating it from the background. Then use sable on the fairy's dress and the girl's sash, aiming for a golden look. Although the girl's dress is "white," it still needs plenty of color in the shadows. Use jade green, grayed lavender, and cloud blue in the shadows, along with some 30% warm gray.

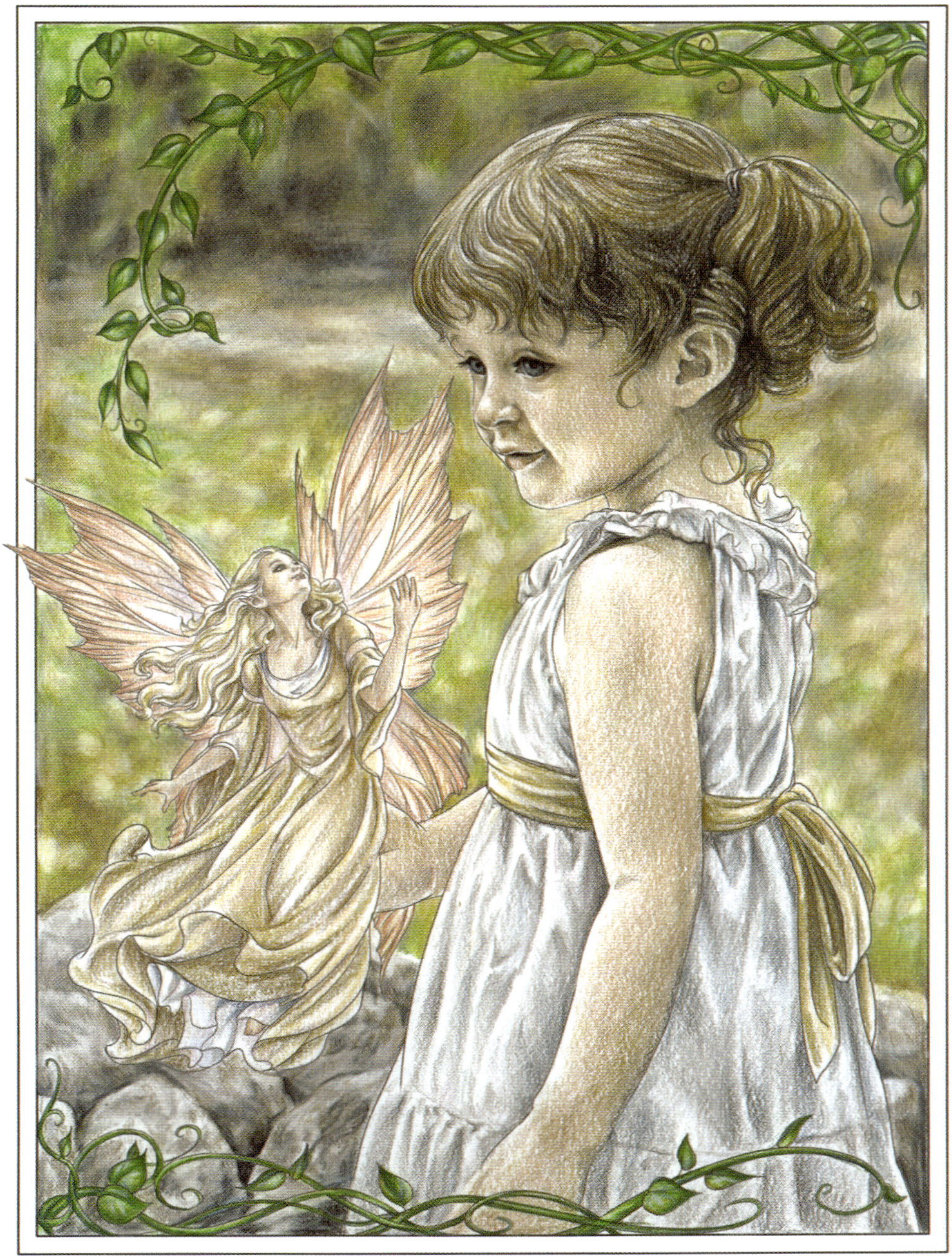

Step 5 Once your are happy with the eyes, use various French gray pencils for dark skin shadows. From there, branch out to the rest of the skin. Use bronze and light umber for some of the flesh shadows. Use peach beige for the lighter areas of flesh, and use bronze and light umber for some of the shadows in the hair and fairy's dress. Then work on the framing leaves using olive green, dark green, indigo blue, and bronze. To push back areas of the background, use a bit of white.

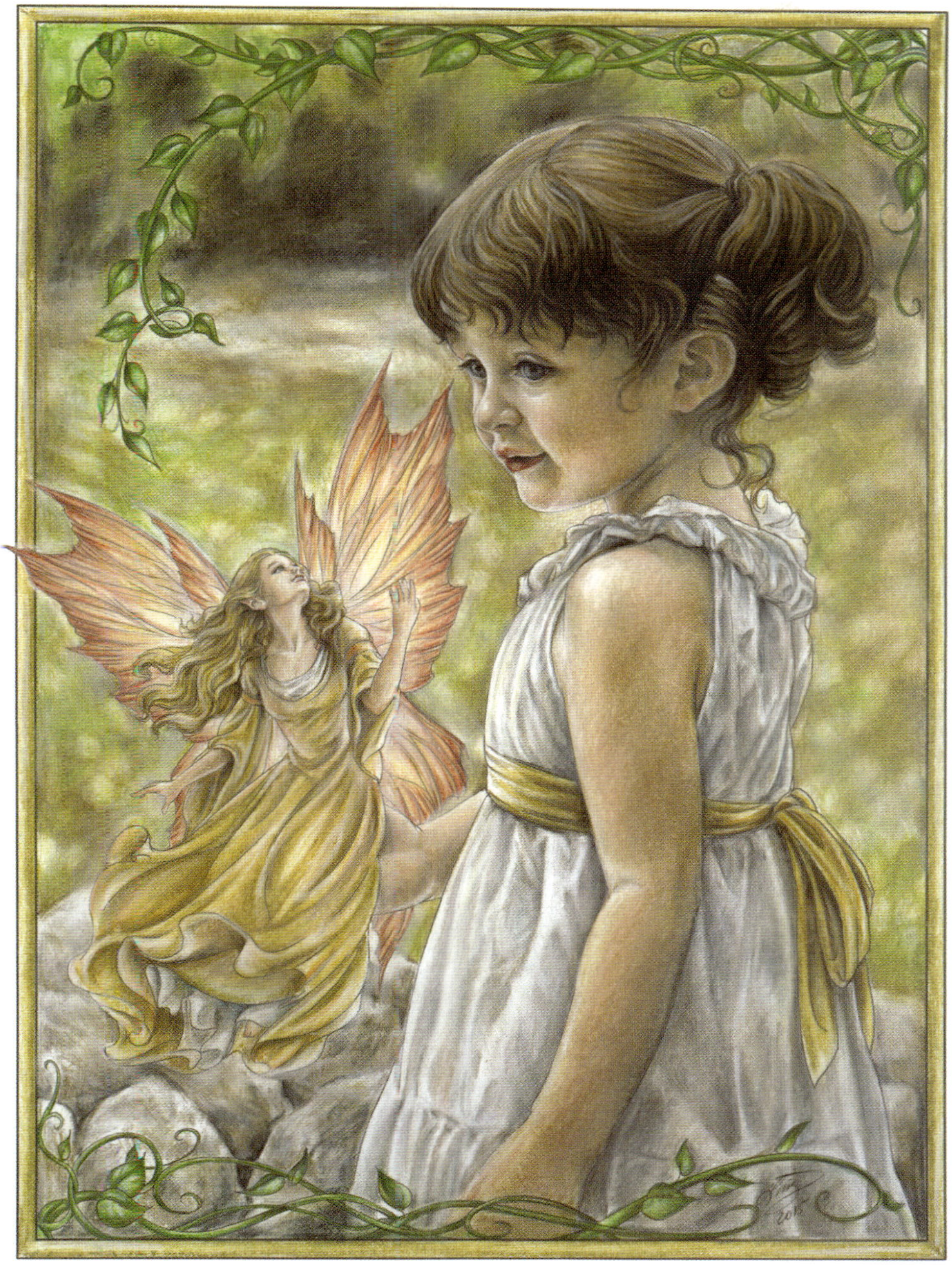

STEP 6 Start off using a colorless blender on the characters. Then layer over previous colors, pushing and pulling the values as needed. To get some of the values dark enough, use very dark grays, such as French and cool grays from 50% to 90%. Reserve black for just a few of the darkest areas, which really gives it dimension. Next, add chestnut to the lips and wing tips. Use goldenrod, sand, and bronze in the fairy's dress and girl's sash, using a colorless blender to smooth the strokes. To finish the piece, use sand and bronze for the gold border. Blend them together and use an eraser to create clean edges.

Knock on Wood

with Lindsay Archer

IN THIS PROJECT, set the vibrant purples and warm wing colors of the fairy against the cool, green leaves and neutral branches of the forest. You'll find that working with just a few dominant colors can simplify a busy composition.

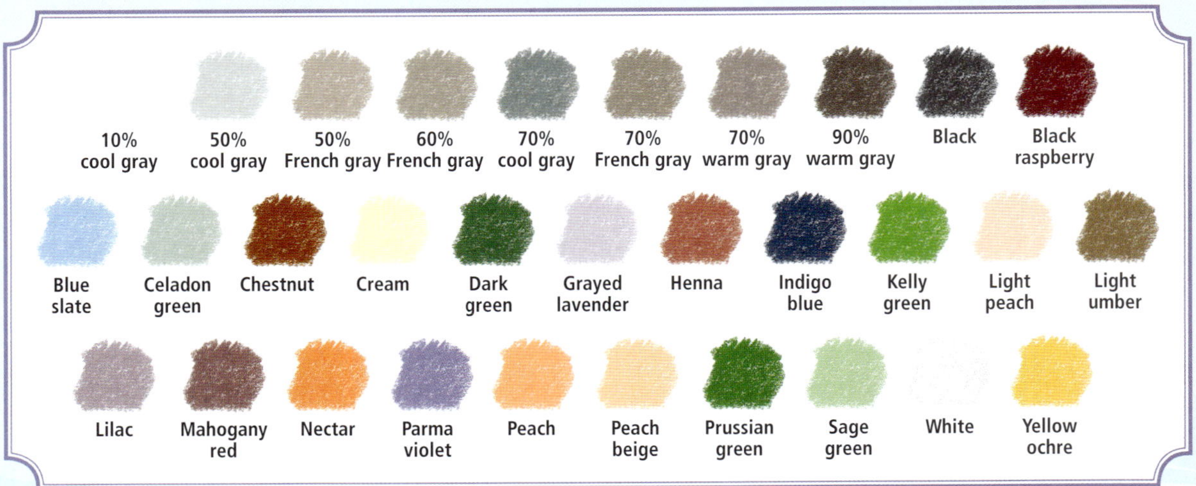

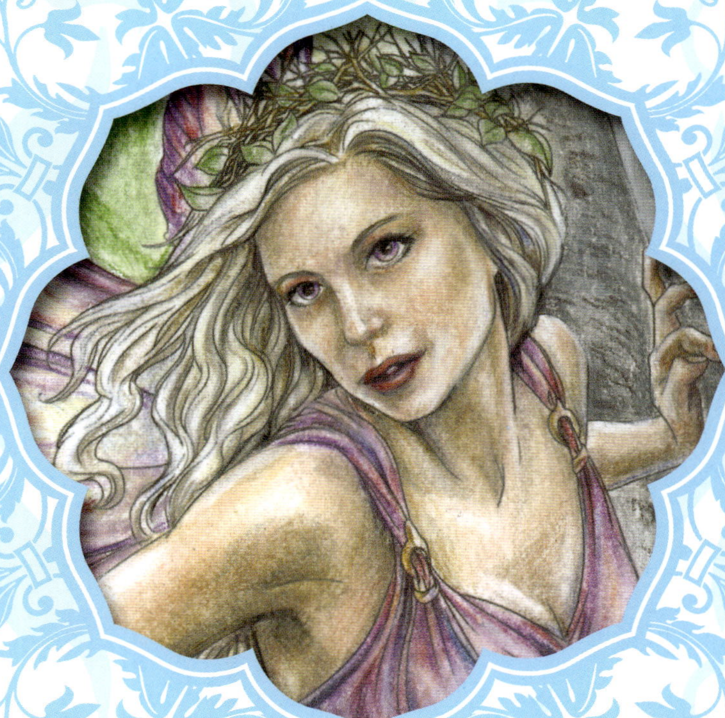

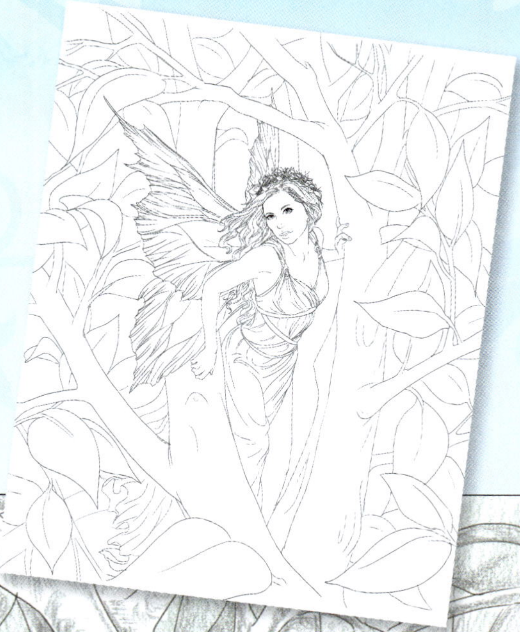

Sketch Begin by creating a line drawing of the scene.

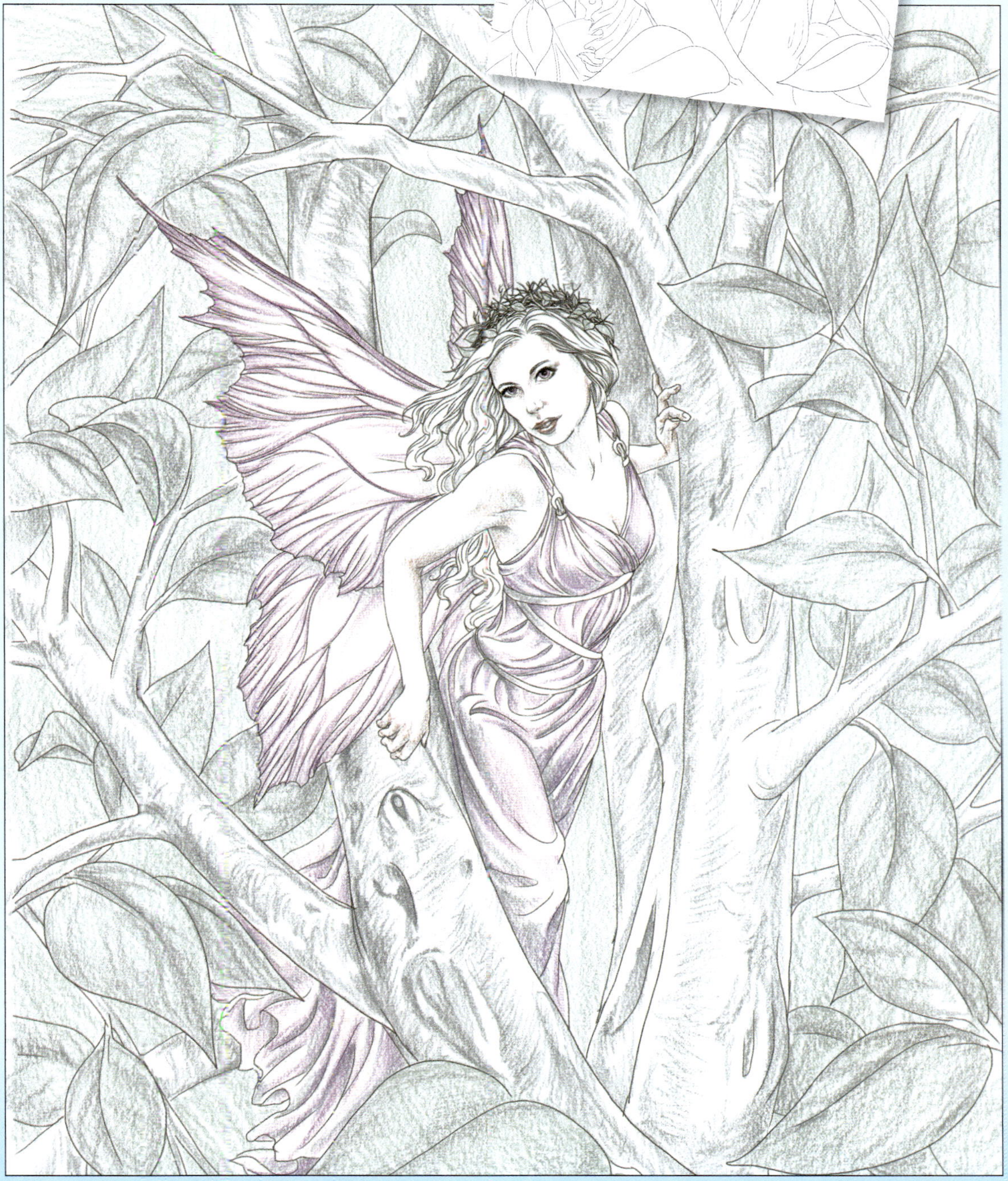

Step 1 Begin working the shadows with 50% cool gray to establish the base. Then use lilac to work the edges of the wings. Pull inward with each stroke, working from heavy to light pressure. Then use lilac to work on the eyes and dress, applying more tone near the lines and folds for depth. Switch to light peach and lightly color the wings, dress, and skin. For the lips and flesh shadows, use chestnut. For the background foliage, lay down a light layer of celadon green, covering everything except the figure and the branches.

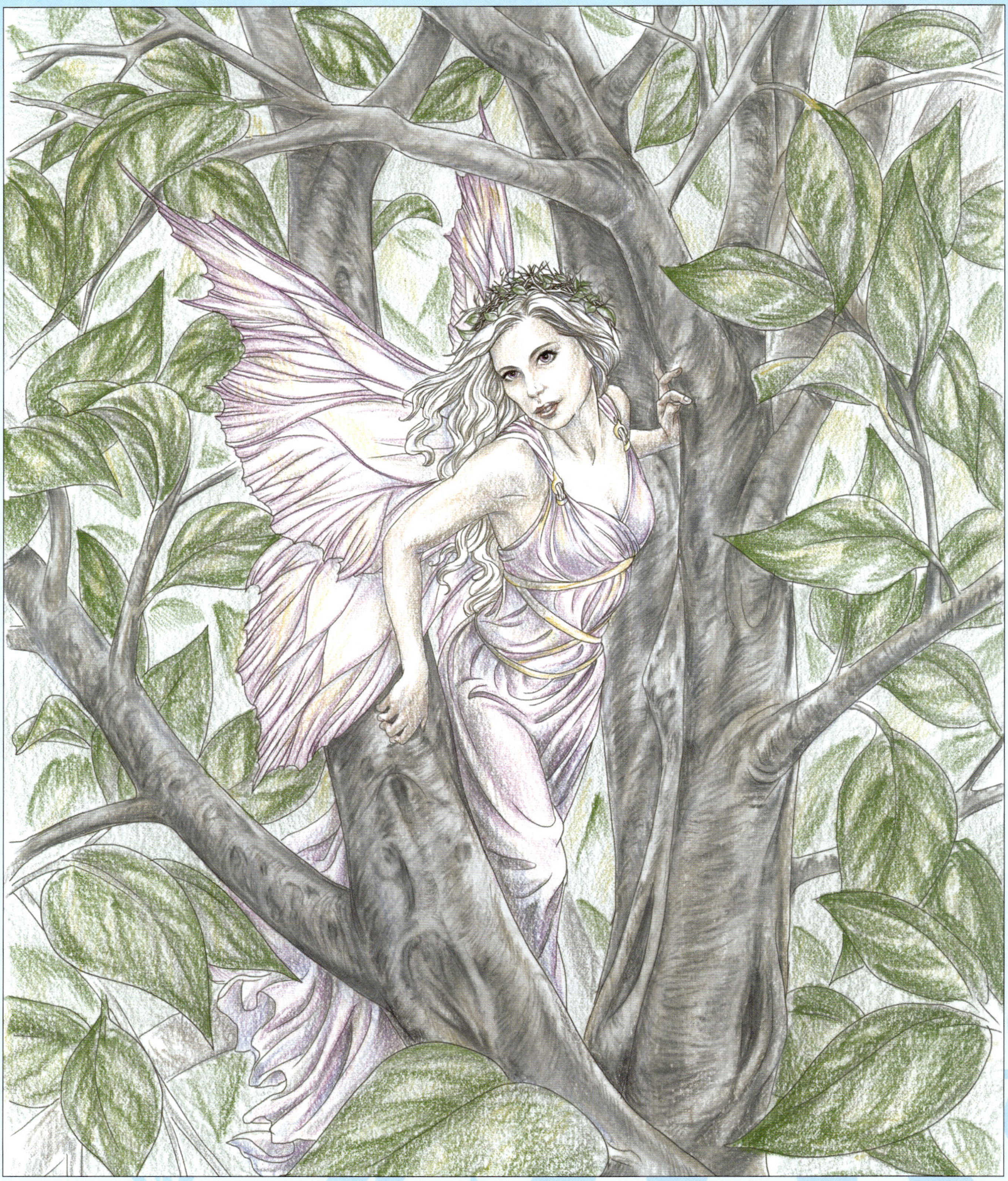

STEP 2 Continue shading, working in 50% French gray for warmth. Then use 70% cool gray for the darks of the branches. Apply a layer of 10% cool gray all over the branches and blend them together, returning with 70% cool gray to create details that "pop." Apply Kelly green over the leaves and use heavy pressure for the darkest areas. Add highlights with yellow ochre to suggest sunlight, adding a bit to the wings and dress. With blue slate, accentuate the figure's shadows. Then use peach beige to add more definition and depth to the flesh.

Step 3 Develop the shadows with blue slate. Then cover the leaves with a layer of sage green, blending with a colorless blender. Apply Kelly green over the leaves, followed by Prussian green and dark green for depth. Return to the leaves with a layer of cream and press firmly for highlights. Then add chestnut, which complements and tones down the green a notch. Using white and firm pressure, add highlights to the branches. Complete this step by adding details with 90% warm gray.

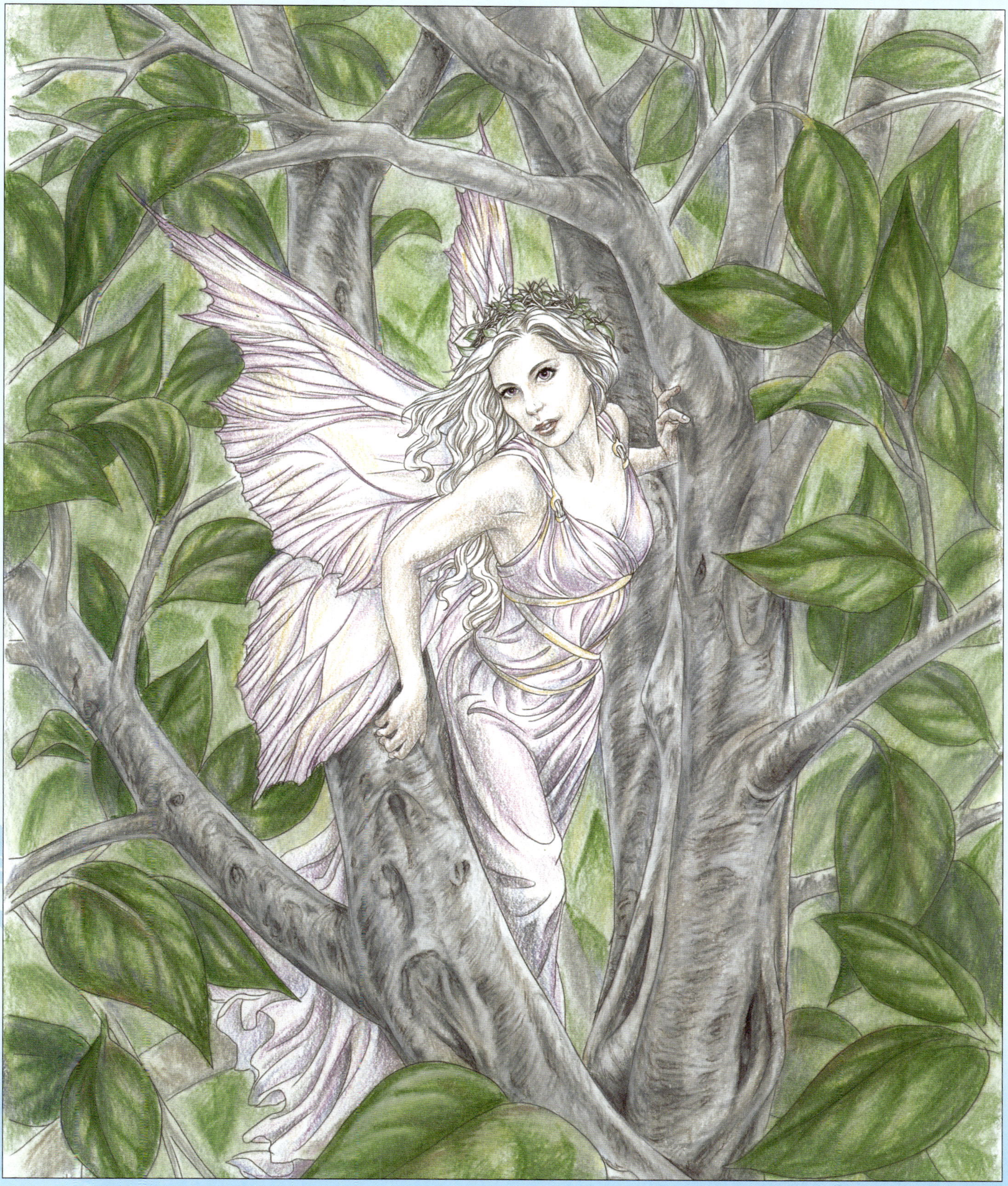

Step 4 Focusing on the wings, work from the outside inward. Use dark colors on the edges, including parma violet and mahogany red, and pull in the colors using henna and nectar. Switch to peach and cream for the wing centers and blend the wings with a colorless blender. Use white to lighten the veins, shading beneath with nectar or grayed lavender. With mahogany red, accent the corners of the veins.

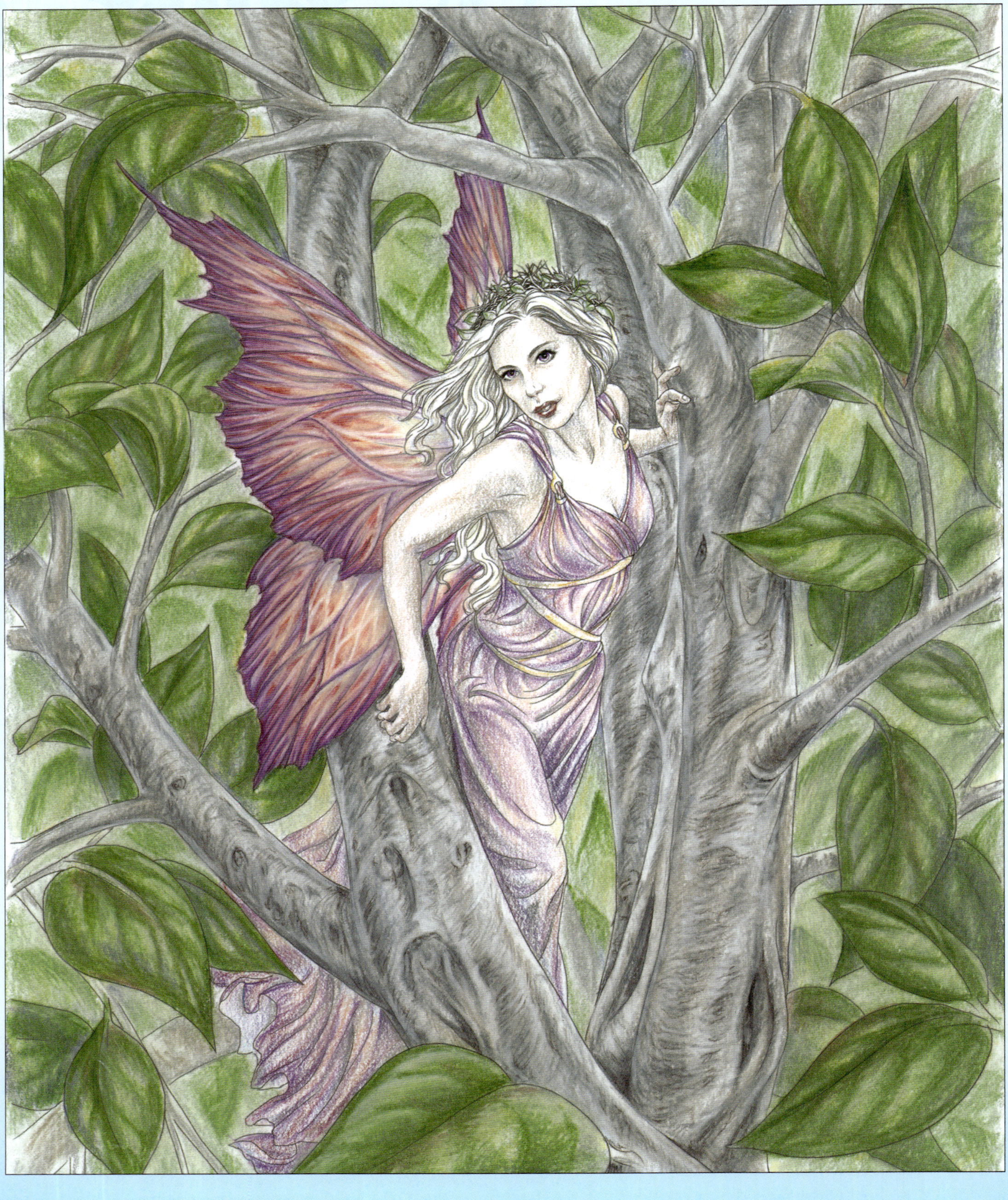

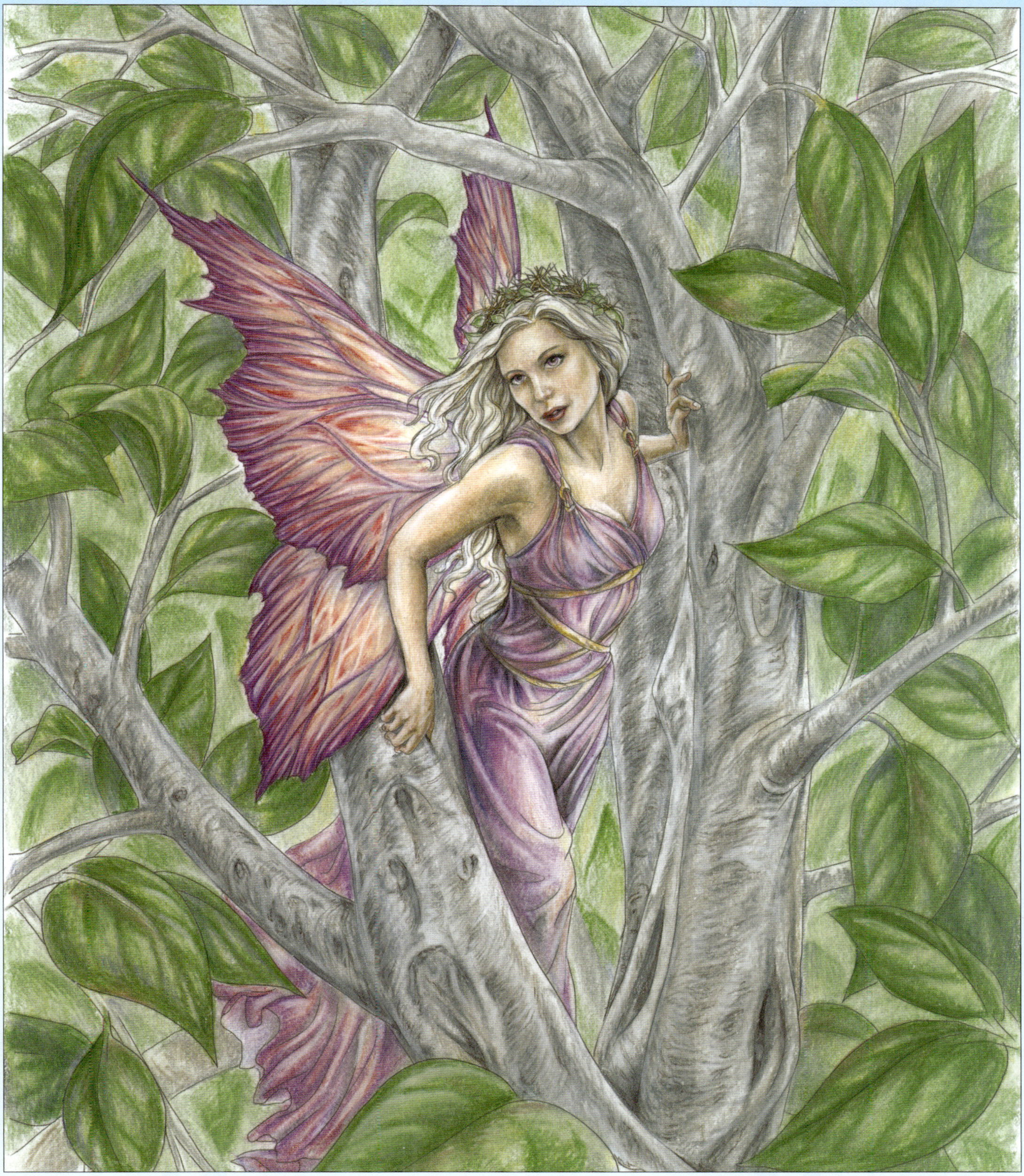

STEP 5 Blend within the dress using grayed lavender over the midtones and white over the highlights. For the shadows, use 60% and 70% French gray along with 70% warm gray and black. In some areas, use indigo blue to cool and black raspberry to darken. For the face, use a mix of light peach and cream for the lightest areas, peach beige for the midtones, and light umber with 70% French gray for the darker flesh tones. Apply shadows to her blonde hair with light umber. To finish, use nectar to add color to her face and black to darken the eyes.

Templates

PAGES 121 THROUGH 127 CONTAIN TEMPLATES for select projects in this book. You can use these templates to transfer guidelines to your drawing surface, which will speed up the sketching process. Simply follow the steps below.

1. Trace the template onto a sheet of tracing paper, or make a photocopy of the template onto a sheet of copy paper, scaling it to your desired size.

2. Coat the back of the paper with a layer of graphite using a pencil. (In place of this step, you could purchase a sheet of graphite transfer paper.)

3. Now place the template graphite-side down on top of your art paper or canvas. Using a pencil, ballpoint pen, or stylus, trace the lines of the template.

4. Occasionally peel back the corner of the template to make sure the lines are transferring well to your drawing surface. The result will be a light guideline for creating your sketch!

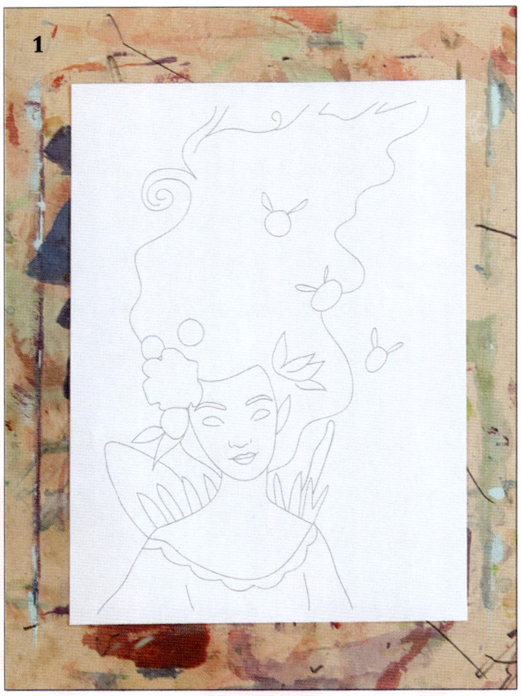

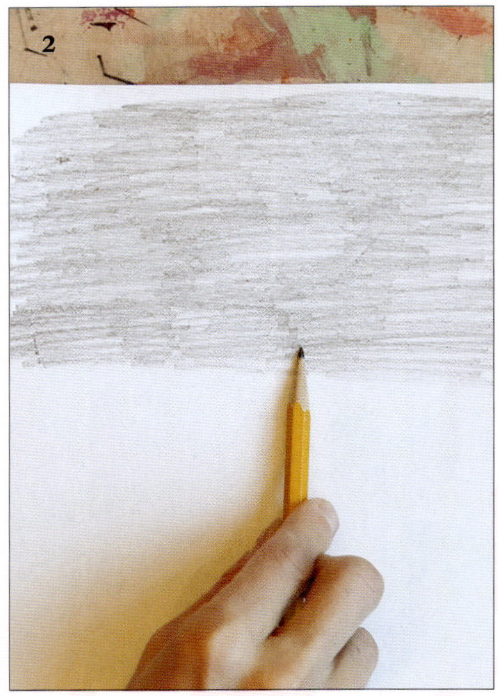

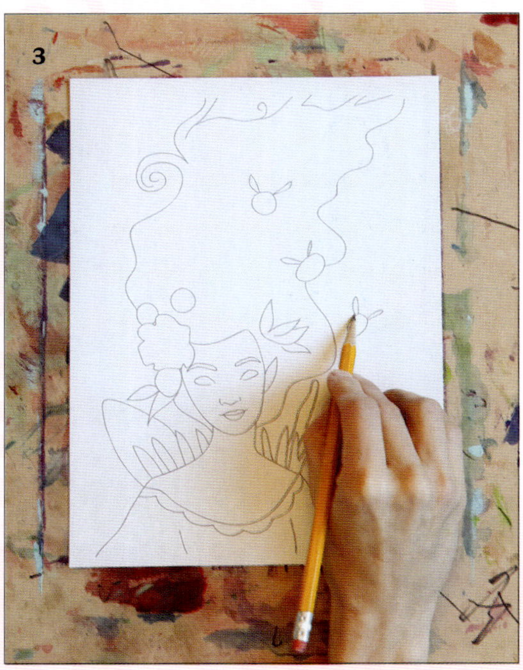

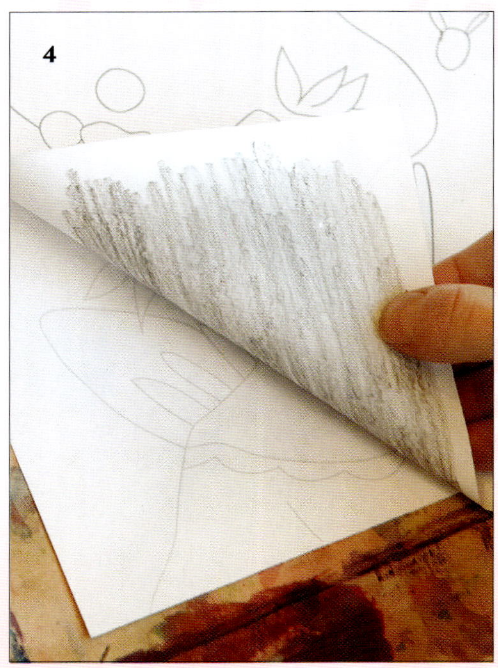

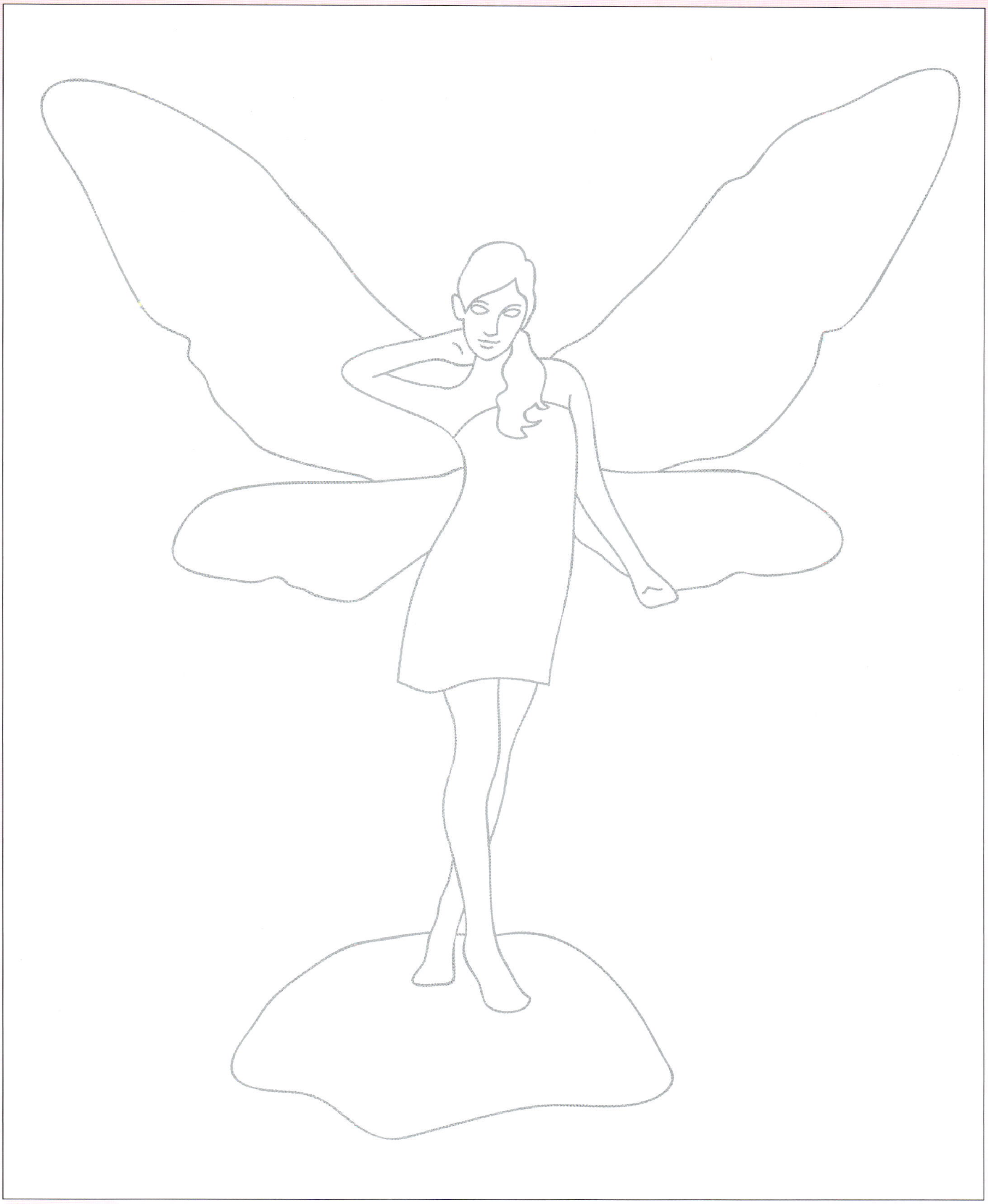

Water Fairy

Project on page 26.

Fire Fairy

Project on page 34.

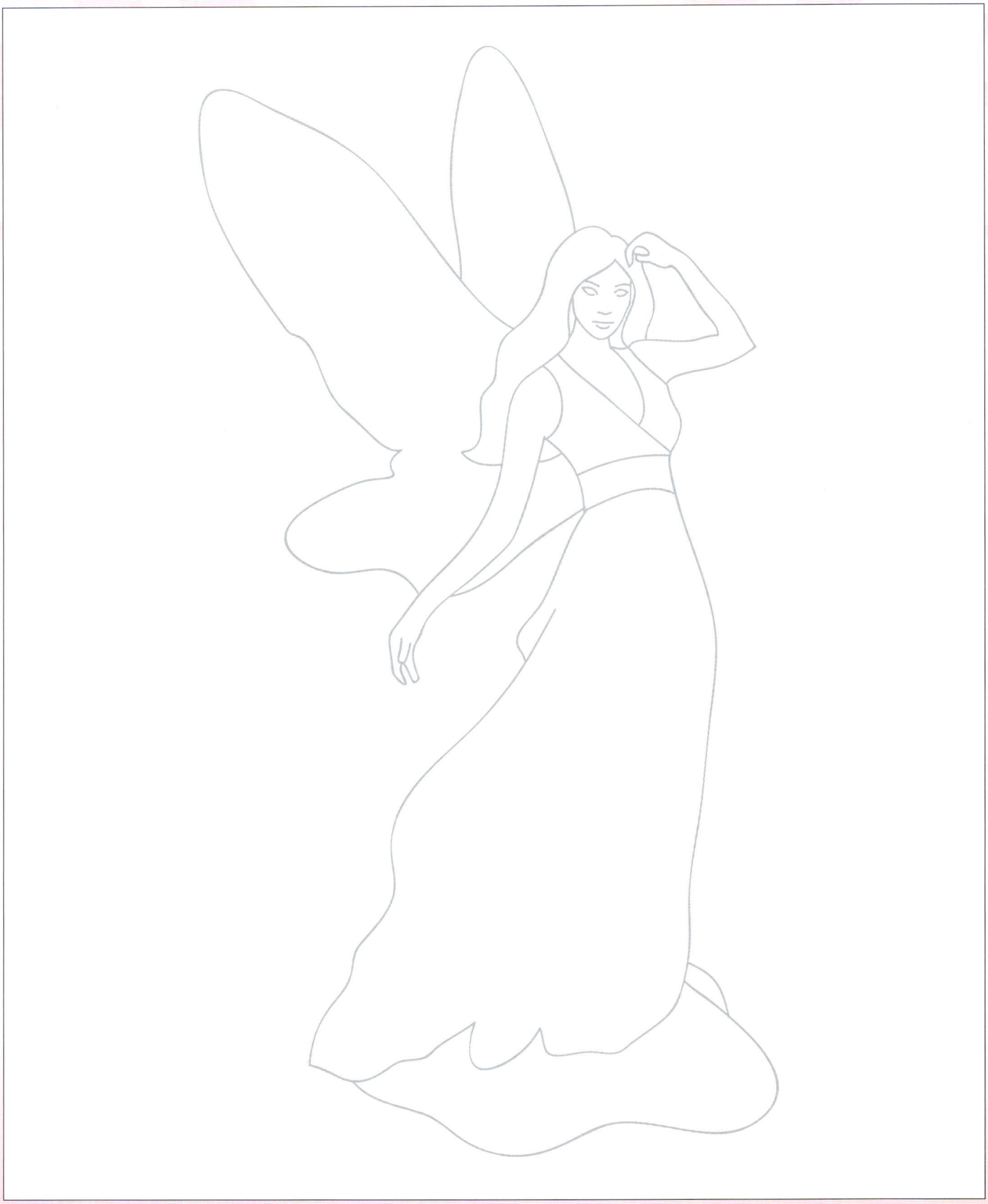

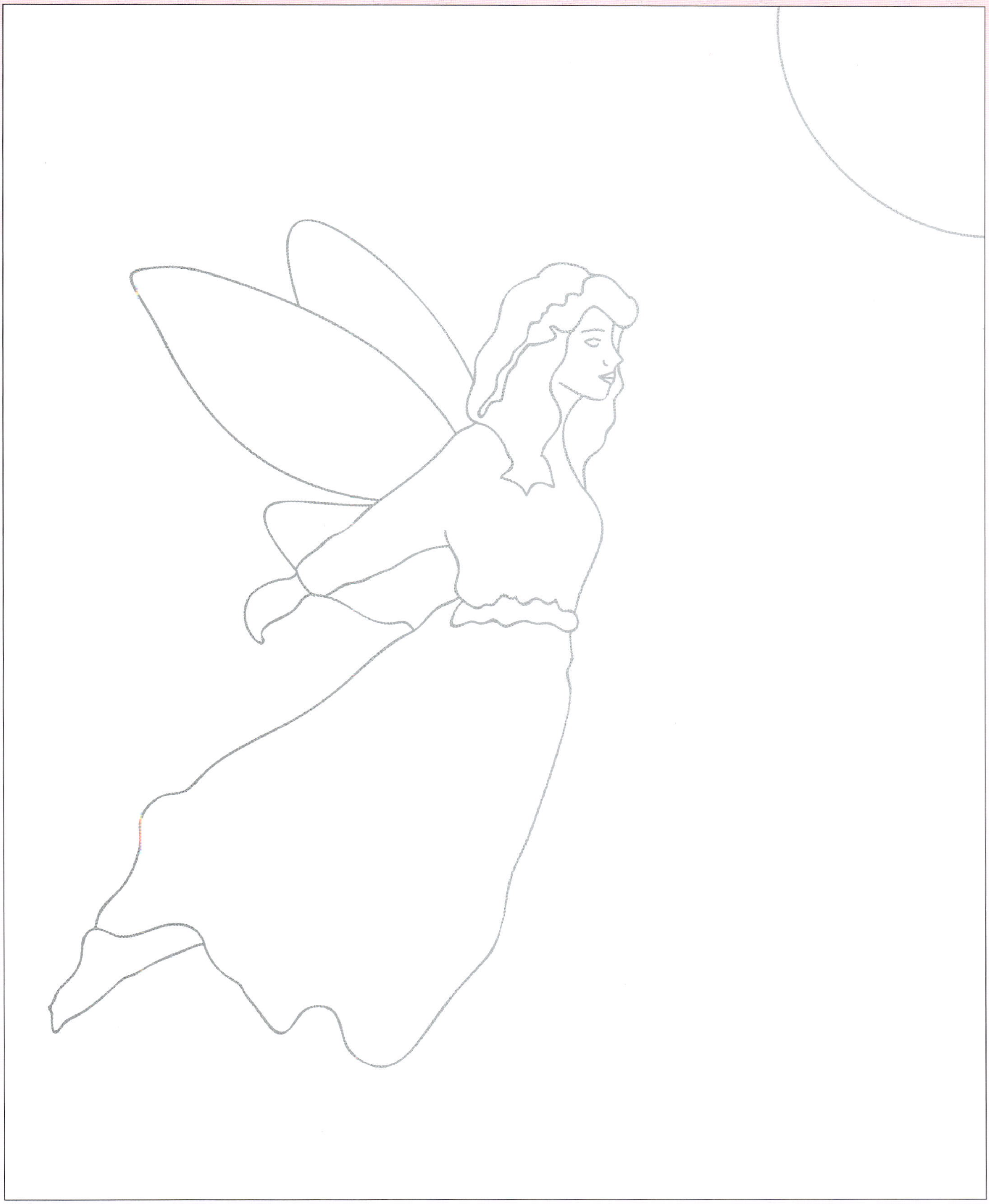

Celestial Fairy

Project on page 42.

Windblown Fairy

Project on page 62.

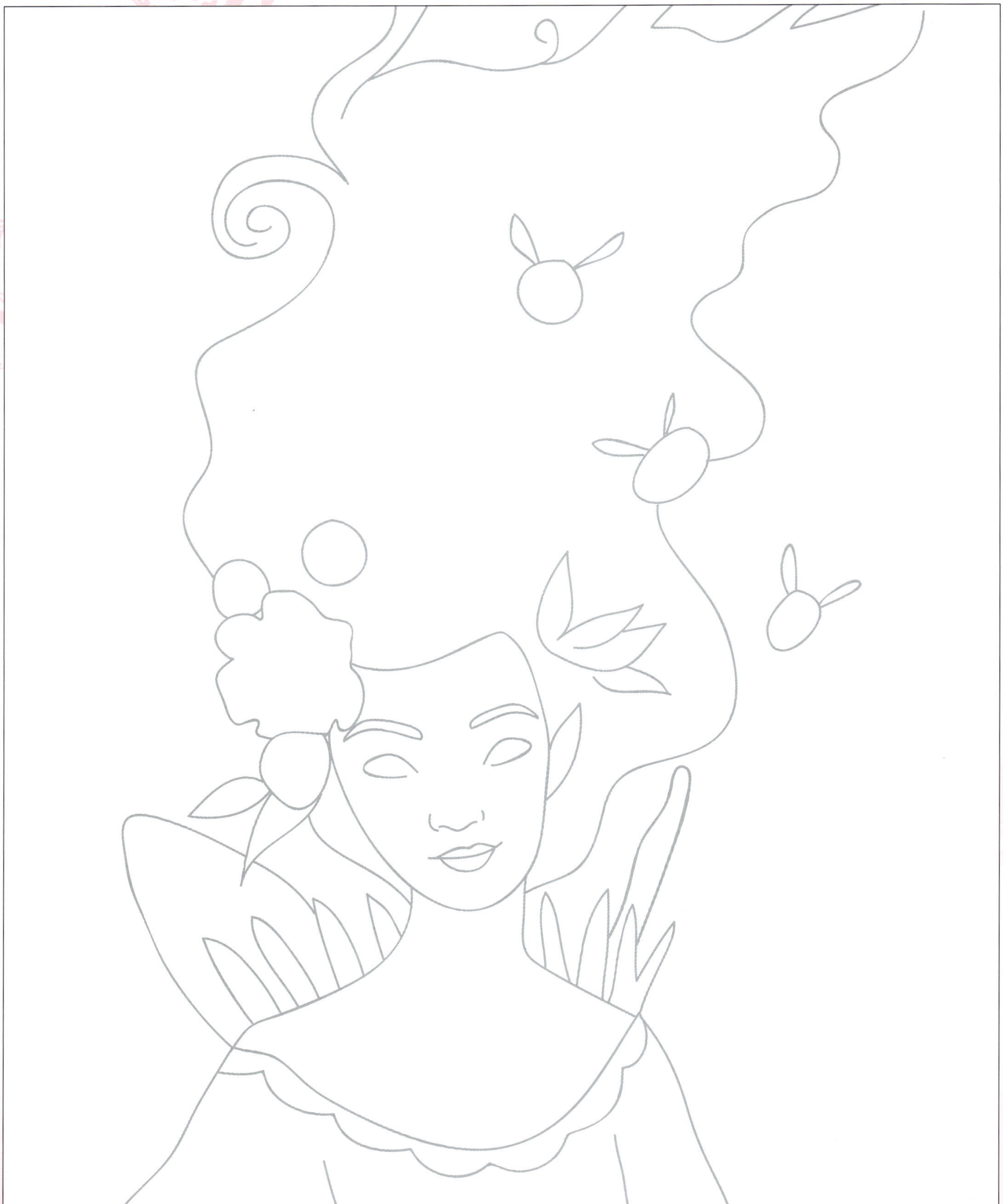

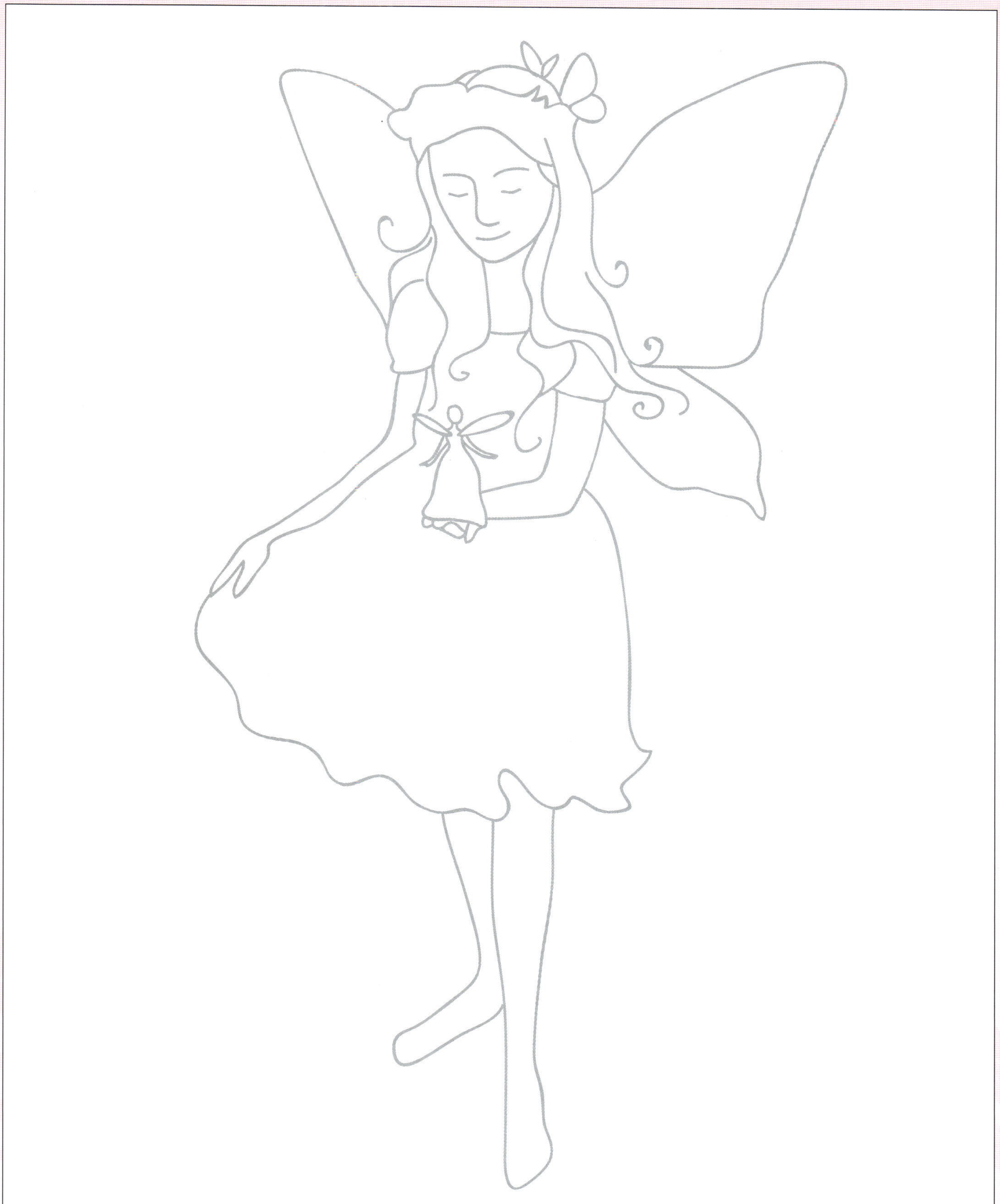

Fairy Circle

Project on page 68.

Butterfly Fairy

Project on page 82.

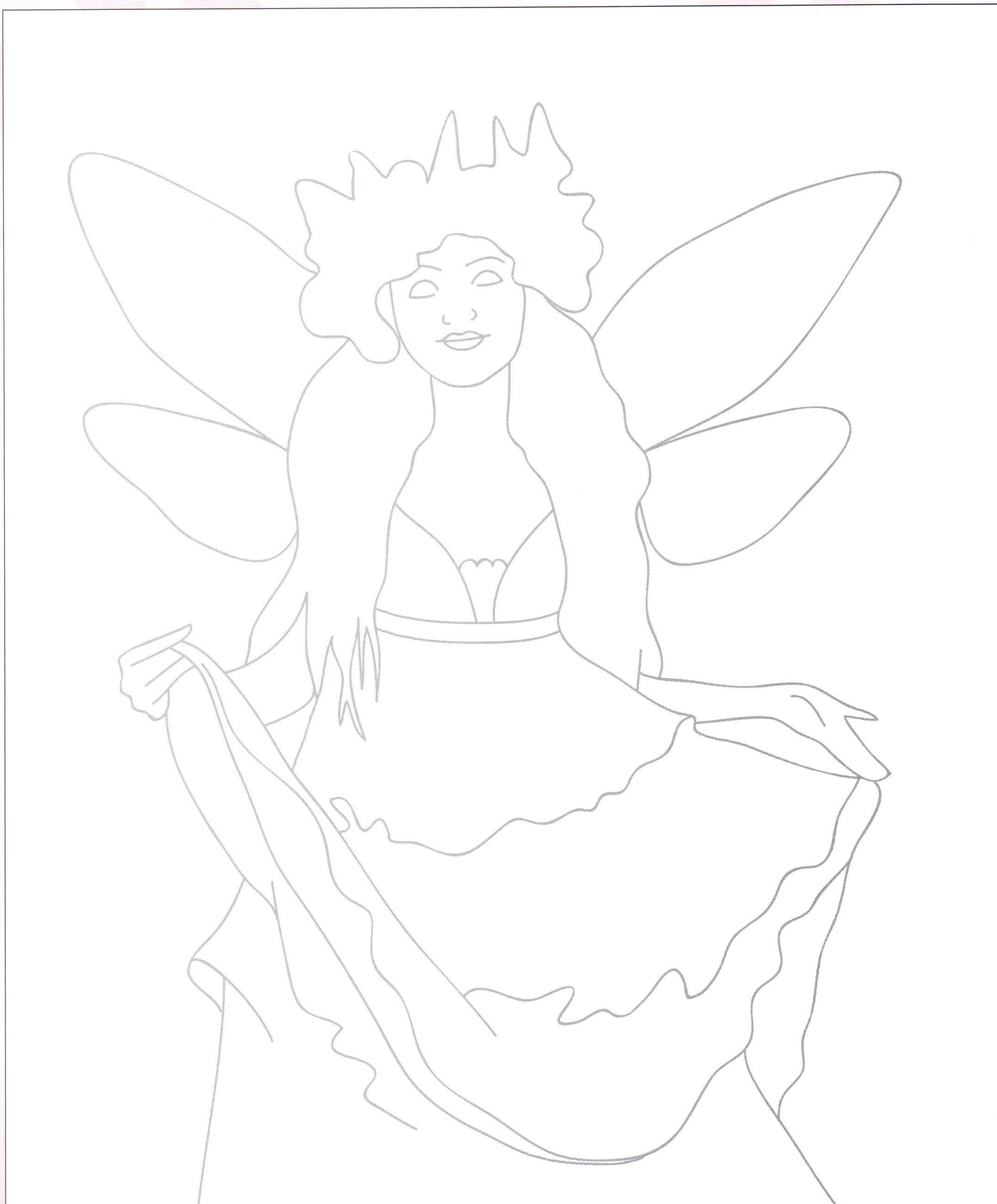

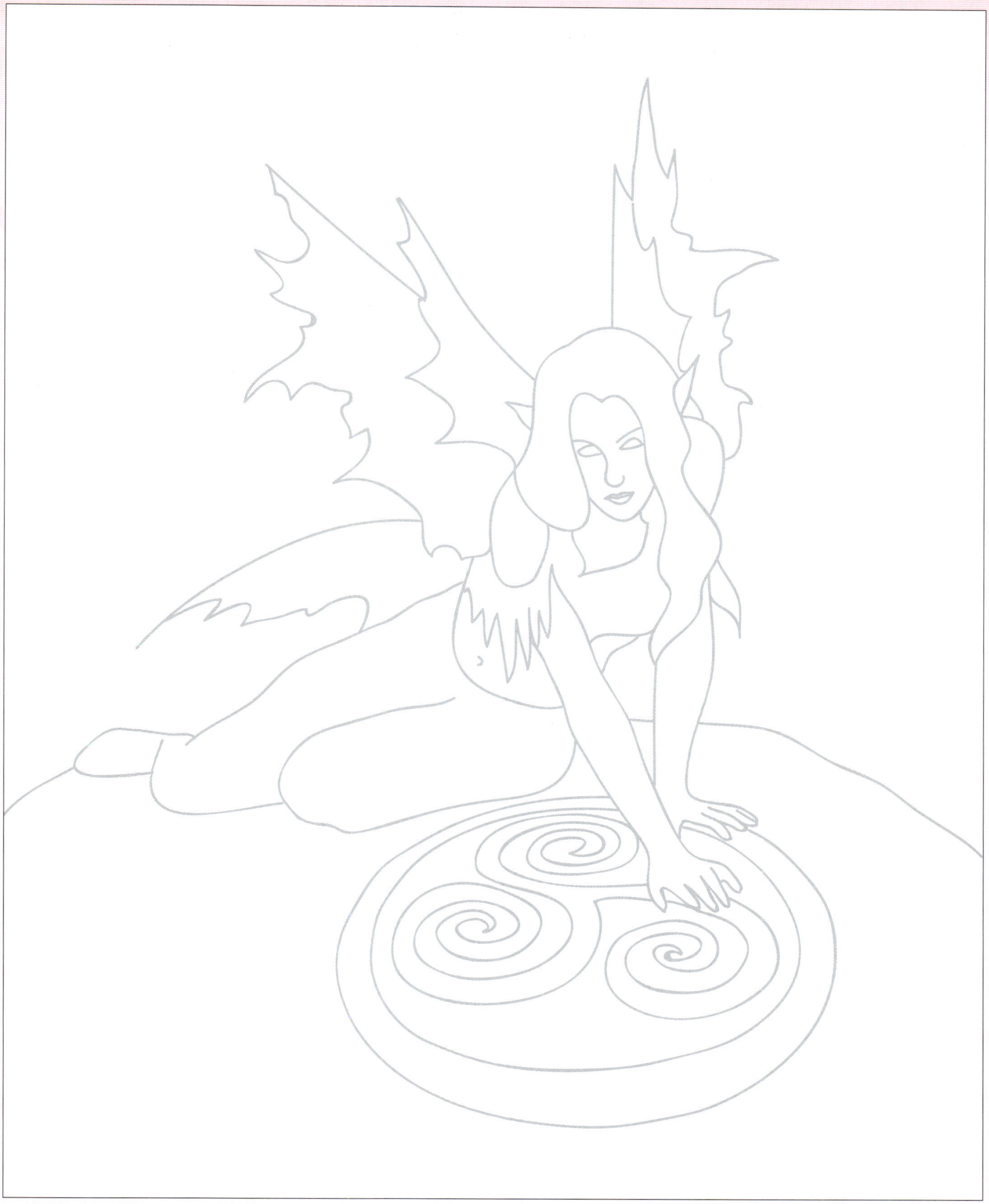

Runestone Fairy

Project on page 96.

About the Artists

Skilled in many mediums and subject areas, **Lindsay Archer** is an accomplished professional artist in the gaming industry with well over a decade of experience. Lindsay has illustrated for such role-playing games as Serenity™, Supernatural™, Dragonlance™, Battlestar Galactica™, and Cortex™. Through the years, she has been prolific in both illustration and her own fantasy artwork. To learn more about the artist and her work, visit *www.lindsayarcher.com*.

Sara Burrier discovered early her love for fairies, mermaids, and the fairytale realm. It wasn't until college that she learned how impactful and whimsical fairytale imagery could be. She received a BFA in illustration and moved back to her hometown, where she began teaching art to children. Over the next several years she built her own freelance studio, Sara B Illustration, and licensed her images for puzzles, greeting cards, and other merchandise. Sara is always looking for the next challenge for her work, and how it can help others find their light. The best parts of her job are selling her work in person, giving out smiles and encouragement, and writing books to teach others how to do what she loves. When Sara isn't creating art, she is cooking, spending time with her friends, or taking walks with her family. Visit *www.sarabillustration.com*.

Cynthia Knox is an award-winning artist who specializes in works of traditional realism. She is a Signature Member of the Colored Pencil Society of America, a juried member of the International Guild of Realism, a commissioned portrait artist, and an occasional art instructor. Her artwork is in shows, private collections, and on her website. Cynthia credits her passion and inspiration for art to a deep love for God and encouragement from her parents and family. She currently lives in upstate New York with her husband, Jeff, and their two daughters, Katharine and Abby. Visit *www.cynthiaknox.com*.

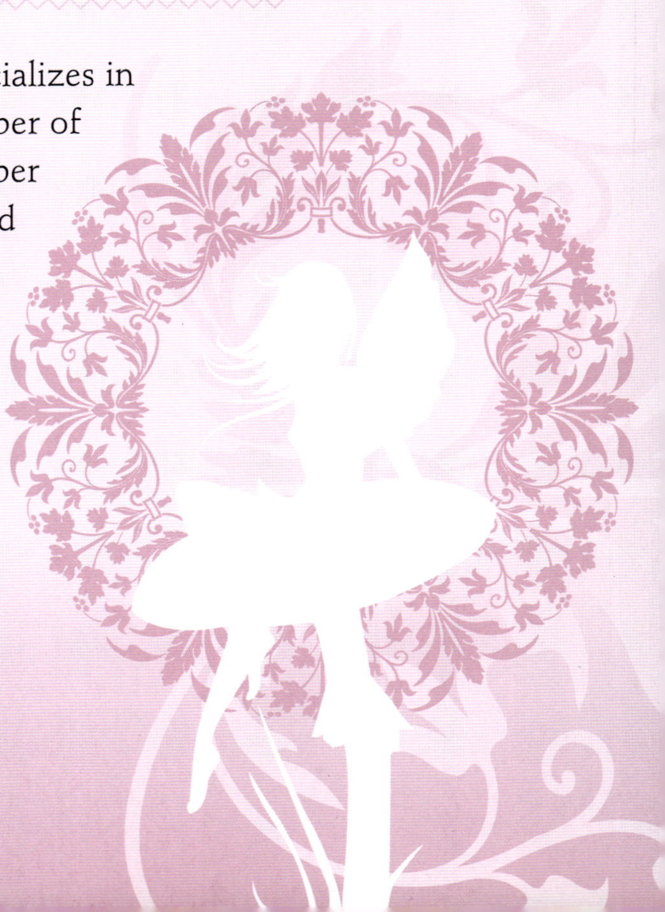